THE ORIGINS OF LOUISVILLE'S OLMSTED PARKS & PARKWAYS

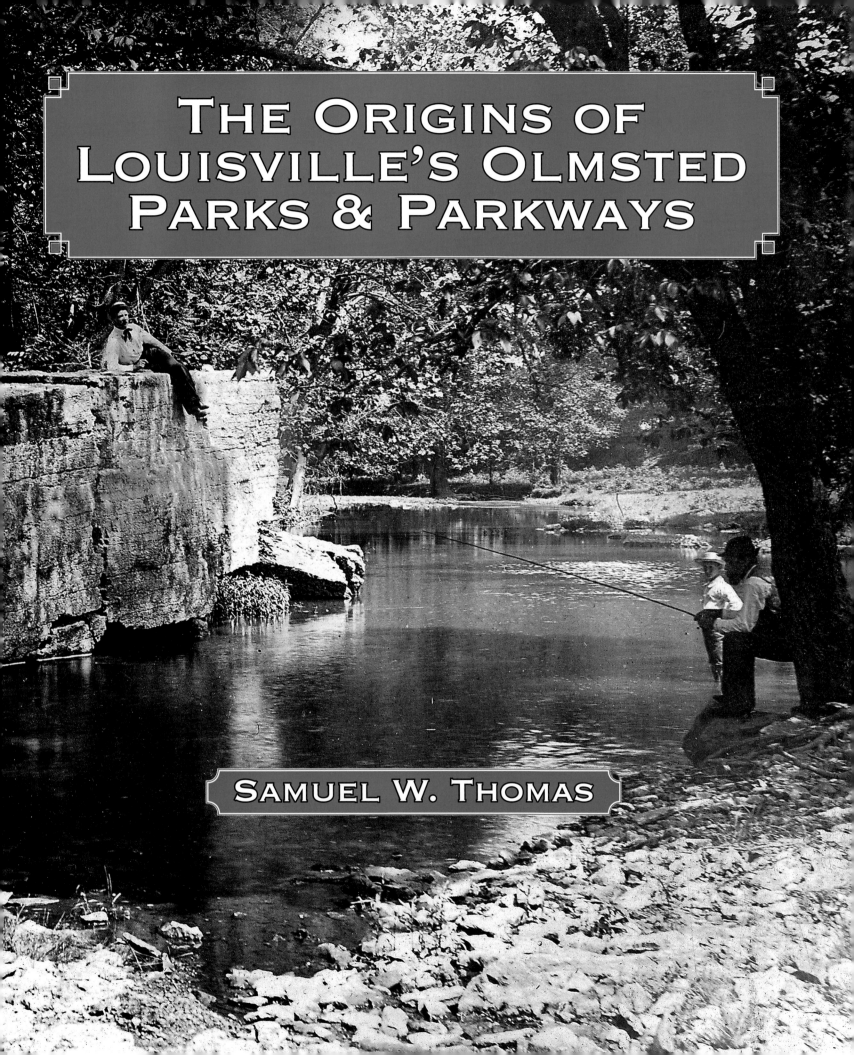

The Origins of Louisville's Olmsted Parks & Parkways

Samuel W. Thomas

Dedicated to the memory of Edmund Francis Lee and Benjamin Grove, who paved the way for Louisville's park system; Emil Mahlo and Cecil Fraser, who assisted Frederick Law Olmsted and his firm; and Carl Berg, who continued in their tradition.

> We hope, for the credit of our rich, vigorous, and expanding city, that our park will be not only commensurate with the present greatness of Louisville, but that its founders will regard the brilliant future of the Falls City, and do that now which future generations will be grateful for…. Let us have a park which will vie with any in the country. Let it be the jewel in the crown of the city.
>
> "Our Parks." *The Louisville Daily Journal*, 4 August 1866.

Editor: Deborah M. Thomas

Book Design and Production: Wm. Knox Gunn and Samuel W. Thomas

Published by Holland Brown Books

Printed in China

HOLLAND
BROWN
BOOKS

hollandbrownbooks.com

Page 1: Postcard, "Autumn in Jacob Park," about 1890.
Pages 2-3: Outing at Big Rock about 1890. Griswold Collection, University of Louisville Photographic Archives.

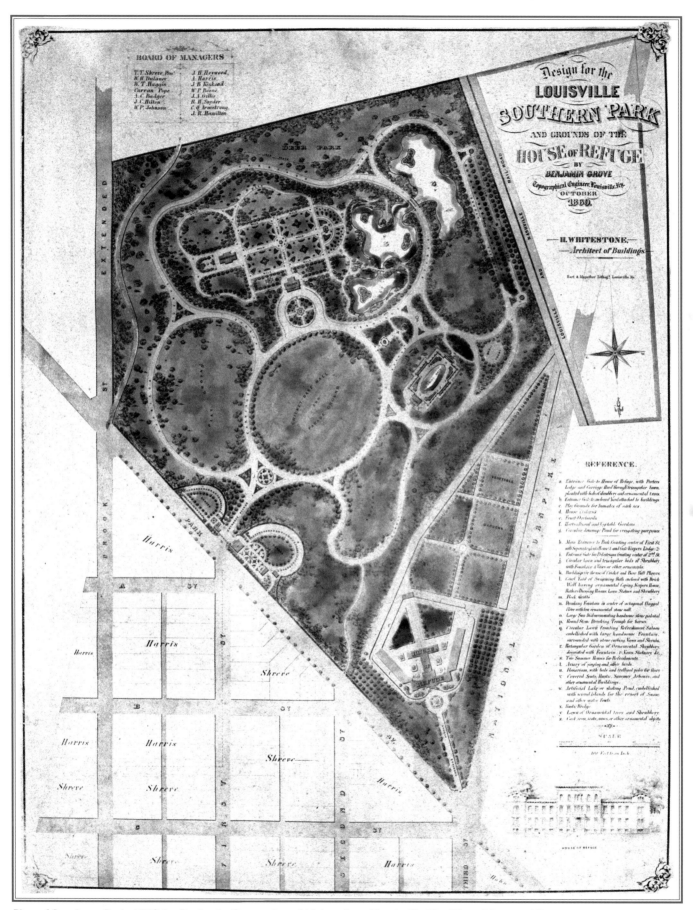

Plan of Southern Park, 1860, by Benjamin Grove, site of University of Louisville. The Filson Historical Society.

FOREWORD

I WAS INTRODUCED TO SAM THOMAS before even moving to Louisville through *Views of Louisville Since 1766*, which some family friends in the Highlands had given to my parents. It was, and still is, a fascinating historical document of a city I did not then know. Later, I was lucky enough to meet Sam and even benefit from his research for one of our properties in the Portland neighborhood, and also learned of Kenton Place (an Olmsted park on East Market Street).

When I heard that before he died last year Sam had nearly completed a years-long effort to produce a book about the origins of the Louisville park system, I knew I wanted to help. Stephanie Brothers and I at Holland Brown Books are honored to have worked with Sam's widow, Debbie Thomas, to release this book on the one-year anniversary of his passing.

As a proud member of the Board of Trustees of the Frederick Law Olmsted Parks Conservancy, I realize there are some points made in this history that will surprise some Louisville Olmsted purists. Folks must realize, however, this is a book less about Olmsted himself and his work here, and more about what happened in Louisville before, during and after Olmsted came, from the early days of George Rogers Clark and his park plan that Sam debunks, to the work of locals Benjamin Grove, Emil Mahlo, General John Castleman and the "innovator of urban parks" Joseph Paxton. Specific chapters on many Louisville parks, such as Central Park, are inspiring and edifying. There is also much research on the parkways and parks Olmsted was building in other places and learning from.

Holland Brown Books will be releasing another book a year from now which will focus more on Olmsted himself and his team, especially his nephew and stepson John Charles Olmsted, who worked until 1915 in Louisville. Despite one of Sam's theses that Olmsted's work in Louisville has been "overstated," I believe that the Louisville park system remains Olmsted's life's masterpiece, which alas remains unrecognized to many nationally.

Sam's thorough research in this book highlights all the great parks-related work the ever-industrious and civic-minded citizens of Louisville undertook before Olmsted first came to Louisville to work on the parks in 1891 at the request of Andrew Cowan and the Salmagundi group. Sam documents earlier Olmsted trips to Louisville as well. It is clear this civic engagement is still going strong today!

Using vivid archival photos and drawings and his always eloquent prose, Sam evokes an era of self-improvement that continues today. We discover bipartisan collaboration in long-term planning for Louisville, and are inspired today to continue the discussion of how parks and trees impact our quality of life.

–Gill Holland
Holland Brown Books

PREFACE

The 1874 creation of the Louisville Jockey Club and Driving Park Association, which became known commonly as Churchill Downs, prompted a reader of *The Louisville Daily Commercial* to propose an alternative. "The main object in view should be the establishment of a park by the rich men of Louisville, which…might be made a source of health and pleasure to the poor man who has no carriage and horses to insure needed and beneficial exercise in the fresh country atmosphere. Some of the most charming spots visited by the writer in Europe have been small parks of thirty to fifty acres in extent, beautifully and tastefully embellished with flowers and groves, lakes, and walks, wherein 5,000 or more persons daily congregate, and for several hours thoroughly enjoy themselves."[1]

The unidentified letter writer pointed out that one of Joseph Paxton's park designs had been presented to him and "has been laid away for several years waiting for an opportunity to use it." While noting only that Paxton received large sums, "sometimes $10,000 or $15,000" for his park designs, no further identification was offered of the prominent landscape architect. The writer undoubtedly thought that among the paper's readership he was addressing, Sir Joseph Paxton was well enough known, perhaps more for his famous Crystal Palace in London's Hyde Park and the grounds of the Duke of Devonshire's estate, Chatsworth, than his urban parks. His first urban park was Prince's Park, opened in the outskirts of Liverpool in 1843. Four years later, his more impressive park opened in Birkenhead, a few miles away just across the River Mersey.

While touring England as an observer and journalist in 1850, Frederick Law Olmsted visited Birkenhead Park. It was the first park the 28-year-old Olmsted had ever seen. It "broke on him like a revelation," biographer Laura Wood Roper would say. Olmsted wrote glowingly of his observations in A. J. Downing's magazine, *The Horticulturalist, and Journal of Rural Art and Rural Taste*, in 1851. Downing, who was considered America's leading authority on horticulture and domestic architecture, began to campaign for the creation of a similar park in

Boathouse, Birkenhead Park by Samuel W. Thomas, 2010.

New York City before he died in 1852. When requests for proposals were made for Central Park in 1857, Downing's former architecture partner, Calvert Vaux, asked Olmsted to join him in making a submission.

Downing and English native Vaux had met in London in the summer of 1850, and when Downing returned to Newburgh, New York, in the fall, Vaux accompanied him. Sailing to New York from Liverpool, they surely inspected Paxton's Birkenhead Park before embarking, if they had not already visited the grounds.

Downing and Vaux became partners in Downing's architectural practice. Olmsted visited Downing, whom he already knew, and Vaux in Newburgh in 1851. As Vaux's biographer Francis E. Kowsky noted, when it came time to submit a design for the Central Park competition, Vaux asked Olmsted to join him mainly because Olmsted was then working on the park site and was familiar with its topography. While Olmsted had no professional training or experience in park design, Vaux was a gifted artist and trained architect who had traveled on the Continent studying parks and gardens. This experience, observed Professor Kowsky, along with his ever-so-short partnership with Downing, provided Vaux with "a command of the Romantic tradition of design that in the early 1850s surpassed that of any of his contemporaries on this side of the Atlantic."[2]

Despite Vaux having the lead in Central Park's design, Olmsted garnered most of the recognition and praise. The two remained partners and friends for some time, but Vaux continued to be galled by his less than equal credit for the joint venture that began the public park movement in America. Although when questioned Olmsted acknowledged Vaux's role, he seemed content to allow the public's perception of his dominant role stand. In time, Vaux's participation would be all but forgotten.

Olmsted's role in the development of Louisville's park and parkway system has also been overstated. This book places Olmsted's Louisville work in the context of the longstanding intentions and plans already in motion when Olmsted came to Louisville in 1891 to advise the elected Board of Park Commissioners about its work.

Paxton died in 1865, but he lived long enough to see the influence of his innovative park designs in America and elsewhere through Frederick

BOOKS on Architecture, Horticulture and Farming.—Ranlett's Architecture, a series of original designs for Domestic and Ornamental Cottages, connected with Landscape Gardening, adapted to the United States; illustrated by drawings of ground plots, plans, prospective views, elevations, sections, and details, together with estimates of costs, &c. This is universally acknowledged to be the best book on Architecture extant. In 2 vols. Price $10.

Downing's Horticulturist and Journal of Rural Art and Rural Taste, devoted to Horticulture, Landscape Gardening, Rural Architecture, Botany, Pomology, Entomology, Rural Economy, &c. In 4 vols., bound, at $3.75.

The Farmer's Guide to Scientific and Practical Agriculture, detailing the labors of the farm in all their variety, and adapting them to the seasons of the year as they successively occur, by Henry Stephens, author of the Book of the Farm, &c., assisted by John P. Norton, Professor of Scientific Agriculture in Yale College, New Haven. Published in 20 numbers at 25 cents. The whole set for $5. Nos. 1 and 2 now published.

All for sale by   [m10]   GEO. W. NOBLE.

The Louisville Daily Journal, 11 May 1850.

Law Olmsted and others, including Benjamin Grove of Louisville. Grove was a native of Birmingham, England, only a hundred or so miles east of Liverpool. Certainly he would have been aware of Paxton's parks before coming to Louisville. Two of Grove's known Louisville plans of 1860 follow Paxton's tenets in every detail. These comprehensive plans by Grove begin the 30-year odyssey that resulted in a Board of Park Commissioners that would invite Frederick Law Olmsted to put his seal of approval on its initial efforts and then to guide and design the creation of Louisville's parks system, which has grown into one of the country's largest.

The sesquicentennial of Frederick Law Olmsted's birth in 1972 refocused national attention on his achievements and influence. "The reason for this new recognition of an unsung genius may well be," Joan Riehm wrote in *The Courier-Journal & Times*, "that to a nation trying frantically to make cities livable and conserve the natural environment, Olmsted is particularly contemporary." She noted as part of the celebration the recent publication of *Frederick Law Olmsted and the American Environmental Tradition* by Albert Fein, director of Urban Studies at the Brooklyn Center of Long Island University.[3] The book was published by George Braziller of New York in a series called Planning and Cities, under the general editorship of George R. Collins of Columbia University, who noted that the illustrations in Fein's book "make up what is probably the most complete representation to date of Olmsted's projects: they have been arranged in a thematic fashion, so as to acquaint the reader with the various categories of Olmsted's design activity." Of the 104 illustrations, the seven depicting Louisville projects were obtained by Dr. Fein while doing research in the city.

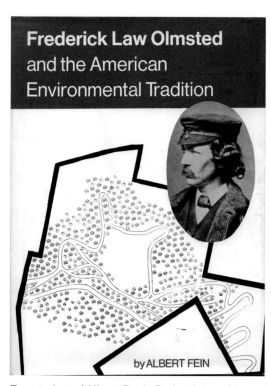

Frederick Law Olmsted and the American Environmental Tradition

by ALBERT FEIN

Dust jacket of Albert Fein's *Frederick Law Olmsted and the American Environmental Tradition* (New York, 1972). Strangely, the background map was not an Olmsted work, but rather Ransom Scowden's plan for Jacob Park that Fein had used as illustration 64.

Two years after Olmsted's revival, his Louisville masterpiece, Cherokee Park, was virtually destroyed by the April 3, 1974, tornado. Restoring the park brought Olmsted back into the local limelight. On the heels of the disaster, *Courier-Journal & Times* writer Barry G. Jacobs reviewed a new book, *FLO: A Biography of Frederick Law Olmsted* by Laura Wood Roper, whom Dr. Fein had characterized as "the principal Olmsted scholar." "Unfortunately, the Louisville park was a relatively minor episode near the end of Olmsted's career," Jacobs pointed out, "and receives only brief mention in this work, with no details on its planning given."[4] Only weeks later, Jacobs traveled to the Brookline, Mass., headquarters of Olmsted Associates, where the firm's plans remained stored. He interviewed the firm's senior partner, Artemus P. Richardson, who would come to Louisville to direct the restoration of Cherokee Park.[5]

When the National Association for Olmsted Parks met in Louisville in December 1981, author Sam Thomas presented a slide talk on "Louisville's Olmsted Park System." Some of that research was melded into a more comprehensive audiovisual program, "Louisville's Parks: An Olmsted Legacy," that premiered in Louisville at the 36th annual meeting of The National Trust for Historic Preservation in October 1982. This production was part of The Olmsted Festival, masterminded by Eleanor Bingham Miller in association with C. J. Pressma and Nancy Comstock, that included an exhibition of Olmsted's Louisville parks and gardens, as well as the renovation of one of his local projects, Boone Square.

The Friends of Olmsted Association was formed in 1986 and was soon renamed the Louisville Friends of Olmsted Parks, which produced *Louisville's Olmstedian Legacy: An Interpretive Analysis and Documentary Inventory* in September 1988. The Friends sponsored a conference on Olmsted in Louisville, keynoted by Charles C. McLaughlin, editor-in-chief of the Frederick Law Olmsted Papers. Prior to the meeting, McLaughlin told art critic Diane Heilenman that there was particular interest among scholars in tracking down two Louisville Olmsted firm projects: Alta Vista for J. B. McFerran and Castlewood for J. B. Castleman. Both dated to 1898 and were the only Kentucky projects that the firm made lithographs of to market its subdivision work.[6]

In fact, the plat of Alta Vista may still be displayed prominently at Fairstead, the firm's headquarters and Olmsted National Historic Site in Brookline, Mass., on a wall dividing the family residence from the workroom. Another featured speaker, Arleyn Levee, pointed out to Diane Heilenman that "too often, people credit the man [Frederick Law Olmsted] when they mean the firm…. John really should be given his due in Louisville and in Lexington."

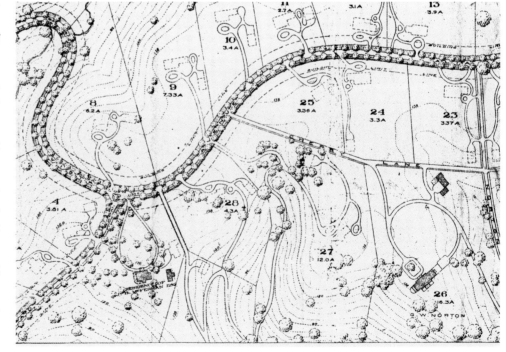

Section of *Design Map for Alta Vista*, Olmsted Brothers, March 1900, based on topographical map by Cecil Fraser. University of Louisville Archives.

John Charles Olmsted, the nephew and stepson of Frederick Law Olmsted, had more to do with the Louisville projects than anyone in the Olmsted firms. The son of John Hull Olmsted was not yet seven years old when his widowed mother, Mary Cleveland Bryant Perkins, married Frederick Law Olmsted in 1859. After spending two summers as a surveyor and graduating from Yale, John C. Olmsted joined his stepfather as a draftsman in 1875. He became a partner in F. L. Olmsted & J. C. Olmsted in 1884. Working in the office were Charles Eliot, a graduate of Harvard, where his father was president, and Henry Sargent Codman, a graduate of the Massachusetts Institute of Technology. Codman directly assisted Frederick Law Olmsted in the Louisville work until his untimely death early in 1893. His role in landscape planning for the Chicago World's Fair and the Vanderbilt estate, Biltmore, at Asheville, North Carolina, was significant, as Witold Rybczynski has recently brought to light.[7] Codman's place at Olmsted's side was taken by Eliot, and the firm of F. L. Olmsted & Co., formed in 1889, became Olmsted, Olmsted & Eliot. Eliot died suddenly 24 March 1897.[8] Between Codman's death and that of Eliot, Frederick Law Olmsted made only one visit (1894) to Louisville. He became mentally incapable of conducting business and retired in 1895. Following Eliot's death, the firm became Olmsted & Olmsted, reflecting the partnership of John C. Olmsted and his stepbrother, Frederick Law Olmsted, Jr., who had graduated from Harvard and had been working for the firm since late 1894. Although Louisville's Board of Park Commissioners was forced to suspend the firm's planning process after bond monies were exhausted and the 1893 financial panic followed, future park projects would be under the purview of John Olmsted with the help of colleagues Warren Manning and later James F. Dawson.

The Louisville Friends of Olmsted Parks was superceded by the Louisville Olmsted Parks Conservancy as the group took on the task of developing a Master Plan for the Louisville Olmsted Parks and Parkways in 1991, marking the 100th anniversary of the hiring of Frederick Law Olmsted. The Halvorson Co. of Boston was selected to produce the master plan for Iroquois, Cherokee, and Shawnee parks and their connecting parkways. "The focus will be on passive uses, mainly green space," Bill Samuels, Jr., chairman of the organization noted.[9] In conjunction with the master plan, two invaluable resource documents were also prepared for the Louisville Olmsted Parks Conservancy in 1992. Charles E. Beveridge and Arleyn A. Levee drew from material in all the Olmsted repositories "the most important statements" by Olmsted firm members "concerning the design, construction, and maintenance of the principal elements of the park system that they planned for Louisville beginning in 1891" for *Olmsted Documentary Resource for Louisville's Park Legacy: Cherokee, Iroquois and Shawnee Parks and The Parkways*. Arleyn Levee then produced an equally helpful booklet, *Louisville's Olmsted Park Legacy: Selective Chronology of Cherokee, Iroquois and Shawnee Parks and The Parkways*. In June 2002,

Arleyn A. Levee, Elizabeth Barlow Rogers, and Charles A. Birnbaum made "reflective remarks" as part of "An Olmsted Odyssey," celebrating Louisville's landscape legacy. Waterfront Park and the new Floyds Fork greenway carry that tradition forward.

This book is an account of the local efforts that led to the day in 1891 when Frederick Law Olmsted first laid eyes on the rolling pasture land along Beargrass Creek and deemed it highly suitable for park purposes. It outlines the procedure the Olmsted firm took in developing the Louisville park system and how the parkways came about later. The genesis of this book first appeared in a lengthy article for the Forum section of *The Courier-Journal*, 15 September 1991, "Louisville Parks: The Olmsted myth."

A number of people have helped shape this work. After obtaining a copy of my book about Cave Hill Cemetery, Thomas W. Byers wrote from Gloucester, Mass., in late 1990. He was looking for a suitable repository for a book of reduced landscape plans by his great-grandfather Benjamin Grove, who had designed much of the cemetery. The collection, which he gave to The Filson Historical Society, is an indispensable record of Benjamin Grove's work. Another descendant of Benjamin Grove, Mrs. Katherine Mason Orr of Louisville, gave The Filson Historical Society a blueprint of her great-grandfather's 1857 map of Cave Hill Cemetery. She also provided helpful family information to the author.

The author thanks Elizabeth Milroy, Ph.D., professor of Art History and American Studies at Wesleyan University, for information about Fairmount Park and Christopher R. Dougherty of the Fairmount Park Commission for confirmation of Emil Mahlo's employment.

The author also wishes to acknowledge the interest and research of Eleanor Bingham Miller, Carl Kramer, Ph.D., Douglas Stern, Patricia A. Clare, Jack Trawick, Anita Solodkin, Herb Zimmerman, Allen J. Share, Ph.D., Susan M. Rademacher, Grady Clay, George H. Yater, Thomas A. Courtenay, M.D., Mary Jean Kinsman, James J. Holmberg, Robin Lynn Wallace, David Morgan, and Bill Carner. Mike Heitz, director of Metro Parks, and Mimi Zinniel, president & CEO of the Olmsted Parks Conservancy, have made their records and plans readily available.

Morton Venable Joyes and Caroline H. P. Barr Joyes at Big Rock, December 1888. The Filson Historical Society.

PRELUDE
BIG ROCK IN BEARGRASS CREEK

Beargrass Creek, which is one of the many beautiful streams of the highly cultivated and happy State of Kentucky, meanders through a deeply shaded growth of majestic beech woods, in which are interspersed various species of walnut, oak, elm, ash, and other trees, extending on either side of its course. The spot on which I witnessed the celebration of an anniversary of the glorious proclamation of our independence is situated on its banks near the city of Louisville.

John James Audubon, "A Kentucky Barbecue." 1809. Maria R. Audubon, ed., *Audubon and His Journals* (New York, 1897, reprinted 1960), 2: 486.

THE MOST STRIKING AND DISTINCTIVE NATURAL FEATURE of all the Louisville parks is Big Rock. As the first surveyors made their way up the Middle Fork of Beargrass Creek in 1774, they surely took note of this huge limestone block that somehow had come to rest in the creek bed. It has been a picturesque landmark ever since, a park emblem, the most painted and photographed site in the all the parks. Who gave Big Rock its rather unimaginative name so long ago is unknown. Even the naming of Beargrass Creek remains a mystery.[10] The earliest map of the Falls of the Ohio made in 1766 simply noted it as "Creek 15 Yards wide." However, Lewis Evans' map of the same year called it "Rotten C. or Bear Grass C."[11] Dr. John Mitchell's map of 1755 shows a Bear Grass Creek in an area in southwestern Virginia that would have been familiar to explorers and surveyors passing into Kentucky. One of those was Dr. Thomas Walker, who referred to Beargrass River in his 1750 journal. Two decades later, the name was changed to Powell's River.[12]

Dr. Walker's journal of his party's exploration into Kentucky in 1750 was published by a descendant, William Cabell Rives, in 1888.[13] A vital part was missing: Walker's account of ten days from 10-20 April 1750 during which his party reached Beargrass River and he described Cumberland Gap. Rives was able to find the missing pages, and in 1894 he sent J. Stoddard Johnston copies for his research on the first exploration into Kentucky. Johnston, vice president of The Filson Club, published Dr. Walker's complete narrative in 1898. On 12 April, Dr. Walker recorded, "we rode four miles to Beargrass River.... On the Banks is some Bear Grass." In a footnote, Johnston identified Beargrass as *Yucca filamentosa*. This designation has been repeated in the local historical literature.[14] In 1991, Lawrence J. Fleenor, Jr., M.D., of Big Stone Gap, Virginia, published *The Bear Grass, A History*, in which he chronicled the region surrounding Powell's River, first identified as Beargrass River by Dr. Walker.[15] The bear grass described and illustrated by Dr. Fleenor is not yucca, but giant cane. There are a number of pioneer references to cane breaks, but no mention of yucca. In addition, in his 1819 *Sketches of Louisville*, Dr. Henry McMurtrie listed great cane in his "Florula Louisvillensis," but yucca was not included. One can conclude that the bear grass that lent its name to the local creek was a member of the giant cane family.

"Few of the present generation would have to be told where Big Rock reposes," *The Courier-Journal* observed in 1899. "Mr. Henry Gray, now eighty-five years old, who was born in that vicinity, says he remembers Big Rock as a great resort as far back as 1819.... For many years the Speed family had its annual reunions and picnics here on the Fourth of July, and it has always been a favorite place for outing parties."[16]

Former US Attorney General James Speed wrote about Big Rock, located near his cherished country home he called The Poplars.[17] On a Sunday after weekend guests had returned from various church services in town, Speed was asked which church he had attended. "I went to the oldest church of them all," he replied.

Big Rock in Beargrass Creek about 1895. Griswold Collection, University of Louisville Photographic Archives.

Years ago, when Louisville was an insignificant village, Fortunatus Cosby, one of the sweetest poets Kentucky ever produced, frequented the locality, and many of his best verses were composed while stretched out on the old moss-covered rock under the drooping branches of the old beeches, still casting their shadows in the limpid stream below.

"New Homes." *The Courier-Journal*, 2 March 1902.

Partial foundation of Ward's Mill near Big Rock about 1890. University of Louisville Photographic Archives.

I spent the whole morning on Beargrass Creek at Big Rock, and I was the only man in the congregation. The sermon was not spoken in words, it was merely felt; but the church in which I sat had a wonderful ceiling that was an intricate mosaic of delicate green, with small splashes of pale blue showing through, and floating down the long, dim corridors that were carpeted with the softest green, came the voices of the choristers. It wasn't a trained chorus, but in some way all of the voices of the feathered songsters seemed to blend wonderfully with the sounds that came from the leaves and with the hoarse undercurrent of melody that came from the water, as it rushed over the stones above Big Rock.[18]

"There is situated the big rock, known to every artist in the city," *The Courier-Journal* observed in "Gems Of Scenery," 10 May 1891. "Standing on 'Big Rock' the view compels admiration. Above are the rapids of the creek, where the stream flows over solid, moss-covered rocks dashing from under the heavy shade of beech trees."

And so on at every turn the onlooker is held spell bound by nature's work. Here it was that Clarence Boyd loved to sit and sketch.[19] It was here that he painted his masterpiece when he placed 'Big Rock' upon the canvas with the hand of genius. August Carl, who appreciated the beauties of the spot, was a favorite visitor.[20] 'Big Rock' was also the resort of Carl Brenner, who took much of his material from this neighborhood.[21] During pleasant weather, there is not a day but some ambitious artist sets his easel upon the broad back of 'Big Rock' where, in future, the city's weariest people will find rest and recreation.

Big Rock was not part of the lands assembled in 1891 for Cherokee Park. Its site and the nearby ruins of Ward's Mill were part of 17 acres adjacent to Cherokee Park given to the Board of Park Commissioners in late 1899 by Mrs. Sallie Rutherford Carter, whose father, George L. Douglass, had purchased a considerable holding in the area in 1874.[22] General John Castleman, president of the Board, secured the gift on a visit to Mrs. Carter in Biloxi, Mississippi.[23]

Access to Big Rock from Cherokee Park had been made possible by an earlier gift of Col. Morris B. Belknap who offered a "goodly sum of money" to extend the park road eastward along Beargrass Creek and to erect a "monumental bridge" across the creek in memory of his wife, Lily Buckner Belknap.[24] When Col. Belknap formally presented the project to the Board of Park Commissioners in May 1899, he admitted it was contrary to proper park practice to indicate "monuments or memorials," but he conditioned his offer by requesting that the road honoring his wife be named Glen Lily Road "so long as this property is under the control of the Board."[25]

Park work in 1900 focused on the Glen Lily development. "The beauty of the glen will never be known until the present improvements are completed and it is fit for public entrance," *The Courier-Journal* reported. "Then it will be the most popular place in the city for picnic parties. In this little valley lies the famous Big Rock, an immense block of stone, which fell ages ago from the rocky bank of the creek, and which lies across the stream in its picturesque spot. A little farther stands the ruin of an old stone mill, which has not been other than a ruin for sixty years. Near it, covered with moss and soil, is the old millstone."

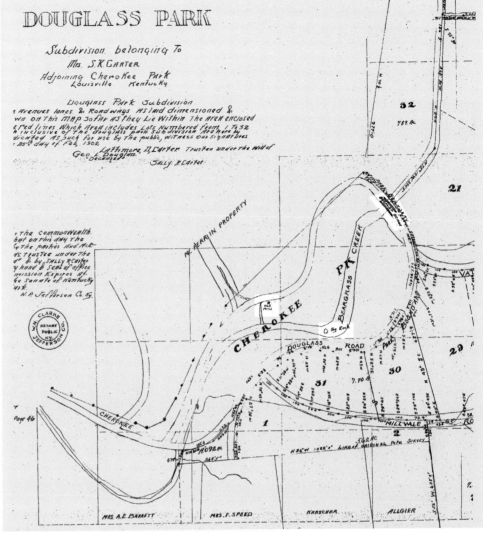

Section of plat of Douglass Park by Cecil Fraser with highlighted locations of Big Rock, Ward's Mill, and Belknap Bridge, dated 25 February 1902. Jefferson County Plat and Subdivision Book 1, p. 46.

An incredible amount of work is now done in this glen under the superintendence of the able park engineer of the city, Cecil Fraser. The entire creek bed has been turned aside, and a retaining wall built for hundreds of yards. The approaches to the bridge will be easy, and on the other side of the creek, along the hillside, the road is again walled up and will afford an easy ascent and drive along the miniature bluff over Big Rock and the creek ways.[26]

"The biggest work here has been the extension of the drive up Beargrass Creek and macadamizing it," John C. Olmsted noted during an inspection with Cecil Fraser 11 November 1900. "This is done in payment so to speak for 17 acres of land in the valley given by Mrs. Carter and has to be done by 29th of this month according to the

PRELIMINARY SKETCH FOR
BELKNAP BRIDGE
        CITY OF LOUISVILLE   PARK COMMISSION
        SHEPLEY, RUTAN AND COOLIDGE, ARCHITECTS

Preliminary rendering of Belknap Bridge about 1900 by Shepley, Rutan & Coolidge. Courtesy of Shepley Bulfinch Richardson and Abbott Architects, Boston.[30]

Below: Belknap Memorial Bridge. *Art Work of Louisville, Ky.,* 1903, Part 5.

Beargrass Creek above Big Rock photographed by Alex W. Nettelroth, 24 December 1889. University of Louisville Photographic Archives. Nettelroth was assistant surveyor for S. J. Hobbs & Co.

agreement." He added, "Mrs. Carter has graded one (narrow) road up a ravine S. from the park drive and has big signs 'villa lots for sale.'" Olmsted happened to meet the Morris Belknaps "and had a few words about the bridge." At that time, Beargrass Creek was forded at the site across rough stones.

The Belknap Bridge, which connected Alta Vista and Cherokee Drive (Lexington Road) with Douglass Boulevard and Bardstown Road, was designed by the Boston architectural firm of Shepley, Rutan & Coolidge and erected in 1901.[27] The bridge over Beargrass Creek was part of a master scheme by Peyton N. Clarke to tie his Douglass Park development to Cherokee Park.[28] The plat of Douglass Park was prepared by Cecil Fraser.[29]

The subdivision of Douglass Park in 1902 by Mrs. Sally Rutherford Carter provided some prime residential building lots along the south side of Beargrass Creek in the area of Big Rock. Board of Park Commissioner Andrew Cowan purchased the lot overlooking the creek that included the Belknap Bridge. About 1906, he engaged Philadelphia architect Wilson Eyre, a founder and editor of *House and Garden,* to design Alloway, a Tudor Revival house, completed in 1908.

Outing on Beargrass Creek about 1905 appears to be east of Belknap Bridge on land owned by Andrew Cowan. Griswold Collection, University of Louisville Photographic Archives. Area later became part of connector between Cherokee and Seneca parks.

We are glad to learn that Colonel Cowan is disposed to abandon the road up the hillside. His original requirement that there should be such a road, giving him a direct entrance upon the park border road at the foot of the hill near the Belknap bridge, was a source of much regret to us at the time and we persuaded him to permit the entrance to be partly at the branch valley instead of on the park border drive as he first demanded it. We are glad to learn that he is coming to appreciate the ugliness of it. Those great rounded Bluegrass spurs projecting into the valley of Beargrass Creek are particularly fine landscape features and their character is such that it is extremely objectionable to cut into their surface and break them up with roads, fences, hedges and other artificial structures. Fortunately, the right-of-way up the little branch valley northeast of the house site has all the appearance of a private drive and is well located in the landscape sense, and although roundabout, and therefore inconvenient, the advantage of doing without the more direct drive much more than overcomes the disadvantage of this roundabout route.

John C. Olmsted to Wilson Eyre, 4 September 1906. Olmsted firm papers, Library of Congress.

1
George Rogers Clark's 1779 Park Plan Is a Fraud

"One thing the first settlers at the Falls of the Ohio forgot was to make provision, when the town of Louisville was laid out, for an esplanade along the river front," a *Courier-Journal* editorial observed in 1882.

> This was a terrible oversight. It was a wrong beginning whose effect is seen in the absence of parks through the present metropolis. No provisions for a delightful public park having been made in the original town, the subsequent owners of additions did not think it worth while to give any ground for such a necessary public purpose. Thus Louisville is to-day in the summer one of the dryest-looking cities in the country…. If the parks had been provided for a hundred years ago in the original plot and in each addition to the original town as it was laid out, we would have our parks at comparatively little expense. Now the ground has become costly, and the parks must be made further from the center of the city.[31]

Within months of the editorial, Louisville historian Reuben T. Durrett began informing colleagues that he had discovered a 1779 map that included provisions for parks delineated by none other than the town's recognized founder, George Rogers Clark. A myth was thus born that has proved impossible to extinguish.[32]

"More than one hundred years have elapsed since the first unsuccessful effort was made to have public parks in Louisville," Board of Parks Commissioner Durrett wrote for the board's *First Annual Report* in 1891. "When the first settlers at the Falls of the Ohio were in 1779 preparing a petition to the Virginia Legislature, to establish a town by the name of Louisville at this place, General George Rogers Clark, then fresh from his conquest of the Illinois country, prepared a plan of the contemplated town…. Had this plan been carried out and the noble old forest trees left on the grounds, Louisville would have been one of the handsomest cities in the world."

In his chapter, The Public Parks and Parkways, for the 1896 *Memorial*

Engraving of George Rogers Clark by James Barton Longacre after portrait by John Wesley Jarvis. *The National Portrait Gallery of Distinguished Americans* (1856).

History of Louisville, Andrew Cowan was apologetic for the city's slow start in providing these public amenities.

It is not surprising that the founders of this beautiful city, at the Falls of the Ohio, more than a hundred years ago, should have failed to realize the great importance of providing large areas for the health and comfort of a population that now numbers over two hundred thousand souls. These early settlers scarcely dreamed of the brilliant future of their town. They had traveled over the mountains and through the wilderness, or floated their boats down the rivers from the older settled country, and here where the beautiful river flowed deep and broad, before its calm surface was broken into rapids at the "Falls of the Ohio," they built their pioneer homes, surrounded by the primitive forest.

The broad and fertile plain over which the present city is spread was then a virgin forest. The mighty sycamores and giant oaks, the great beech and the lofty walnut trees, crowded upon the soil that was needed for sowing and planting, and were therefore but cumberers of the ground, to be cut down and destroyed. Many of these noble trees that escaped the axe are yet standing, singly or in groups, upon the land that was so recently acquired for public parks.

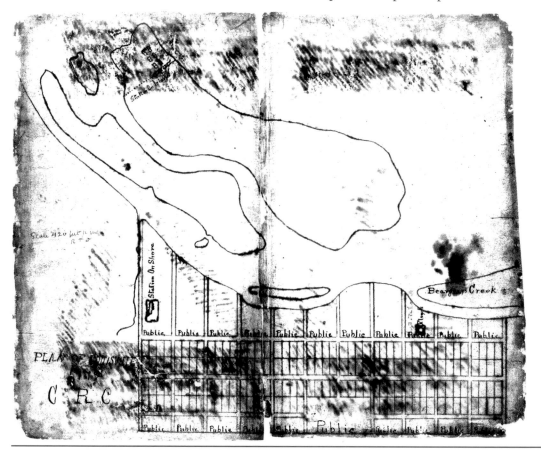

1779 Plan of Louisville. Durrett Collection, University of Chicago Library.

Cowan continued to rely on Col. Durrett, who besides being a parks commissioner was president of The Filson Club, Louisville's historical society. "When Louisville was first laid out as a town at the Falls of the Ohio, in 1779, there was one of its citizens who had the forethought to suggest that public grounds or parks be reserved for the benefit of its future inhabitants. This great and farseeing man was Gen. George Rogers Clark. He made a survey and map of the town in 1779, which has been preserved and is now in the possession of R. T. Durrett."

Cowan then, as Durrett had done, pointed out that "General Clark's plan was never officially adopted by the trustees so far as their records show." This part at least is true. No mention of General Clark's 1779 plan or map of the town of Louisville can be found in the Trustees' minutes or anywhere else for that matter. In fact, there is no mention of any such plan in George Rogers Clark's own vast collection of papers.

The map was first published by Col. Durrett in a *Courier-Journal* article, "Ancient Louisville," 2 August 1883. Durrett had noted in an 1880 paper to the Southern Historical Association that the "original plan of Louisville…provided for public lots, and but for a great neglect of the Trustees we should now have parks in which noble trees of the original forest would be preserved, and in which the pure air of heaven could be breathed by our citizens."[33]

"And when ordinary surveyors were laying off the Town of Louisville, in 1779, the stern old warrior [an interesting characterization, as Clark then would have been only 27] drew a plan which if it had been adopted, would have made Louisville the most beautiful city on the continent," Durrett wrote Lyman C. Draper 19 April 1883. "He projected Main Street along the river bank at the top of the second bank, and laid off building lots only on its Southern side, then leaving all the ground between this street and the river as public ground. Then back of Jefferson Street, he laid off a park half a square in depth, extending the whole length of the city from east to west. This park he connected with the Court-house lot, which of itself embraced two whole squares. No man who had not an eye for the beautiful, and a touch of poetry in his soul, could thus lay off a city, &c."[34]

This description would have surprised Draper, who, as corresponding secretary of the State Historical Society of Wisconsin, had been accumulating information about Clark and other western pioneers for nearly 40 years and had assembled the largest collection of Clark papers, including a trunk's worth gathered from Locust Grove in 1846.

Durrett told Draper that the 1779 map and others by Clark of the Falls area "fell by pure accident into my hands." In copying the maps for Draper, he pointed out that the plan of Louisville made by Clark in the fall of 1779 "indicates the taste and genius of its maker in the plan it presents of Louisville…. No engineer but one of taste, and a little of the poetry of nature, would thus lay out a city. And I think Genl. Clark had something of both these qualities beneath the rough garb of the soldier which he outwardly wore."

The 1779 plan of Louisville is clearly a fraud with a number of telltale errors that prove that point. The plan's title block and place identifications are printed, a practice George Rogers Clark is not known

On the 7th of May, 1828, we reached Louisville, a large handsome town in Kentucky…. Nothing delighted us more at this beautiful spot than the rich, fresh, genuine greensward–the honest grass, in short–upon which we could sit down with comfort.

Basil Hall, *Travels in North America* (Edinburgh, 1830), 3: 375.

to have employed. Certainly he would not have initialed the document "CRC." The row of public spaces shown on the document along the north side of Main Street had already been distributed as lots in the 24 April 1779 lottery, a fact George Rogers Clark would surely have known even though he remained in the Illinois territory following the recapture of Vincennes. Likewise, the row of public spaces depicted on the document on the north side of Green (later Liberty) Street actually had been set aside on the south side of the street. Finally, Clark would not have drawn Floyd's Station on the south side of Beargrass Creek between Third and Fourth streets, because it did not exist.[35]

Who could imagine anyone contemplating a town with parks at a time when Dr. William Fleming provided the following description of the Falls? "At this place are about 500 people who mostly look like ghosts, daily dying, especially the Young, and Young and Old to my surprise frequently infested with dangerous eating ulcers in the Mouth & face. The affects of Bilious & intermitting disorders and Agues infest them all. This they ascribe to the lowness of the river which is dried up one half of its channel, and the water they drink, draining through a pond which runs of the back of the town."[36]

In an extraordinary admission to Draper, Durrett wrote that there was nothing on any of the maps to confirm they had been made by Clark. "It accords with my wishes to have made them by the old hero, and hence the assumption. What can prove the contrary? Nothing, unless some other finding of papers hereafter teaches a different view."[37] It appears, from Durrett's known use of artists to prepare sketches of people and places, that he had the maps drawn from information he supplied and wanted to illustrate. Despite the lack of corroborating information that Clark drew any maps or ground plans as Durrett reported, the assertion that General Clark planned Louisville's first parks was continued by Andrew Cowan and has been given further significance and credence by its inclusion in John W. Reps' *Town Planning in Frontier America* (Princeton, 1965), 277.

"And so we went on after the first effort for parks in 1779," Durrett concluded, "until one hundred and ten long years have passed, before we had really gotten down to the successful work of acquiring them." Wrong again. Much thought, debate, and planning had taken place beginning in the 1850s to produce the satisfactory result of the 1890s.

2

LANDSCAPED ESTATES AND PLEASURE GARDENS—JACOB'S WOODS; CHATSWORTH; REPTON; FREDERICK LAW OLMSTED'S VISIT TO HAYFIELD IN 1853; IVYWOOD; EVERGREEN AND RIVERSIDE NURSERIES; AND ELM TREE AND WOODLAND GARDEN

INTEREST IN NATIVE PLANTS BEGAN WITH THE FIRST EXPLORATIONS in the West. In 1783, George Rogers Clark wrote Thomas Jefferson at Monticello that he would "receive a few seads of what the Kentuckyns call sd Coffee Tree. It makes a beautiful shade and I believe will flourish with you."[38]

The first formal listing of indigenous trees and plants was published by Henry McMurtrie, M.D., in his 1819 *Sketches of Louisville And its Environs*. The appended catalogue, "Florula Louisvillensis," contained 600 species of plants "that grow in the Vicinity of the Town, exhibiting their Generic, Specific, and Vulgar English Names." Men of means embellished their estates with such plant material, augmented by exotic varieties they could obtain elsewhere by purchase or trade.

Few early descriptions of landscaped residential properties in Jefferson County exist. Charles Anderson's reminiscences of Soldier's Retreat, established in the early 1790s by his father, Col. Richard Clough Anderson, is the most detailed. The homestead and Anderson family burying ground are now part of Hurstbourne Estates. Col. Anderson's first wife was Elizabeth Clark, and like his brothers-in-law, George Rogers Clark and William Croghan of Locust Grove, he became a surveyor following Revolutionary military service. His son, lawyer Charles Anderson, became governor of Ohio and had a longstanding interest in history.

> The yard was a parallelogram of about three acres immediately around the house. It contained only some half dozen trees. One of these was the largest Catalpa I have ever seen, a primeval forester. My father, from fear of sheltering black gnats etc., would suffer no vines upon his house nor any tree so close to still the air currents....
>
> A little over a quarter of a mile from the house, there stood another very Monarch of the Forest, a huge Yellow Poplar. It was said to be about 8 feet in Diameter and to rise on a clean, clear shaft more than 110 feet, without one limb or knot. My father so ardently admired it that he not only left it in his first "clearing"

A Treatise on Landscape Gardening, adapted to the United States, with a view to the improvement of Country Residences; comprising historical notices and general principles of the art, directions for laying out grounds, arranging plantations, the description of hardy trees, decorative accompaniments to the house and grounds, the formation of pieces of artificial water, flower gardens, &c., with Remarks on Rural Architecture. Fourth edition, enlarged, revised, and newly illustrated. By A. J. Downing, author of Designs for Cottage Residences, etc. Price $3.50. For sale by Beckwith & Morton.

"Landscape Gardening, new edition," *The Louisville Daily Journal*, 26 June 1849.

LOUISVILLE'S FIRST PARK was located on the southern outskirts of downtown, on the extensive holdings of successful merchant and banker John I. Jacob. Known as Jacob's Woods, this tract extended south of Broadway to Breckinridge from Fifth Street east to Preston Street, but at its core was the Jacob residence. "I am going to ask that you close your eyes...and visualize if you possibly can a very extensive public park, in which are large forest trees, artistically arranged flower beds and here and there clusters of shrubs of various kinds, all of which added to the charm of this large area which extended from Walnut to Chestnut and from Third to Fourth Streets," William C. Kendrick wrote to *The Courier-Journal*, 4 June 1933 under the heading "Old Louisville." "The home in the center of this woodland was built by [John I. Jacob] about 1810. He occupied it until his death in 1852." After the civic-minded Jacob died, family members continued to live in the house. They were in Europe in 1854 when the house burned to the ground. By that time, for the most part, Jacob's Woods had been built over.

The honors paid to the memory of La Fayette on Saturday, by our citizens, were highly creditable to themselves and to the memory of that illustrious patriot. The procession was the largest ever seen in our city.... The procession was formed on Jefferson street, and extended upwards of three quarters of a mile... to a grove on Mr. John I. Jacob's lot.

Daily Louisville Public Advertiser, 21 July 1834.

as an outpost or sentinel of its forest. But most careful by his compass and Theodolite and other guides of measurement, he so located his Soldier's Retreat House that the bolt holes in his pairs of Folding doors should be in a perfect dead-due-south line from the center of that wonderful (to me) adorable creature of God!

Leading the vision to this central spectacle, an Avenue of Locusts and Walnuts, about 150 feet in width extended from the roadside along the front line of palings around the yard to a parallel road along the Farm Fence which ran between it and the Poplar with its forest, just behind it. This grand avenue was always clad, except at its two tree lines and the middle road way in a well grazed Bluegrass sward. On the right hand as we looked towards the Tree (the cynosure of all eyes) there extended the whole distance of this lane our vineyard. This was one of my father's early Bucolical hobbies and extravagancies. A cold water zealot in all his drinks (except of Coffee and Tea) in moderation he had become an ally of the Swiss immigrants at Vevay, Indiana, in their attempts to introduce light wines into our feasts as a moral reformer....

The other side of the avenue was blessed by one of the very largest and very best private apple orchards, ever grafted, planted and cared for by a master in pomology.

❧ ❧ ❧

JOHN EDWARDS'S REASON FOR CALLING HIS PLACE CHATSWORTH is not known, but the name was even then deeply embedded in landscape gardening history. The gardens of the English estate of the dukes of Devonshire in Derbyshire called Chatsworth had long been recognized. In time, they would be improved by Joseph Paxton, whose Birkenhead Park outside Liverpool became the inspiration for Olmsted and Vaux's Central Park.

Chatsworth displayed the art of the gardener at a perfect pitch.... The gardens were a fine example of the mixing of the new "gardenesque" style of gardening with the "natural" and "picturesque" parklands of Capability Brown and Repton. Here, nature was subjected to cultivation, a love of plants demonstrated in mass plantings, specimen trees and shrubs displayed to their greatest advantage and matched by ostentatious botanical collections. Chatsworth was not only the most excellent garden in England to visit, it had become effectively the finest school of gardening in Europe.

Kate Colquhoun, *A Thing In Disguise: The Visionary Life of Joseph Paxton* (London, 2003), 161.

Alfred Edwards wrote *The Courier-Journal* in 1894 that his grandmother, Mary Montgomery Geiger Edwards, had received a large parcel of land east of Louisville from her father. She married John Edwards and they built a brick residence before 1806.[39] "My grandfather named the place Chatsworth and commenced the improvement of it…and at the death of his father he inherited the place. My father married Miss Taylor, the daughter of Mrs. Gibson Taylor, then a widow, in 1830. They continued to improve and beautify Chatsworth until it was regarded, even among the beautiful places of the neighborhood, as one of the most beautiful."

NOT FAR FROM LOUISVILLE'S CHATSWORTH, which marked the western edge of Crescent Hill, was another fine estate called Repton. Here again was a name steeped in landscape gardening lore—Humphry Repton—the most noted English designer of his day and the author of *Observations on the Theory and Practice of Landscape Gardening*. The property overlooking Brownsboro Road had been embellished by Norborne Alexander Galt, M.D., and his father, naturalist and physician William Craig Galt, M.D., who arrived at the Falls of the Ohio in 1802. His first beautifully landscaped residence was on the northeast corner of Second and Main, the site of the first Galt House in 1835. The younger Dr. Galt died in 1844 of injuries suffered from being thrown from his buggy; his father died in 1853.

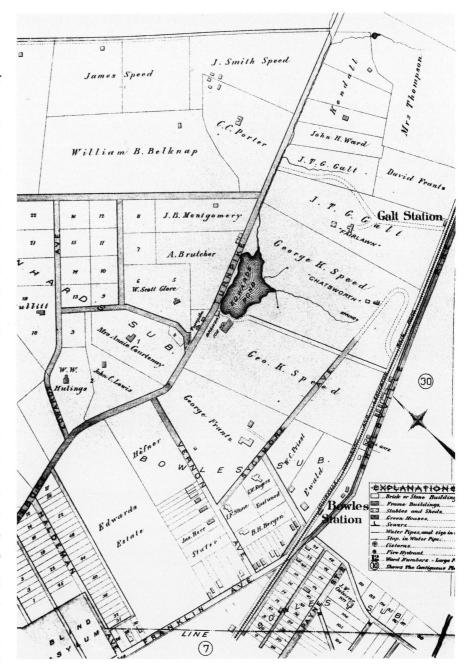

Section from the *Atlas of the City of Louisville. Ky.,* 1884.

> Died, in Jefferson county, on the 22d inst., at the farm of the late Dr. N. Galt, Dr. W. C. Galt, in the 77th year of his age…. Throughout life Dr. Galt had the love of a devotee for the cultivation of fruits and flowers. In the midst of his most engrossing cares this love of nature was conspicuous. Those who resided here before the erection of the Hotel, which bears the

William Craig Galt, M.D., by Matthew Harris Jouett. Huntington Library and Art Gallery, San Marino, CA.

name of Dr. Galt, remember the floral beauty of the grounds around the dwelling of Dr. Galt, which occupied the space now filled by the Hotel. When the property was devoted to hotel purposes, Dr. N. Galt completed the improvement of his farm, a few miles from the city, and thither his venerable father often escaped in the summer season, for the enjoyment of his early tastes. And when he felt himself finally released from the cares of business, Dr. Galt entered upon the cultivation of fine fruits and green house flowers, with the zeal and delight of youthfulness.

The Louisville Daily Courier, 24 October 1853.

"I have spoken of Repton many times, but never have attempted to describe it," Selena Gray Ingram wrote about 1910, "so I shall try to tell something of it now."[40]

In my great-grandfather's [William Craig Galt] time, it was so beautifully laid out and the greenhouses were so wonderful, that it was quite a show place, and people came from far and near to see it. Every kind of rare tree and shrub that could be procured anywhere, my grandfather [Norborne Alexander Galt] made grow at Repton. There were orange and fig trees (most carefully protected in the winter time) smoke trees, fringe trees, tulip trees, and the most beautiful magnolia grandiflora I have ever seen anywhere. One hot house was devoted entirely to azaleas....

The driveway formed a circle at the back of the house, while the greensward came right up to the foot of the steps of the front porch. As the house was on a beautiful, rolling hill, the smooth green lawn swept away from it in a gradual slope, for a long distance, without a break, so that nothing interrupted the lovely view. The orchard was at

Repton overlooking Brownsboro Road after being rebuilt about 1902. Courtesy of Ella Garth Choate Woodward.

the foot of the hill, at least the pear orchard was there, while the apple orchard was way off at one side. On either side of the clear stretch in front of the house were clumps of magnificent forest trees—oaks, elms, maples, &c, while in several places the beech trees had been entirely covered with a rank growth of wild grape vine, forming a wide cool tent, beneath where on the hottest day all was dark and sweet. What fun it was to swing in those grapevines! On both sides of the house were glorious beds of flowers of every description, while ornamental trees and shrubs of every kind gave variety to the landscape. No outhouses were visible from the house, but winding paths led to them. Hedges of "box" separated the stable yard from the garden, while osage orange hedges separated the orchards from the pasture. On one side of the house at a little distance, were lofty pine trees, and beyond these were the greenhouses…. Still further on, the rambling walk led to the loveliest of old orchards with a high wall around it.

"Repton was the showplace of the neighborhood, situated at the top of the hill and wonderfully planted with rare imported shrubs and flowers," Mary Ormsby Gray Nalle recalled. "At one point the hill-side was terraced and a series of ponds, each flowing out into the one next below, was established. One of these ponds was fenced in with wire screening and stocked with gold fish. Once there was a severe storm and afterwards it was discovered that the fish pond had overflowed and nearly all the gold fish had been washed out to Edward's pond over by the Blind Asylum. What fun we did have fishing for them."[41]

❧ ❧ ❧

DR. GALT HAD JUST DIED WHEN FREDERICK LAW OLMSTED visited Louisville in late 1853. Olmsted, who had studied scientific agriculture under Benjamin Silliman at Yale and was particularly interested in plants, sought out America's preeminent botanist, Dr. Charles Wilkins Short, Emeritus Professor of Materia Medica and Medical Botany in the Medical Department of the Louisville University. Also teaching medical chemistry and toxicology in the Medical Department was Benjamin Silliman, Jr. Olmsted was traveling with his brother, John Hull Olmsted, on his second tour of the South in an effort to document the effects of Slavery. The 31-year-old wrote from Louisville 1 December 1853, "we called on Prentice…an elderly, bright, keen, sorrowed looking man." George D. Prentice was the well-known editor of *The Louisville Daily Journal*. "We also called on Dr. Short, a wealthy old hunker at a beautiful place 5 miles out from town."[42] Short, who had received his medical degree from the University of Pennsylvania in 1815, resided on the Bardstown Road at Hayfield, which he had purchased in early 1847 for his son after inheriting a substantial fortune from his uncle.[43]

The Hayfield property on the South Fork of Beargrass Creek was used as a retreat called Sans Souci by John Thruston before David L. Ward purchased the land and erected a substantial dwelling on the ridge overlooking the creek. George Hancock purchased the Ward place in 1834 after his wife, Eliza Croghan Hancock, died at Locust Grove. He

An idea that early should be allowed to have weight in connection with these parks…is the idea of the educational ends which the parks may be made to subserve. What we have, in so far at least as all the larger and finer trees and plants are concerned, ought to be named, both the technical and common names being attached. It is unfortunate, but it is a fact…that the place of the sciences, especially of the natural sciences, is not recognized here as it should be and is in all the larger and some of the smaller cities in this country and throughout civilization. Why, to our discredit, are we without a natural history society or any scientific organization? A generation or so ago Louisville had a society of the sort under consideration; and Louisville certainly has had, possibly even now has, great botanists and other naturalists; and surely we are not dead to these important features of an advanced civilization.

"Louisville Parks." *The Louisville Post*, 30 June 1893.

Scene at Hayfield in the 1850s by an unknown artist. Courtesy of Thomas A Courtenay, M.D.

added a Greek Revival residence in front of the old, and erected outbuildings north of the house. When Hancock advertised the property for sale in 1840, it was called the Haylands, "containing 454 acres, 230 of which are in a high state of improvement and cultivation, the balance in timber."

This estate is admirably suited for hemp, grain, grass, a stock or dairy farm, and is offered the cheapest bargain in the State. The improvements have cost nearly $30,000, consisting of a splendid new brick and cut stone mansion, brick negro houses, stables, carriage house, ice house, &c., one of the best springs and dairies in the State, large apple and peach orchard, a terraced garden and yard filled with choice fruits, shrubs, &c., which (with the grounds around the house containing some 10 or 12 acres) is enclosed with a stone wall, durably and tastefully constructed, making it altogether, for its beauty, health, fertility, neighborhood, convenience to market, and price, one of the most desirable situations in the State.[44]

Haylands may have been a newspaper error or the name may have been changed to Hayfield by subsequent owner Moses M. Rawlings or by Dr. Short himself.

The editor of the two-volume *Memorial History of Louisville* (1896), J. Stoddard Johnston, was raised at Hayfield by George Hancock. Johnston, who was born in 1833, graduated from Yale, as had Hancock. He recalled the place in a 1908 *Courier-Journal* article. "There was a terraced garden at Hayfield sloping toward Beargrass creek, with broad walks and well-kept avenues lined with roses, syringas, snowballs and calycanthus, making its rear a quiet and secluded spot. In those days dueling was in vogue, and I remember well seeing Gen. Preston and my uncle, Albert Sidney Johnston, practicing with dueling pistols just before the duel between Robert Wickliffe, known as the young Duke, and Cassius M. Clay, in which Johnston was Wickliffe's second."[45] The duel was held at Locust Grove in May 1841.

Dr. Short's botanical collection was considered one of the most comprehensive in the country. In his will he bequeathed his "Herbarium or collection of dried plants to the Smithsonian Institute of Washington City upon the condition that the collection be carefully preserved and subject at all times to the inspection of those in pursuit of Botanical Knowledge."[46] The collection ultimately was given by his

Charles Wilkins Short, M.D., by James Reid Lambdin about 1834. Courtesy of Thomas A. Courtenay, M.D.

heirs to the Academy of Natural Science of Philadelphia.

Dr. Short's daughter, Mary Churchill Short, married William Allen Richardson in 1841, and in 1859 they purchased land adjacent to Hayfield, retaining Henry Whitestone to design a country house in the Italianate style, called Ivywood. Here, according to his obituary, Richardson "could also indulge in his love of trees and fruits and flowers; and under his guidance and handiwork, and with the intelligent assistance of his wife, what had been wildwood and canebrake soon blossomed into a picturesque landscape garden."[47]

Ca. 1860 Italianate mansion designed by Henry Whitestone and landscaped grounds of W. A. Richardson. *History of The Ohio Falls Cities and Their Counties* (Cleveland, 1882), opp. 48. Engraving of Ivywood was misidentified as the residence of L. L. Dorsey.

Ivywood was purchased by distiller Frederic W. Adams, who moved there from his bachelor apartment on Main Street. He called the place Woodleigh.[48] Later it was owned by the Charles Claggett family before being torn down in 1954 by the Methodist Hospital Commission. Atherton High School now occupies the site.[49]

In assessing the nursery business in late 1853, *The Louisville Daily Courier* pointed out that "the *habit* which the people of the South-West have always had, of sending East for articles of home consumption, has heretofore interfered very materially with experiments in the nursery business in the Ohio Valley."

> For a quarter of a century past to our own recollection, nurseries have been established, some of them of large size, but it is only within the last twelve or fifteen years that the demand for young fruit trees has been regular and considerable in this region, and lower prices and greater varieties East, added to the old habit of sending in that direction for supplies of nearly all necessaries, have continued to induce the people of the West and South-West to pass by our own nurseries, and get their supplies from abroad....
>
> The gentlemen who have been best known here, for their efforts to introduce and disseminate good varieties of fruits are, Lawrence Young, G. G. Hikes (and his father long before him), A. & E. Thompson, Arthur Peter, and a few such amateurs as Ormsby Hite, the late W. Weissinger, and the late Dr. Galt.[50]

As the demand for fruit and ornamental trees and plants increased, nurseries were formed to supply them locally. Edward Dorsey Hobbs and James Wilson Walker formed a partnership in 1852, creating the Evergreen Nurseries on land that Hobbs owned in Anchorage, where they could take advantage of the new Louisville and Frankfort Railroad for distribution.

> They are now ready to fill orders for almost any number and variety of apple, peach, cherry, pear, plum, apricot and quince trees, and have for sale specimens of by far the largest and most various collection of evergreens and other ornamental trees in this vicinity…. Not only the fruit trees, but the ornamental trees and shrubbery in the nursery of these gentlemen, are well worth examining by all persons who have gardens and lawns to stock, or intend to establish orchards. Mr. Hobbs is quite an enthusiast in the production of good fruits, and the embellishments of grounds with evergreens and deciduous trees, while Mr. Walker is a practical nurseryman, from the great nursery of Messrs. Elwanger & Barry, near Rochester, New York, and of course thoroughly understands his business.
>
> Mr. Hobbs…during the past season visited the principal eastern nurseries, and ordered trees of all the good old varieties, and all the best new ones, from which to propagate for stocking their grounds.[51]

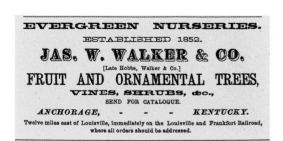

Advertisement. 1872 Louisville directory.

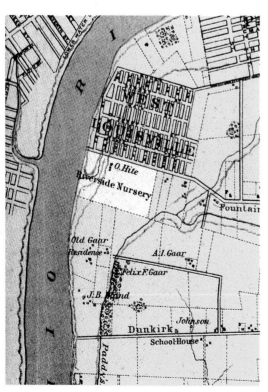

Section from *Louisville and Its Defenses* map, 1865.

ORMSBY HITE'S RIVERSIDE NURSERY is shown on the south side of the Fountain Ferry Road fronting the Ohio River on the 1865 *Louisville and Its Defenses* map. Hite built his residence Fontainebleau on the property about 1848, but landscaping the grounds had begun under a previous owner, Col. Aaron Fontaine. The tract had been called Carter's Ferry before Fontaine purchased it from William Lytle in 1814. According to a family descendant, Charles Thruston Johnson, "the place was laid out in orchards, lawns and grass lands. The house, of substantial construction, faced the Ohio river, where a boat was kept for pleasure and service. A fine cypress avenue opened on what is now Main, and the old 'Fontaine Ferry Road' was a famous drive leading into the country seat."[52] When the road was improved in 1882, *The Courier-Journal* declared, "This will be one of the most beautiful drives for the citizens of Louisville…. The citizens of the county are building the road at their own expense, and its use will be free to those who drive over it…. But few of the citizens have an idea of the excellent qualities of this drive and the beauty of the land."[53] After completion, Jefferson County Court would take over the road's maintenance.

Ormsby Hite died at Fontainebleau in 1876 at the age of 70. The

Fontainebleau about 1870. Files of Samuel W. Thomas.

site was purchased in 1887 by Tony Landenwich and made into a summer resort.

Fontaine Ferry Park had a wealth of choice shade trees when Mr. Landenwich became its owner, and to these he has added over 800 trees of maple, fox-elder, buckeye, North Carolina poplar, oaks, elms, ash, cedars, dogwood, pines, redbud, imported English ash, linden and other favored lawn trees. The Scotch elms forming a great row on the high bank facing the river were planted forty five years ago by Mr. Ormsby Hite. Near the house, which has become popular with summer boarders, the shade is densest and is supplemented with long grape arbors, beneath which are tables, chairs and rustic seats. The handsomely laid out winding walks and drives are of tanbark, giving no dust and becoming, if anything, all the better from falling weather, as this packs the material harder than it is in a dry state. Mud and dust have no place here….

Fontaine Ferry Park is the gateway to the Western Park, which embraces some 170 acres, in addition to some forty acres of river front. A walk or drive of an eighth of a mile from Fontaine Ferry house puts it within the Western Park and lays open before you a tract of land to which nature and topography have given wonderful charms.[54]

Fontaine Ferry Park came into prominence in 1896 as a bicycle racing track.[55] It was being transformed into the amusement park that opened as Fontaine Ferry Park in 1905, when a writer to *The Evening Post* lamented, "It will be a matter of some sentiment and regret that this once beautiful river estate of a Virginia gentleman should end its

Fontaine Ferry Bicycle Track and Grandstand. *The Courier-Journal*, 12 August 1896. Louisville was hosting the League of American Wheelmen.

existence as an up-to-date resort for 'hoi polloi.'"[56] In 1916, the old concrete bicycle racetrack was broken up for construction of a new driveway connecting Shawnee Park with Western Parkway.[57]

⇛ ⇛ ⇛

WOODLAND GARDEN, ONE MILE FROM LOUISVILLE.

THE proprietor of this beautiful Summer Retreat, is now enabled to announce to the public, that the extensive improvements making in the establishment, will be entirely completed by the first of June, at which time he will be prepared to receive and accommodate regular boarders or transient visiters. Since the close of the last season, he has been engaged in improving and erecting additions to the buildings, and in ornamenting his gardens and grounds; and he flatters himself that there is now no establishment of a similar character in the State, that presents greater attractions as a Summer residence, than the WOODLAND GARDEN.

He will be prepared to accommodate about 25 persons during the Summer months, with Boarding and convenient rooms, and has engaged, for the season, the assistance of one of the best French Cooks in the Western country.

His BAR will be at all times supplied with a choice assortment of liquors, and will be attended by a French gentleman, whose time will be devoted to furnishing company with any refreshments required.

He would also inform the public, that his BALL ROOM will be completed on the 31st of the present month, on which occasion a BALL will be given, at 3 o'clock, P. M. under the superintendence of *MR. MATTHIEU.*—On the same evening at half past seven o'clock, there will be a very beautiful exhibition of FIRE WORKS by *MR. MATTHIEU,* which will be repeated every other Tuesday during the season.

Tickets can be obtained at the Hotels of *Major Langhorne* and *Major Throckmorton,* at *Mr. Lynch's Coffee House,* and the Bar of the Woodland Garden.

The Ball Room will be ready for Parties at any time.

The Proprietor has made engagements to give a BARBECUE at the Woodland Garden, on the FOURTH OF JULY next, and every effort will be made to make it equal to any ever given in this State.   J. OLIPHANT.

may 20, 1831.

The Louisville Daily Journal, 26 May 1831. J. Oliphant must have been a representative of William Pickett.

SEVERAL NOTABLE PLEASURE GARDENS attracted visitors, especially in the summer months. In 1827, former blacksmith William Pickett created Woodland Garden, his long-lasting enterprise at the head of Main Street on eight acres of leased land. Hugh Hays would later declare "it was the first pleasure garden in all the Western country."[58]

> He built nice booths all through the grounds, and a beautiful suit of rooms, with a porch or gallery in front for a promenade…. The garden was patronized by first-class citizens. Men, women and children flocked to see the Woodland Garden…. In 1834 Mr. Pickett built a railroad around his Garden, upon which he ran a miniature locomotive, and charged five cents a ride.

In the 1832 Louisville directory, Pickett acknowledged his Woodland Garden: "The Proprietor has the satisfaction to present this to the citizens of Louisville, and transient persons, as not only the nearest retreat from the city, but as the most extensive; affording many acres of land under high cultivation, Groves of native trees and a Garden abounding in all the necessaries and luxuries of life." According to Hugh Hays, Pickett sold out about 1838 to a "Down East sharper" named Lindsey. Under Lindsey's management, Woodland Garden featured an elderly black woman he claimed was 127 years old and had been George Washington's nurse. Lindsey had trained Joyce Heath (or Joice Heth) to carry on a conversation with him about Washington and also placed her on exhibition at the Apollo Hall on Third Street. "The greatest showman on earth, P. T. Barnum, made his appearance at Woodland Garden," Hays recalled. "He heard of Joyce, and found her well-trained by Lindsey and bought her, paying a good sum for her. Joyce Heath was the first traveling show Barnum ever had on the road." Years after she died in 1836, Barnum acknowledged she was only about 90 years old and had never known George Washington. It should be noted that Ralph W. Lindsey was listed in the 1838-1839 city directory at Woodland Garden. He was not listed in the next directory in 1841.

In later years, as nearby Butchertown grew in size, Woodland Garden's clientele became increasingly German. At a reception for General Willich during the Civil War, the garden "presented a beautiful sight, fully lighted as it was with jets of gas beneath the umbrageous elms and primeval trees which grow there."[59]

"While nearly all the larger cities have the advantage of [over] Louisville in the possession of public parks for their crowded population, Louisville has an equal advantage in the possession of numerous and elegant pleasure gardens. There is no place of resort, of a similar character, in any of the Eastern cities to be compared with Woodland Garden for its beauty and accommodations," *The Courier-Journal* related in 1877, when the retreat was under the new ownership of Nellis Borden. "Every vestige of old landmarks has been removed, and in their place has sprung up every improvement that can be desired for the pleasure and comfort of the visitor."[60]

❧ ❧ ❧

Woodland Garden, 1875. George H. Yater, *Two Hundred Years at the Falls of the Ohio*, 107.

TAKING ADVANTAGE OF THE COMPLETION of the Louisville and Portland Canal, Joseph L. Detiste established Elm Tree Garden near his boarding establishment in Shippingport. In May 1829, a young surveying draftsman, Increase Allen Lapham, working on the canal recorded: "Leveled for Mr. Detiste the place for the posts of an amphitheatre or summer house which he is building in a large elm tree near the Bridge which Capt B. Hall requested should be called 'Hall's Tree.'"[61] The

ELM TREE PAVILION.

THE subscriber respectfully informs his friends and the public, that he has erected an establishment at the foot of the canal bridge, as a branch of the Orleans' Coffee House, where they can be accommodated with all kinds of refreshments, ice creams, &c.

Shippingport, june 6—1113ow   J. L. DETISTE.

Louisville Public Advertiser, 6 June 1829.

Basil Hall, "Study of a Forest of Kentucky near Louisville," 10 May 1828. Courtesy of the Lilly Library, University of Indiana. "The trees, also, round Louisville were incomparably finer than any we had seen elsewhere, especially the sycamores. They were not only taller, but, have plenty of space…have grown up with singular beauty." Basil Hall, *Travels in North America* (Edinburgh, 1830), 3: 375.

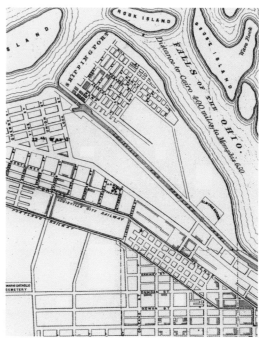

Section of *City Directory Map of Louisville…1866* showing Elm Tree Garden and Shippingport.

Bridge over canal with flag and perhaps the signature tree of Elm Tree Garden at right. By John B. H. Latrobe, 1832. Amon Carter Museum, Fort Worth, Texas.

stone bridge crossing the canal connected Shippingport with Louisville at Eighteenth Street. Lapham noted on 25 June 1829, "Henry Clay rode across the bridge today although it is not entirely finished." According to the *Memorial History of Louisville*, Elm Tree Garden was the site of "amusements of almost any kind, such as horse racing, foot racing, wrestling, shooting at the mark, gander pulling, and if desired, a rough and tumble fight could be had at a moment's notice for the asking."[62] The facility was later improved, but remained subject to flooding.

LYNCH'S GARDEN WAS ESTABLISHED IN 1833 between Main and Market streets, Second and Third streets on a large lot that had belonged to the late Dr. Richard Ferguson, the prominent surgeon who had amputated George Rogers Clark's leg. According to Hugh Hays, the property included Ferguson's "home garden, which was full of choice trees and fine shrubbery.... Mr. Lynch built on the Main-street front a large brick building with a broad entrance to the garden, a number of private rooms, an office, ball-room, billiard-room, parlors, etc.... This garden was only patronized by the upper classes and no commonly-dressed person was allowed to enter."[63] When the proprietor's beautiful wife ran off in 1837, he closed the garden, moved away, and soon died.

MAGNOLIA GARDEN WAS ANOTHER PLEASURE SPOT formerly belonging to a physician, Dr. James Chew Johnston, who had graduated from Princeton and the University of Pennsylvania. His late Greek Revival house was located on the north side of Jefferson Street between Brook and Floyd streets. Reportedly, "the doctor was something of a horticulturist, and the extensive grounds around the Jefferson Street house blossomed with scores of fruit trees and many flowers."[64] "Mr. Sutphen has fitted up the garden on the property of Dr. Johns[t]on, at the head of Jefferson street, in a very comfortable style," *The Louisville Daily Journal* reported. "Mr. Sutphen is particular to exclude all improper persons from the grounds, as his object is to offer inducements to none other than genteel persons. An entrance to the garden has been opened from Market street."[65] The site was adversely impacted when the depot of the Louisville, Cincinnati & Lexington Railroad was built across Jefferson Street in 1850. After the railroad moved to the waterfront, the Johnston property faced the Haymarket.

MAGNOLIA GARDEN.
The undersigned has, during the past year, been engaged in fitting up for the accommodation of the public the handsome Garden formerly belonging to Dr. Johnson, situated near the rail road depot, at the upper end of Jefferson street. The Garden is one of the most delightful spots in the country, and will furnish a most fine and agreeable resort for the ladies and gentlemen of the city. All kinds of refreshments, such as Ice-Creams, Sherbets, Lemonades, and all other Confections and delicacies of the season will always be kept on hand.
may 7 d1m&w4   J. SUTPHEN, Proprietor.

The Louisville Daily Journal, 13 May 1850.

❧ ❧ ❧

"WE URGED UPON THE PUBLIC ATTENTION, sometime ago, the importance of planting trees in the streets as a sanitary measure," *The Louisville Daily Journal* stated in May 1850. "As a measure of scarcely less importance, we urge upon our readers now the great value of ornamenting the grounds about dwellings with beautiful shrubbery."[66] With this introduction, the *Journal* began a report on local florist Edward Wilson and his recent trip to England to purchase roses and dwarf fruit trees from Thomas Rivers, the recognized horticultural authority. "Mr. Wilson…purchased of Rivers only such as were not in this country, and is engaged now in propagating these new varieties…. Roses of Rivers's collection, obtained by Mr. Wilson, are some fifty varieties, which, added to his previous collection, makes one of the finest assortments of the rose to be found in this country."

The *Journal* pointed out the recent introduction of Japanese lilies "among the beautiful gems" for ornamenting property. "No front grounds of dwellings should be without these floral beauties." To ensure that the buyer was receiving the variety "true to that name," the *Journal* admonished, "The proper place to buy plants is at the garden of one we know. If a mistake is made there, it may be rectified."

Edward Wilson had leased his garden location near the Louisville Marine Hospital, on the southwest corner of Floyd and Walnut streets from Henry Clay, Jr., beginning in 1839.

E. WILSON'S GARDEN,
Between Floyd and East, on
Walnut Street,—Louisville, Ky.
Where he keeps for sale a choice collection of EVERGREENS, TREES, GRAPE VINES, SHRUBS, &c. and a great variety of ROSES and GREEN HOUSE PLANTS.
☞ All orders sent through the Post Office will be promptly attended to.

Louisville directory for 1851-1852.

EDMUND FRANCIS LEE INTRODUCES RURAL CEMETERY CONCEPT (1838); DESIGNS CAVE HILL CEMETERY (1847); IMPROVES BEARGRASS CREEK (1855); AND PLANS FOR WHARF AND HARBOR (1856)

AMERICA'S FIRST PASTORAL PARKS WERE PICTURESQUE cemeteries, attractive destinations established in rural settings, funded by proceeds from sales of rights to bury. The acknowledged prototype for such cemeteries is also the most famous in the world. The Cemetery of Père-Lachaise opened on the outskirts of Paris, France, in 1804.[67] The first American town plan incorporating a cemetery acknowledged to be based upon Père-Lachaise was designed for William Bullock, who intended to create a new town around Elmwood Hall, his estate on the south side of the Ohio River, now the small town of Ludlow, Ky. John B. Papworth prepared the layout of Hygeia in 1827, four years before the first rural American cemetery.[68]

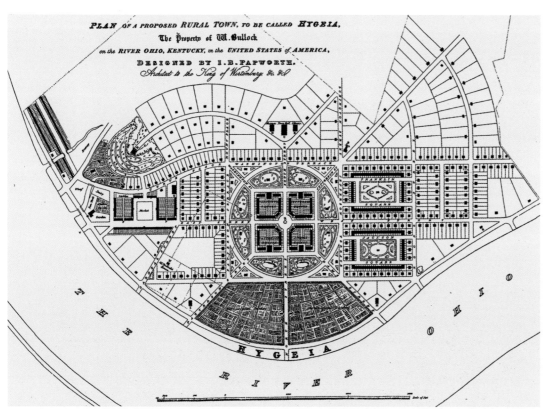

Plan of Hygeia by J. B. Papworth. *Sketch of a Journey through the Western States* (London, 1827).[69]

Beginning with Mount Auburn outside Boston in 1831, rural cemeteries took advantage of the topography in creating scenic places for burial and contemplation of the departed. They were this country's first parks. Laurel Hill in Philadelphia (1836) and Green-Wood in Brooklyn (1838) followed the creative pattern of burying in nature.[70] Remarkably, in 1838, civil engineer Edmund Francis Lee published a pamphlet, *Walnut Ridge Cemetery, near Jeffersonville, with some Rules, and Regulations, and an Essay on Public Rural Cemeteries.*

A place of burial may be made a delightful place of resort, and an embellishment to a town of no ordinary character, by being located in the midst of rural scenery, and by affording susceptibilities for the tasteful display of works of art and offerings dedicated to the memory of the dead. Such a place would become, by these means, an object gratifying to the pride of citizens and attractive to strangers; but what is of vastly greater importance, it would become in due time a school of virtue, teaching by the examples of the dead, a nursery of all the pious and tender emotions of the heart, on the due cultivation of which, the preservation of social order of religion, and of our dearest privileges mainly depend.[71]

Lee was born in Hartford, Connecticut, in 1800, and nothing is known of his upbringing or education.[72] While in Cincinnati in 1835, he published a *Map of the Mammoth Cave, accompanied with notes*, which stimulated interest in developing the natural phenomenon near Bowling Green, Kentucky, as a tourist attraction.[73] The civil engineer was first listed in the Louisville directory of 1845-1846.[74] In May 1846, the Louisville Common Council selected Lee as City Architect over prominent architect John Stirewalt.[75]

In November 1846, the City of Louisville set aside a portion of Cave Hill Farm, which it had purchased in 1832 anticipating the future need for burial ground in the eastern expansion of the city and the potential revenues from rock quarries on the property. The designated site was on the north side of Bardstown Road adjacent to the Eastern Burying Ground, established in 1843. The new cemetery's design was expected to be set out in the conventional grid manner.[76] The committee appointed to establish the cemetery was authorized "to call upon the City Engineer or elsewhere" to survey the property set aside.[77] Lee prepared a detailed report of his cemetery proposal and a plat, which the committee requested the mayor to have "placed in a frame, for its preservation." The layout of the cemetery was like none other in Louisville. The concept for perpetual maintenance was

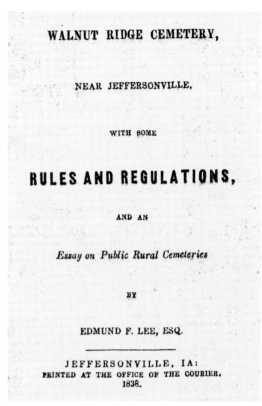

Title page of Edmund F. Lee's 15-page pamphlet on Walnut Ridge Cemetery. The Filson Historical Society.

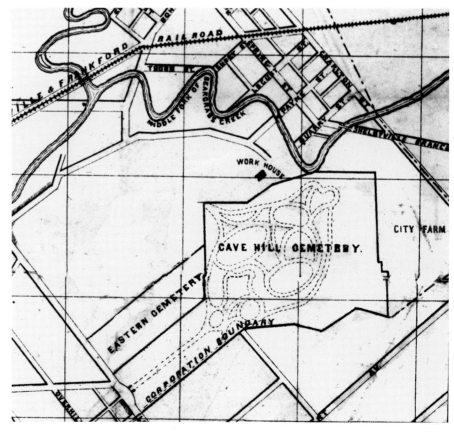

Edmund F. Lee's layout of Cave Hill Cemetery as depicted on W. Lee White's *A New Map of Louisville* (1856).

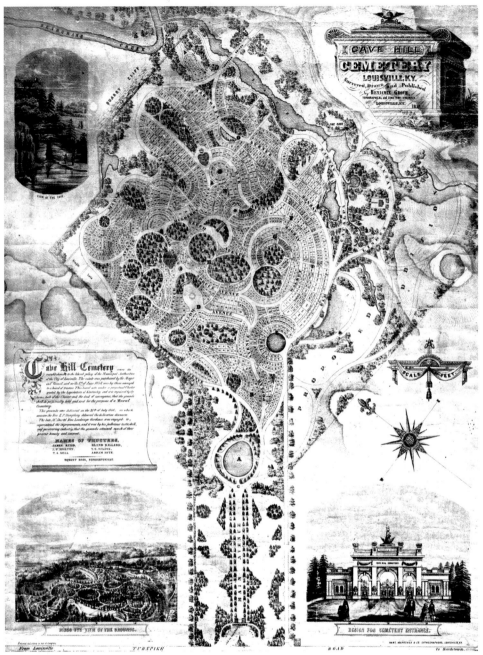

New map of Cave Hill Cemetery published by Benjamin Grove several months after Edmund F. Lee died. Lithographic print, courtesy of Cave Hill Cemetery.

novel also. Families could set aside large plots for future need, with part of the funds from their acquisition of burial rights being invested for the eventual time when the cemetery was full and income from burials ceased. Heretofore, when cemeteries filled up, they soon became derelict, overgrown, and an eyesore.[78]

By the time Cave Hill Cemetery was dedicated 25 July 1848, burials had already taken place. The first superintendent, David Ross, did not report to work until August, so presumably Lee supervised the laying out of the cemetery.[79] Little is known about David Ross, who was born in Scotland in 1811, and while in Ohio had married Nancy Clarke.[80] She returned to Cincinnati after Ross died 21 August 1856. He was replaced by his younger brother, Robert, who reportedly had been trained at Chatsworth, the estate of the sixth duke of Devonshire.[81] Quite possibly, David Ross had also come under the tutelage of Joseph Paxton, Chatsworth's famous landscaper whose Birkenhead Park in Liverpool influenced Frederick Law Olmsted's Central Park.[82]

One must look elsewhere for Greensward's [Central Park's] precedents. They are found among the picturesque rural cemeteries. Brooklyn's Green-Wood and Philadelphia's Laurel Hill introduced landscaping features such as winding paths, naturalistic ponds, and secluded groves. The other precedent was Paxton's Birkenhead Park, with its carefully contrived vistas, its contrast of meadows and copses, its subordination of artifice to the scenic effects of vegetation and water, and above all, its being a single, unified design.

Witold Rybczynski, *A Clearing in the Distance* (New York, 1999), 168.

Edmund F. Lee was appointed to fill a vacancy as Louisville's city engineer in the summer of 1855.[83] For decades the waterfront entrance to the city had been fouled and made unattractive by Beargrass Creek's confluence with the Ohio between Third and Fourth streets. "There is scarcely a village of ten thousand inhabitants, on any Western river, which does not offer a better presentation than Louisville," noted the Chamber of Commerce's *Commercial Review*. "A few miserable shanties, occupied by mock-auctioneers and clothiers, alternating with board-yards and filthy coffee-houses, make the river front of a great city; and convey to the traveler anything but a pleasant view, or an agreeable idea of the port at which he has arrived.... A little while since, it was necessary to thread dirty alleys and clamber over muddy hills, in an unpaved part of the city, in order to reach the only landing place for steamboats. For a city which professes to be the half-way house between the North and South; and which hopes to reap the pecuniary reward of its geographical position, this is certainly shameful."[84] By the end of 1855, Lee had completed construction of the Beargrass Cut-off, which diverted water from the three courses of Beargrass Creek into the Ohio River east of the city. While the Cut-off was intended to allow the wharf area to be improved, little was accomplished, although Lee did make the necessary plans.

Lee was elected for a one-year stint as city engineer the following January. He tendered his resignation 6 November 1856; less than a year later he died of cholera.[85] His obituary said he was 45 years old, while his headstone indicates he was slightly older.[86] In either case, his early demise was a loss to the community.

Section O, Cave Hill Cemetery. 2011 by Samuel W. Thomas.

A decade after his death, the *Louisville Daily Courier* reported:

> We have recently looked over a plan of improvement for the city wharf, prepared by the late Edmund F. Lee, an able civil engineer of this city, and we must confess we were struck with admiration of its simplicity, its boldness, its economy and its perfect adaptation to the wants of our city in its greatest possible future expansion.
>
> The plan of Mr. Lee is truly grand. It proposes to make a noble wharf, suited to all stages of water, extending from Preston street down to about Tenth or Eleventh, removing a portion of the upper end of the canal and bringing into play several squares of wharf front which have been nearly entirely abandoned and are practically worthless. Instead of our present disgraceful, irregular, contracted front of the city, it gives us over a mile of as noble a wharf as the country contains, always ready for the requirements of business at any stage of the river.

Lee's concept also called for the creation of a harbor. The stone quarried in that process would be used to wall off the harbor and to pave the wharf. While the newspaper enthusiastically endorsed the project, it did not go forward.

Above: J. T. Palmatary's 1855 bird's-eye view of Louisville, made just before Beargrass Creek was diverted, depicts a Third Street bridge that does not appear on contemporary maps. Below: The Second Street bridge to the east (left) was illustrated in Oscar Comettant's journal of his 1859 trip to America.

4
PRESTON'S WOODS (1852) AND CORN ISLAND (1853): EARLY PARK PROPOSALS

AN EARLY LOUISVILLE PARK PROPOSAL was an area at the head of Broadway commonly known as Preston's Woods. The area was in the middle of Col. William Preston's 1,000-acre land grant, on land inherited by his son, Maj. William Preston, and his son, Gen. William Preston.[87] By 1852, its reputation had been sullied to the extent a writer calling himself Randolph suggested in *The Louisville Daily Democrat* that the city purchase the site and convert it into a park.[88]

There are many people in this city, among whom, no doubt, are most of the councilmen, who are not aware of the bacchanalian festivals held every Sabbath in Preston's woods. Parties of young boys, from ten years old and upwards, resort thither once a week to swill beer and guzzle gin and brandy, until they are unable to get home in the evening without help. We need not say one word of the evil effect such proceedings will have on the morals of the rising generation. The top of the hill is crowded with men, women and children drinking, while oaths and obscene language seem to be the natural mother tongue…. It is fast becoming the resort of drunkards, strumpets, and others of the lowest portion of the community, to the total exclusion of respectable people; and these collect there who think of nothing but satisfying their own hellish appetites, regardless of others. We want to see a stop put to these proceedings….

We think it would be an excellent plan for the city to buy all that portion north of Broadway, turn it into a park, and adopt the regulations necessary to make a park a place where innocent pleasures can be enjoyed. If the city does not see proper to buy and make the park, then we hope the mayor, as the head of the police, will cause these proceedings to be stopped. We judge it only necessary to call his attention to the fact—knowing that he lives too far down Broadway to visit the woods—to have him use effective means for suppression of this evil. [James S. Speed, whose term as mayor had begun several weeks before on 26 April 1852, resided on the south side of Broadway between Eighth and Ninth streets.]

I can recall, when there was no street pavement on Broadway except each side of a nice little park in that street, between Sixth and Seventh Streets.[89]

Alfred Pirtle, "Reminiscences of Louisville," a paper read before The Filson Club, 1 March 1917.

Preston's Woods highlighted on section of G. T. Bergmann's *Map of Jefferson County, Kentucky*, 1858. The Phoenix Hill Park and Brewery later occupied part of Preston's Woods.

Preston's Woods as developed, about 1903. Samuel W. Thomas files.

Preston's Woods continued as a public gathering place. In his unsuccessful campaign for the presidency in 1860 against Abraham Lincoln, Senator Stephen A. Douglas spoke at Preston's Woods, where "the people thronged…by the thousands. For two hours the people continued to gather, and when Senator Douglas alighted at the outskirts of the dense assembly he could hardly penetrate to the stand, to which he was lifted by the willing hands of his friends, when he at last reached it." Douglas was welcomed by James Speed.[90]

Early in 1861, an estimated 8,000-10,000 persons gathered at Preston's Woods to witness the execution by hanging of David Caution, a slave convicted of attempting to rape Catherine Swanson. "It was not a pleasant scene, but was barbarous and a morally unhealthy exhibition, the like of which we trust may never again be enacted in Louisville…. We must say, for the credit of the city," the *Daily Louisville Democrat* reported, "the major portion of the crowd was of the lower classes—the ignorant and depraved…. But the most disgusting part of the scene was the presence of hundreds of women, come to witness the death struggles of a man condemned for a foul outrage upon one of their own sex."[91]

William Carnes Kendrick, who was born in 1852, recollected the location of Preston's Woods.[92]

> Suppose we place ourselves for the time being at the bridge that spans Beargrass Creek on Broadway, just at the foot of the rise in the land toward Cave Hill Cemetery…. This hill or rising ground was then a thickly wooded tract known as, "Preston's Woods." Through the center a deep cut was made, with clay-bank sides. At the bottom of this cut was a real country dirt road, just wide enough for the passing of two vehicles, side by side. This road led to the entrance of Cave Hill and on to the country beyond.
>
> Preston's Woods remained as a public gathering place until the area was developed.

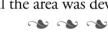

ACCORDING TO ANDREW COWAN, young City Councilman and lawyer Reuben T. Durrett urged in 1853 that a park be created on Corn Island in order to protect its trees from being cut down and that trees be planted and a retaining wall built to save its soil from continued erosion.[93] Unfortunately no formal resolution to that effect can be found in the Common Council minutes before Durrett resigned in October 1853. Several years later, the *New Map of Louisville* (1856) showed Corn Island as the proposed location of the Louisville Water Works. Neither idea was feasible, and the island continued to erode.

Section from *New Map of Louisville* (1856). "I observed the little island of about seven acres oposite to whare the Town of Lewisville now stands seldom or never was intirly covered by the water." George Rogers Clark observed in his Memoir when he landed with troops and some families late in May 1778. Before the families moved to the mainland, a crop of corn was planted, providing the place with a lasting name. Later the outcropping was quarried for stone and excavated for cement before the river's level was raised and the island's remnants disappeared.

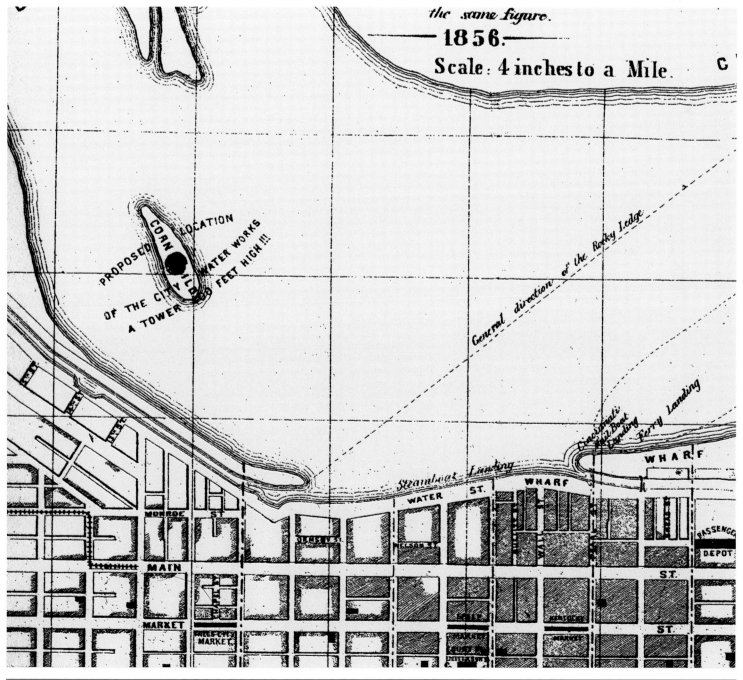

SITE OF THE FIRST CATHOLIC CEMETERY BECOMES AN ATTRACTION: DU PONT ARTESIAN WELL (1857)

THE OLD CATHOLIC GRAVEYARD on the west side of Tenth Street south of Water Street was abandoned in 1835 and bodies were reinterred in the Catholic section of the new city cemetery on Jefferson Street.[94] The old graveyard site was depicted as cleared on Palmatary's 1855 bird's-eye view of Louisville.

Section of Palmatary's 1855 bird's-eye view showing the old Catholic chapel and graveyard (outlined in green) in block between Tenth and Eleventh, Main and Water streets above the river bank at the head of the Portland canal.

The site became part of the Cromie paper manufacturing complex that was taken over by Charles Irénée du Pont, Jr., and his cousin, Alfred Victor du Pont.[95] They began boring a 2,086-ft artesian well in April 1857 that rivaled any in the world, producing 230 gallons per minute and a 170-ft high fountain. "The artesian well in this city is daily visited by hundreds," the *Louisville Daily Democrat* reported 26 August 1858. After analysis of the mineral water, Louisville's distinguished chemist J. Lawrence Smith, M.D., confirmed its medicinal virtues, which enhanced the artesian well's regional appeal.[96]

"The crowds of people who daily visit Dupont's famous Artesian well will be glad to learn that the sparkling waters are soon to gush through a graceful fountain," the *Louisville Daily Courier* reported 18 June 1859.

A commission was given some time since to Chas. S. Snead, of the Market street Architectural Foundry, to execute something which should combine utility with grace, and serve to gratify the eye, while conveying the health-giving fluid from earth's deep recesses to upper air. The designer has been highly successful in bending the stubborn iron to his wishes, and as the whole was cast, the difficulties encountered will be understood.

The harmony of the design is perfect.

The structure stands in a basin about twenty feet in diameter, and is tastefully ornamented with lily leaves, frogs and turtles. Surmounting this is a shell-like basin, six feet in diameter, over the scalloped edges of which the water drips in numerous tiny streams. Out of this expands a huge lily cup, which is encrusted with leaves and lesser flowers. Each flower shoots forth a jet of its own, while from the center of the large cup the main stream gushes to a height of sixty feet, and fills the air with diamond spray.

With this beautiful fountain, and famous Uncle Charley [Snead], whose sayings are everywhere quoted, the Artesian [well] will become the rendezvous of the town.

The artesian well was delineated in an open courtyard of the Louisville Paper Company on an 1892 Sanborn map. Sometime later, it disappeared.[97]

Du Pont Artesian Well and Louisville Paper Mill, looking south from Water Street. Richard Deering, *Louisville: Commercial Manufacturing and Social Advantages* (Louisville, 1859). The building at left (east) had recently been erected.

6

THE ORMSBY AND DUMESNIL FAMILIES' CEDAR HILL PARK AND FLORAL PARK (1858)

THE LOUISVILLE DAILY COURIER ASSERTED in the spring of 1854, "The time has arrived for the adornment of the grounds about city residences." The paper was quick to point out the "common mistake" of planting evergreens in the city. While in the country such plants were "an essential appendage to the beauty of the place," in the city where "pure air is exiled" and "where it is loaded in spring, summer and fall with pulverized limestone and at all times with the abominable soot of Pittsburg coal, the evergreen plants should be almost wholly avoided…. In a city these soon become encased with a cement made of Macadamized limestone, ashes and soot and a dreary looking thing this cement makes of the evergreen…. The true embellishments for city grounds are deciduous plants. They shed and renew their leaves often enough to retain a beautiful foliage through the spring, summer and autumn."[98]

While some residents began to take an interest in landscaping their yards, other spaces were becoming sites for outdoor recreation. "The great foot-ball ground for many years was between Fourth and Fifth on Chestnut," lawyer Patrick Joyes wrote in 1868 about times three decades before.[99] "I can't remember back of the days when the old Hope distillery on Main about Thirteenth or Fourteenth was in ruin, though I have often got foot-ball bladders from it when it was a slaughter house and I skated on its ponds."[100]

Our swimming place, when we didn't go to the river, was the "deep-hole" in Beargrass, near Chestnut or Broadway…. We played "shinny" then in the streets, a game now tabooed, perhaps wisely, and as we grew older, rang door bells, changed signs, broke windows, and indulged in all the little refinements of the day, to say nothing about "playing hookey" on all important occasions…. One of the brag skaters of the day who could cut the pigeon wing and all the didoes with the most ease and grace, was Bill Daniel, now one of our amiable city fathers. I saw him at the skating park last winter, and *old* and *stiff* as he is, very few can beat him now…. Do you remember how Jim Chambers used to play "hit-ball?" What a terror he was in the game with that "southpaw" of his.

"The boys of a neighborhood used to play the game of Cricket with a paddle borrowed from somebody's picket fence and a crudely fashioned wicket and a rag ball," R. J. Meaney would recall.[101] It is not known how long the old British game had been played locally, but it was popular in 1866 when reportedly the first match was played in Louisville.[102] The following summer, the Kentucky Cricket Club took on the Louisville Base-ball Club at Cedar Hill Park.

The Louisville Base-ball Club was organized 10 June 1858.[103] "The lovers of this interesting and invigorating game are invited to be present" at "a match this afternoon at the grounds corner of Fourth and Kentucky," the *Louisville Daily Democrat* announced August 26th. The Louisville Base-ball Club and the Eclipse Club, formed shortly afterwards, met in match play in September 1858 at Cedar Hill, a private park provided by the Ormsby and Dumesnil families, bounded by Fourth and Fifth streets, Ormsby and Park avenues, before "a large attendance of spectators, including over one hundred beautiful ladies, who lent the charm of their presence to the exhilarating scene."[104]

The development of the sport was rapid. "If our readers do not suppose that the game of base ball is not an epidemic in this city, we will inform them that it has 'broken out' badly, and is on the increase," *The Louisville Daily Democrat* wrote in the fall of 1866. "Louisville now boasts of upwards of forty regularly organized base ball clubs. The epidemic first broke out among the young clerks, and others who had nothing else to do; but it soon spread far and near, and seems to be confining itself at present chiefly among children."[105] The next summer, when the National Club of Washington came to play the Louisville Club at Cedar Hill, the *Daily Journal* remarked that baseball "has now undoubtedly established itself as the National game of our country." Despite the locals' loss, the newspaper reported that "the game yesterday was the finest ever played in our city."[106] Extra cars were added to the Fourth-Street line, but they could not accommodate the crowd going out. "Inside the grounds there must have been at least seven or eight thousand persons."

Sally Yandell wrote her brother in August 1867: "Base Ball is now the fashionable amusement here & most of the gentlemen belong to some Club & the girls are strong partisans and most of them sport cockades & badges of some Club when on the grounds. Cedar Hill Park is now used for this purpose; the Dumesnils have moved away & the grounds have been much improved.[107] A large swimming pool

We have repeatedly noticed with pleasure the increasing interest being manifested by our young men in manly exercises. It augurs well for an elevated and improved *status* in our future population. Kentuckians, famous once for their remarkable physiques, have been gradually dwindling in size, appearance and activity, until it seemed as if we were approaching a Lilliputian generation. This revival of athletic sports, especially among the youth of our cities, is worthy of the highest commendation. It will change the pallor of the cheek to the roseate hue of health—will give muscle to the limbs—strength and energy to the whole frame, and have a happy tendency upon the intellect. None knew better the invigorating and healthful influence of public games than the old Greeks and Romans, and so long as they cultivated these exercises in the open air, they raised men, not puny and effeminate things.

"Out Door Sports." *Louisville Daily Courier*, 24 September 1858.

Floral Park Concerts.

These promenade concerts, which proved such a delightful feature last summer, will commence again this evening for another season. The music is to be furnished by Prof. Moebius' orchestra.

"Amusements." *The Daily Louisville Commercial*, 12 June 1874.

"The red ball is up!" "The red flags are on the street cars!" Such will be the exclamations this morning of hundreds of our citizens. The pond looked like a sea of glass by moonlight last night, but it was not deemed sufficiently strong to support a large crowd. It will be all right this morning, and the jam on the street will be almost equal to Broadway, New York.

"Skating at Cedar Hill To-Day and To-Night." *Louisville Daily Courier*, 10 January 1868. Justin Martin notes in *Genius of Place: The Life of Frederick Law Olmsted* (Cambridge, 2011), 152, that in 1858 when the ice on the lake in Central Park in New York "was thick enough for skating, a red ball was hoisted."

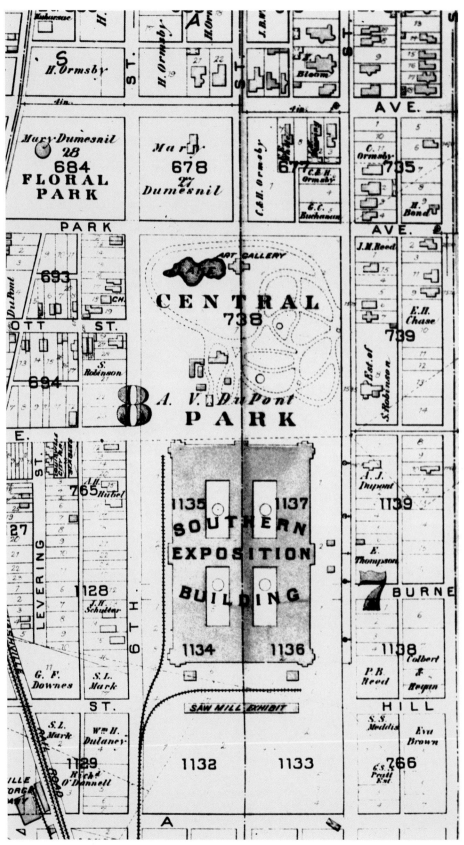

Floral Park and former site of Cedar Hill to the east. *Atlas of the City of Louisville. Ky.*, 1884.

for ladies has been made in the Children's Park & some of the girls are as crazy on the subject of swimming as they were last winter on skating."[108] Only days after Miss Yandell described Cedar Hill Park as the seat of baseball, it was the scene of a cricket match. Despite the loss of the Kentucky Cricket Club to the Louisville Base-ball Club, *The Louisville Daily Journal* thought cricket was quite a worthy game, combining "science, healthful exercise, and rational amusement to a degree unexcelled by any other outdoor pastime. We are glad to note its growing popularity in Louisville."[109]

When the Ormsbys developed their Cedar Hill tract into residential lots, Mary Ormsby Dumesnil and husband Henry A. Dumesnil turned their nearby block between Ormsby and Park avenues and Sixth and Seventh streets into Floral Park, listed for the first time in the 1869 city directory. W. C. Shaw was listed as superintendent and William Ross as horticulturist. The next year Stephen O'Connell had taken over both positions.

By 1875, Cedar Hill Park and Floral Park were not listed in the directory, but may have been open on a limited basis. *The Courier-Journal* described Floral Park after its demise. "In former years, it was the only fashionable resort of the kind accessible, and was one of the most comfortably arranged parks in the country. The grounds were always kept in faultless condition, the trees and hedges neatly trimmed, the lake supplied with pure, fresh water, while an abundance of rare and fragrant flowers made it a most attractive spot."[110] Floral Park reportedly closed about 1880, but in 1887, the city accepted the offer by H. A. Dumesnil for the use of the grounds for five years.[111]

Croquet sets advertised for sale in *The Courier-Journal* in May 1876. Croquet became popular after the Civil War as a lawn sport both sexes could play together.

7
WATER WORKS PARK (1860)

"THE SCENERY ABOUT LOUISVILLE, THOUGH NOT GRAND, is strikingly beautiful," Richard Deering pointed out in his 1859 treatise on the city. During the brief period when Deering and fellow Methodist preacher Drummond Welburn operated a real estate and collections agency bearing their names, Deering authored a little-known but significant monograph, *Louisville: Her Commercial, Manufacturing and Social Advantages*, the city's first illustrated history and contemporary description. "Between the river and the hill, above the city, there is a beautiful plain….The hill back of this plain presents a feature of great beauty, which is much enhanced by farm-houses, improved grounds, and the great reservoir of the water-works. The reservoir crowns the top of this hill, one mile above the city, and when completed will, with its terraced walks, grounds, fountains, and lakes, rival Fairmount."[112]

The centerpiece of what would become Philadelphia's huge Fairmount Park was the classically designed and picturesquely landscaped municipal waterworks established along the Schuylkill River from which water was pumped to reservoirs on top of Faire Mount, now the site of the Philadelphia Museum of Art. Construction of that facility began in 1812, based upon drawings by Frederick C. Graff, Sr., who had served as chief draftsman for Benjamin Henry Latrobe, designer of Philadelphia's first waterworks.[113] After Graff converted the second waterworks from steam to water power in the early 1830s, public gardens were added, along with stairways to viewing areas around the reservoir.

> The south garden was laid out with geometrically ordered walks and plantings, a marble fountain was placed at the center, and ornamental railings were erected along the retaining wall and on the walkway that led up the side of the hill to the reservoir, with a gazebo built on a resting platform halfway up.[114]

Philadelphia's Fairmount Waterworks became a tourist attraction as well as a prototype for municipal systems throughout the country, keeping engineer Graff, and later his son, in demand as consultants.

The City of Louisville authorized the creation of a municipal waterworks in 1832. The first site selected, a sand hill between Main and Market streets, Preston and Floyd streets, was rejected when the city retained an experienced hydraulic engineer, Albert G. Stein, who was building a waterworks in Nashville. Stein had augmented his Prussian education studying in Philadelphia before being retained by Lynchburg, Virginia, to establish its water system in 1825.[115] That led to a similar project in Richmond before moving to Nashville.[116] In Louisville, after taking "the level of the city," he fixed on the square between Washington and Franklin, and Clay and Shelby streets. The desired land was purchased and the city accepted Stein's plan and drawings. The project got underway, but funding for its completion was not forthcoming.[117] "This project was very soon abandoned, but whether from the pressure of the times or from the opposition of many of the citizens does not appear in any record of the period," Ben Casseday wrote in his 1852 *History of Louisville*.

A subsequent plan was devised in 1846 by Frederick Erdmann of Philadelphia, who proposed supplying a district within First and Tenth streets, Water and Walnut streets, from a 22-million gallon reservoir located near the Blind Asylum. Water would be pumped from the Ohio River. The private water company chartered to construct the system wanted the works to use power generated by the Falls. Erdmann rejected the idea and his concept was abandoned.

A decade later, Louisville employed T. R. Scowden, "justly known for his ability and integrity," who had built the system at Cleveland, "said to be the best in the Union."[118]

The site for the Louisville waterworks was finally settled in March 1857, a year after a map of the city showed the proposed location on Corn Island at the east end of the Falls of the Ohio.[119] This area, however, was polluted by Beargrass Creek, which flowed into the Ohio between Third and Fourth streets. Theodore R. Scowden's first smart decision was to select a site along the Ohio River above (east of) the new Beargrass Creek cutoff where polluted water was discharged into the Ohio.

From Scowden's site above the Beargrass Creek cutoff, water was pumped from the Ohio River station at Zorn Avenue to a reservoir on the hill now occupied by the

W. Lee White, *A New Map of Louisville, Ky.*, 1856.

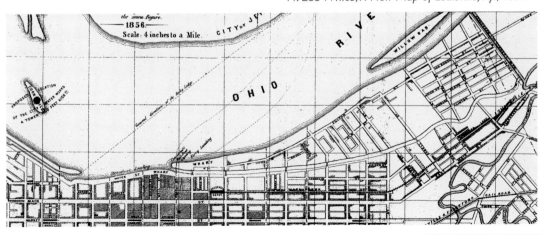

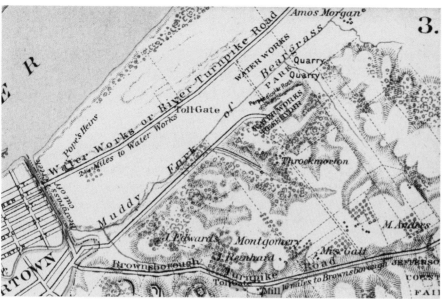

Section showing Water Works Park. *Louisville and Its Defenses*, 1864-1865.

Veterans Administration Hospital. Charles Whittlesey (1808-1886) reported in an 1868 paper to the Association for the Advancement of Science that T. R. Scowden had discovered a cave containing a number of human bones, a stone axe, pestle, and a flint arrowhead while constructing the reservoir. The date of the find, however, was noted as 1853, which predated Scowden's arrival in Louisville by several years. Whittlesey also stated: "Below the cliff there was an ancient Indian burying ground, in which many graves and human bones were exposed while digging the trench for the main inlet pipe of the water-works."[120]

An 1860 description of the Louisville waterworks, by then in operation, noted that "ninety acres of land, including and adjoining the reservoir site, have been reserved for public purposes." A splendid fountain was planned that would "throw a jet of water one hundred feet in height."

View from the reservoir bluff by Joseph Krementz about 1885. Mrs. John Cody Collection, University of Louisville Photographic Archives.

These grounds are to be laid out under the direction of a landscape engineer, and it is contemplated so to ornament the grounds with trees and shrubbery as to furnish a park and pleasure grounds, which will supply a need that has long been seriously felt by our citizens.[121]

According to the Louisville Water Company's *Second Annual Report* (1860):

The Reservoir is located on a perpendicular cliff of rock, ninety feet high, presenting a bold and rugged front of several hundred feet extent, overlaid with ten feet of earth…. Around the Reservoir the lands are undulating, covered with forest trees, and are susceptible of the highest improvement at a comparatively small expense. Thus improved it cannot fail to become a most attractive place of public resort to both citizens and strangers who may be in quest of fresh air, beautiful scenery, and relaxation from the cares of business, and the heat, turmoil, and bustle of a crowded city….

Under the cliff there are forty acres of table land intended for a Park, to be laid out in walks and drives similar to the Engine House grounds, in the centre of which a fountain will be erected that will play a jet one hundred feet high.

The *Fourth Annual Report* (1 January 1862) commented: "Last spring the work of improving the grounds was commenced, by planting trees, sowing the land in grass, laying out and partly grading some of the principal drives, partly excavating two localities for lakes, building a fountain, etc., etc., but for financial reasons, this work was prosecuted only during part of the season, and was left in a safe condition, but far from completion." Even in an uncompleted state, the grounds attracted crowds in the summer months.

In a 23 May 1863 letter to the editor of *The Louisville Daily Journal*, the writer pointed out three places where people would congregate when business was closed—Southern Park, Cave Hill Cemetery, and Eastern Park adjoining the reservoir. He suggested that the reservoir's rocky bluff be made into features supplied by water from the reservoir, using "these basins to be the heads of the fountains at the base of the hill," which would "constitute the entrance to the Park and be adorned with walks, shrubbery, and fountains." He concluded: "Such an addition and improvement would make Eastern Park one of the most beautiful in the country."

One can assume the layout of the park grounds was placed in the

Ca. 1875 view of water works complex. Joseph Krementz Collection, University of Louisville Photographic Archives.

hands of the Water Company's talented engineer, Theodore R. Scowden, who had designed the pumping station, later to be designated a National Historical Landmark. Water Works Park and the "perpendicular rock" bluff were delineated on the 1864-1865 *Louisville and Its Defenses* map. For some reason, perhaps strategic, the pumping station buildings were not depicted.

William C. Kendrick, who was born in 1852, recalled excursions to the area.[122]

> Mellwood Avenue of today was, in the years of which we speak, an ordinary dirt road. Continuing over this road through the low land which lay at the foot of the wooded hill country to the right, we soon came to a sharp turn which leads to the top of the hill, on which was located the first reservoir of the Louisville Water Company, surrounded by a protecting iron fence. From this elevation a marvelous view can be had of the Ohio River far to the right and left, and across the broad expanse of the water can be seen the hills of Indiana. May I stay our trip just here to say that in the groves of the hillside to which I refer, during the summer seasons we had our community outings, the means of transportation then being the old-fashioned furniture cars or wagons, horse drawn. These wagons had placed in them for such occasions long benches, on each side, and could accommodate from twenty to thirty people. You understand, these wagons were used for transporting furniture from one house to another during the moving season.
>
> Again looking from the reservoir we see below us at the foot of the hill what was then called, Reservoir Park. It was one of the three or four small parks in and about Louisville, and was considered quite a beautiful spot.

Reservoir when used by the Louisville Country Club as a swimming pool. Courtesy of William J. Adolph.

8

BENJAMIN GROVE TRANSFORMS OAKLAND CEMETERY INTO SOUTHERN PARK (1860)

WITH CEMETERIES EXISTING IN LOUISVILLE'S eastern and western sections, the City purchased 82.5 acres in the south end from Thomas Browne and his wife, Adelia Shipp Browne, in 1851.[123] In June, the Board of Aldermen examined a plat prepared by surveyor James W. Henning showing "the best disposition that could be made of the ground, laying it off with wide avenues & in hollow squares so that all the lots are easily accessible." The special committee to which the matter had been referred thought "the plan of laying it off in squares" was "preferable to having serpentine or circular walks on the score of economy and at the same time with proper taste in the arrangement of the walks and lots by trees and shrubbery it can be made very beautiful."[124] A sexton's cottage was erected.[125] In April 1854, the mayor was directed "to have the Southern Cemetery opened for Interments and to sell on the best terms a portion of the lots set aside for private use according to the plan made out by J. W. Henning."[126] A receiving vault was designed by the architectural firm of Stancliff & Vogdes, but apparently before it could be built, the Board of Aldermen had reservations about the cemetery's location and its "forming a continuous obstruction for a great distance to the extension of streets or Roads in a Southern direction." The mayor was requested to suspend the sale of lots and to report to the General Council "upon what terms a more suitable piece of ground can be purchased for the purposes of a Cemetery."[127] The aldermen evidently again reversed themselves, however, and in September 1855, the Southern Cemetery was chartered as Oakland Cemetery.[128] The city's attorney and engineer were requested to ascertain the feasibility of opening Third Street from Kentucky Street south to the cemetery. In just two years, though, the Common Council requested the mayor to sell the Oakland Cemetery property. The aldermen, however, were reluctant to do so.[129]

Although no record of burials in Oakland Cemetery exists, the sexton reported on interments to the Board of Aldermen in August 1857.[130] The Common Council kept pushing for the sale, and finally, in 1860, the City "set apart the land known as Oakland Cemetery

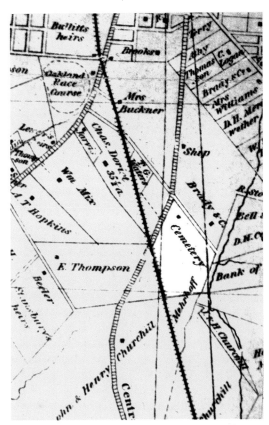

Section of Bergmann's 1858 map of Jefferson County showing cemetery site. Central Plank Road, later known as National Turnpike, became an extension of Third Street. The Oakland Race Course is in upper left.

for the use and benefit of the Louisville House of Refuge," specifying that its managers "shall have disinterred all the persons now buried in Oakland Cemetery and shall have reinterred them in Cave Hill Cemetery," and "ornament and embellish" not less than 40 acres for a public park.[131]

Benjamin Grove's headstone in Section O, Cave Hill Cemetery, 2011, by Samuel W. Thomas.

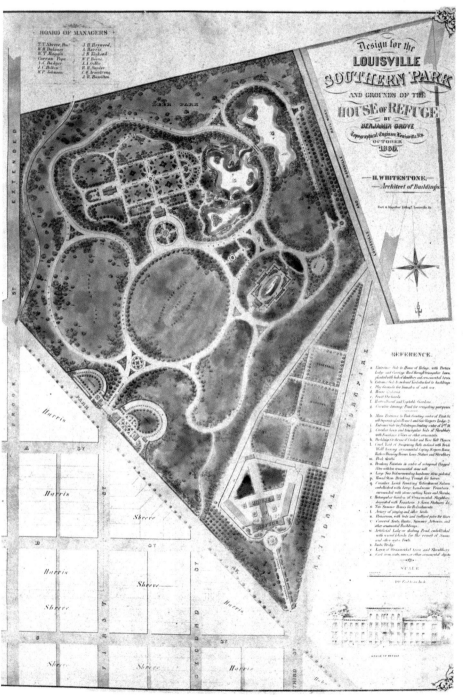

Benjamin Grove's 1860 *Louisville Southern Park and Grounds of the House of Refuge*. The Filson Historical Society. See page 5 for a larger image.

In October 1860, Benjamin Grove created an elaborate layout for the new Southern Park and set off the grounds for the House of Refuge, whose main building the soon-to-be prominent Louisville architect, Henry Whitestone, designed. Grove was born in Birmingham, England, in 1824 and immigrated to New York City in 1851.[132] According to his obituary, he initially settled in New Albany, where he surveyed for the Ft. Wayne and Indianapolis Railroad before working for the Louisville & Nashville Railroad. In his 1858 naturalization petition, he reported that he had been a resident of Louisville for about five years.[133] He spent nearly two years surveying and preparing the first detailed map of Cave Hill Cemetery, which he published in 1857.[134] Grove retired about six years before he died in 1915 at the age of 92.[135]

Roughly half of the 82.5-acre former Oakland Cemetery tract appears to have been designated for park purposes.[136] Grove envisioned the park's entrance at the continuation of First Street. Carriageways led to a large oval designated for cricket, baseball, and a parade ground, on either side of which lay a playground and an archery lawn, behind which was a swimming pool. South of these areas were formal gardens and walks leading to a series of three lakes, each with an island. The eastern side of the park was bordered by Dry Run, the westernmost branch of the South Fork of Beargrass Creek. The western edge was bordered by the L&N RR tracks. A deer park was planned for the southern reaches outside the carriageway that ringed the entire park. A conservatory and a saloon or public hall were the principal buildings planned for the park.

Photograph of Benjamin Grove. The Filson Historical Society.
Below: Grove's business card, about 1865. Inside cover of "Section Maps."

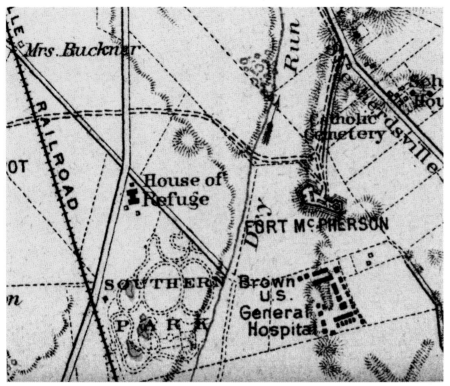

Section of *Louisville and Its Defenses* map, 1864-1865.

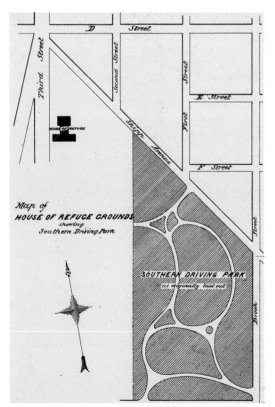

"Southern Driving Park as originally designed," *Third Annual Report of the Board of Park Commissioners* (1893), after p. 63.

Implementation of Grove's design appears to be confirmed by its depiction on the 1864-1865 US Engineers' map, *Louisville and Its Defenses*, which detailed the layout of the Brown US General Hospital immediately to the east.

"This forty acres was used as a public park" until 1866, according to a later report by the Board of Park Commissioners.[137] Then by ordinance, this land was put under control of the board of managers of the House of Refuge and used for farming and gardening purposes. Grove's plan had anticipated extension of north-south streets, including First Street to the park's entrance. When these streets were not extended, the park lacked public access, a factor which may have led to its demise. But Grove's ring carriageway survived as a driving park. *The Courier-Journal* took the opportunity to describe fashionable pleasure driving on Third Street and around Southern Park when a section of Third Street was improved with Nicholson pavement in 1870.

> The completion of the Nicholson to the Park, if this is not a misnomer, will make one of the handsomest and most complete roads in the country…. The grounds belonging to the House of Refuge are susceptible of much improvement, in more senses than one, and it would certainly redound much to the credit of our city fathers to take such improvement in hand. The grounds, it is true, do not possess very extended natural advantages, but a judicious laying out of malls, avenues and drives, added to the one course around the Park, would certainly do much to beautify the Park, and to make it an attractive place of summer resort. In default of this, at least the introduction of a sprinkling cart every afternoon during the hot season.[138]

Watering the House of Refuge park remained an issue well into 1871. While private arrangements were made "to keep the track in order," the House of Refuge was reluctant to allow it. *The Courier-Journal* thought the matter deserved the attention of municipal authorities, concluding: "The park movement of a year or two since was thought worthy of being laid before the people, and it seems somewhat inconsistent that the most should not be made of our present facilities in this direction."[139]

A layout of the grounds of the House of Refuge published in 1878 shows that by then the institution had taken over nearly all the property. Most of the land had been modified for the particular uses of the correctional facility. A large triangular lake south of the administration building may have been a remnant of Grove's planned water features.

In 1886, the House of Refuge was renamed the Louisville Industrial School of Reform. Discussions began in March 1890 about removing the institution's buildings "to cheaper lands farther out." As the *Louisville Commercial* reported: "Whether the present

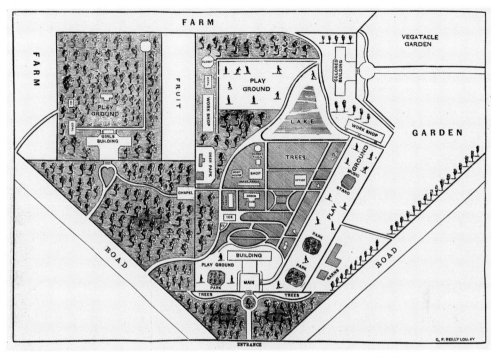

Plat from the *Thirteenth Annual Report of the Louisville House of Refuge…1878.*

grounds will be made into a park, in case of removal, is not being considered for the present, but as there could be no other reason for the change, it is almost certain that a new 'breathing spot' will be the result."[140] In 1891, the Industrial School of Reform was asked to surrender its grounds to the newly formed Board of Park Commissioners.[141] Before any action was taken, however, the park board ran out of money. Three decades later, the Louisville and Jefferson County Children's Home, as it was renamed, moved to Ormsby Village, and the various institutional buildings spread over 47 acres were left vacant.[142]

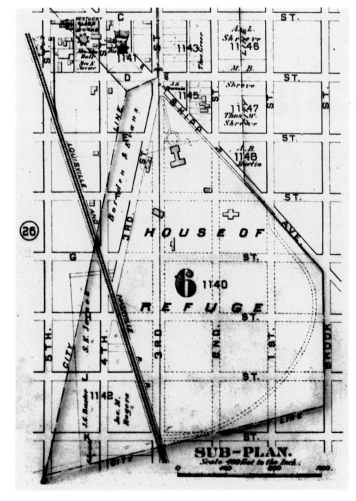

Section of *Atlas of the City of Louisville, Ky.*, 1884, Plate 13.

9

OTHER BENJAMIN GROVE LANDSCAPE PLANS (1860-1890)

Benjamin Grove's 1860 *Design For A Public Park.* The Filson Historical Society.

DESIGN FOR A PUBLIC PARK,
PROPOSED FOR THE CITY OF LOUISVILLE, KY.

A.D. 1860.

BENJAMIN GROVE ALSO PRODUCED A "DESIGN FOR A PUBLIC PARK" that was never implemented. The ambitious 1860 proposal for an urban park ringed by villas and residences with churches at the corners encompassed Rowan Street north to St. Xavier Street and Twenty-first to Twenty-sixth streets. In the park's interior were a gymnasium, tennis court, ground for athletic sports, a girls playground, boys playground, and three lakes. Thomas Slevin owned much of the park's proposed site that he later subdivided as Slevin's Western Addition.[143] No request for a city park in 1860 can be found in the Common Council or Board of Aldermen's meeting minutes. Grove would settle in the area, so perhaps he was simply demonstrating his abilities to lay out a large development. A rectangle of trees was delineated on the 1865 Civil War defenses map just west of Slevin's Western Addition. It became the site of St. Mary's [later called St. John's] Catholic Cemetery, designed by Grove probably in the late 1850s.[144]

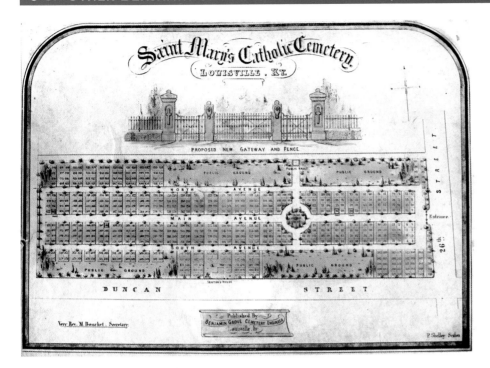

"Saint Mary's Catholic Cemetery," by Benjamin Grove, ca. 1867. The Filson Historical Society.

The city had been expanding south toward Broadway, but this development to the west would have created substantial infill between the city and Portland and was designed to take advantage of the Louisville and Portland Street Railroad. Grove's urban park plan was made two years after Olmsted and Vaux's design for Central Park, but six years before their masterful plan for Prospect Park in Brooklyn. Vaux and Grove were the same age and both were from England. Olmsted was slightly older. The inspiration for Vaux and Olmsted's Central Park was Joseph Paxton's park at Birkenhead, near Liverpool, which opened in the spring of 1847. Certainly, Grove would have been familiar with the park, too, as his native city, Birmingham, was only 100 miles to the east of Birkenhead, a suburb of Liverpool. Paxton biographer Kate Colquhoun wrote that Birkenhead "became the direct model" for Olmsted and Vaux's concept for Central Park. "They followed Paxton's lead in incorporating an outer carriage drive, separate pedestrian walks, open and enclosed spaces, water and architectural ornamentation."[145]

Layout of Birkenhead by Joseph Paxton. George F. Chadwick, *The Works of Sir Joseph Paxton 1803-1865* (London, 1961), 60.

Benjamin Grove also published a survey of Cave Hill Cemetery in 1857 (see p. 40), and would design the two large sections shown on the plan as "proposed additions" in 1868.[146] He more than doubled the size of the cemetery in 1888. Grove also produced a number of Kentucky cemetery plans, including Grove Hill in Shelbyville (1856), Frankfort Cemetery (1857), Lexington Cemetery (1858), Fairview Cemetery in Bowling Green (1864), St. Louis Cemetery, Louisville (1867), Ashland Cemetery (1872), Adas Israel Cemetery, Louisville (1876), and Midway Cemetery (1890), as well as Metairie Cemetery in New Orleans (1873).

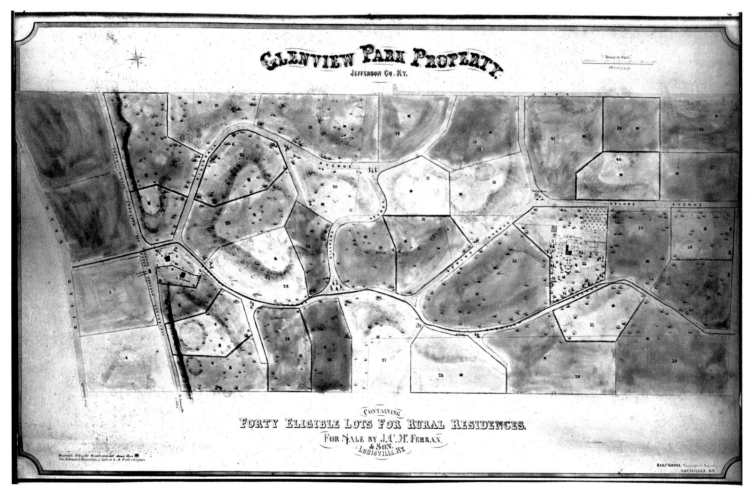

Layout of Glenview Park by Benjamin Grove. The Filson Historical Society.

Grove's plan for James C. McFerran's Glenview Park Property also survives. After James C. McFerran and son John B. McFerran purchased the 640-acre Berry Hill farm from Gerald B. Bate for $117,550 in 1867, the father resided there, breeding and selling fine trotting stock.[147] Sometime between 1874 and 1878, Benjamin Grove laid out the subdivision of their "Glenview Park Property" into 40 lots "for rural residences."[148] J. C. McFerran acquired his son's half-interest in 1881 and the property was sold a year after he died in October 1885.[149]

Extensive additions were made to the old Louisville Marine Hospital on Chestnut Street in the late 1860s. The Louisville City Hospital opened in 1870 and Benjamin Grove landscaped the grounds a year later.[150] The carriage entrances were at the terminations of Floyd Street at Madison Street (north) and Chestnut Street (south).

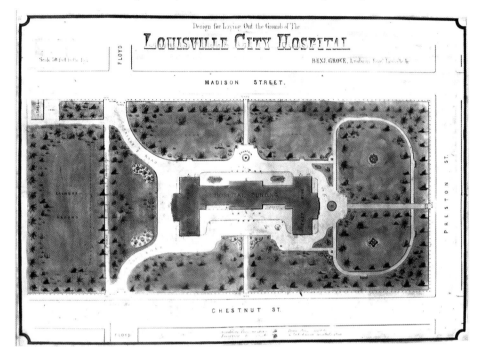

Benjamin Grove's plan for the grounds of the Louisville City Hospital, ca. 1871. The Filson Historical Society.

Below: View of grounds along Chestnut Street entrance to Louisville City Hospital. *Annual Announcement of the Louisville Medical College, Session 1879-1880.*

10

ANOTHER VISIT TO LOUISVILLE BY FREDERICK LAW OLMSTED (1863)

Frederick Law Olmsted about 1860 in heavily layered clothing. Courtesy of The National Park Service, Frederick Law Olmsted National Historic Site.

ON 12 APRIL 1860 IN THE HARBOR at Charleston, Fort Sumter, under the command of George Rogers Clark's nephew Major Robert Anderson, was fired upon. With the beginning of the Civil War, the Falls of the Ohio became a strategic navigational control point to the South as well as the West. Louisville absorbed an influx of Union soldiers sent to protect this transportation artery. Little else occurred in the city for four years that was not related to its virtual occupation. Suddenly, men who were being enlisted from every place and occupation had to be clothed and equipped, fed and cared for. Military camps and hospitals had to be built and staffed in short order under the direction of the United States Sanitary Commission, a new agency created to assist the armed forces. In June 1860, Frederick Law Olmsted became executive secretary of the Sanitary Commission.[151]

According to biographer Laura Wood Roper, Olmsted began a western tour in mid-February 1863, and had two days of meetings in Louisville about the first of March before going on to Nashville.[152] He returned March 10th for another two days of meetings. Unfortunately, there are no accounts of his visit to Louisville in *The Louisville Daily Journal*, which was still being edited by George Prentice, whom Olmsted had called on in 1853. In any event, two hectic days would not have allowed any time to seek out people or places not connected with the work at hand. He resigned from the Sanitary Commission in the fall of 1863 and traveled to Mariposa, California.

Brown US General Hospital just east of Southern Park, now the Belknap campus of the University of Louisville. National Archives.

11

CITY'S FIRST PARK
INITIATIVES (1866-1871)

WHILE OLMSTED EXTRICATED HIMSELF FROM HIS VENTURE in California, Vaux conceived a plan for a large park in Brooklyn, New York, and convinced his old partner to join forces again. The result would be a singular triumph, considered superior in design to Central Park. Olmsted and Vaux were retained in late May 1866 to develop Prospect Park. Joseph P. Davis was appointed engineer in charge; John Bogart and John Y. Culyer were named his assistants.[153] Interestingly, a quarter century later, Culyer would be considered before Olmsted to create the Louisville park system.

Several months after news of Prospect Park spread, *The Louisville Daily Journal* led a lengthy article titled "Our Parks" with a description of the principal features of the Brooklyn concept. "First, a series of green commons, partly separated by groves, but giving an unbroken stretch of greensward three quarters of a mile in length, and over one hundred acres in area; second, a grove or a tract of woodland, free from underbrush, nearly as long and as large as the meadow; third, a lake sixty acres in extent."[154] The *Journal* wanted to show how such amenities were regarded "in cultivated communities," and the "degree of importance" that such cities attached to them. "Experience has shown their utility in a thousand ways, and Louisville, the gem city of the West, is sadly behind-hand, but proposes to redeem its reputation."

At the 8 June 1866 meeting of the Louisville Common Council, president Theophilus C. Tucker introduced a resolution calling for a committee of councilmen and aldermen "to report the locality & cost of a Public Park, which was adopted."[155] Thus, Tucker, who was proprietor of a grocery and produce store specializing in old copper whiskey and apple and peach brandy on East Market Street, may be considered one of the fathers of Louisville parks. By the time the *Journal* brought positive coverage to the initiative, Tucker had received three offers of land by property owners. "Louisville could readily afford a central park," the *Journal* pointed out, "but while we are about it let us have a fine one, if not two or three. The humanizing effect, the healthful pleasure, the educational tendency of a park need not be here dilated upon. Everybody understands these points."[156]

Every one knows the beautiful and picturesque location of the Water-works, and every one has looked with pleasurable emotions from the terrace of the reservoir upon the charming scene spread before him—a panorama of quiet beauteousness.

All about this center of loveliness is land, which, if artistically improved, would make a park of surpassing attractiveness. Below the hills on either side of the reservoir is an undulating plain, with groups of trees here and there, but now mostly covered with luxuriant, tasseled corn. This plain could be made into greensward, with fountains, lakes, conservatories, botanical gardens, aviaries, and the myriad adornments art brings to add splendor to the scene. The knobs afford every means of ornamentation an artist could desire. There are gullies to be bridged with fantastic, rustic bridges, or with elegant carved stone terraces—nooks where wood nymphs might hide—cool grottoes, walks, esplanades, vistas could be prepared, and the whole be made a marvel of taste and elegance.

Mr. James Callahan offers a tract adjoining the Water-works, on the upper side, a tract of land containing 275 acres, stretching back from the river to amongst the knobs.

Major John Throckmorton offers a similar tract of 212 acres, immediately adjoining the Water-works, on the lower side, and also reaching back into the hills.

These tracts, with the already available grounds of the Water-works, would give us a park of about six hundred acres, a very respectable patch, if properly laid out and kept up. Those who go that way should look at the location and see if it is not a pleasant, if not the pleasantest spot about Louisville. Of course we know nothing of the price asked for the land, but if it be not too high, there is *the* place for a park.

The only other land thus far offered is a tract of 44 acres, with 15 acres adjoining which can be secured, the property of Mr. F. G. Edwards. It is situated between the Shelbyville and Brownsboro pikes, three-fourths of a mile east of the city limits. The Louisville and Frankfort railroad runs past this place. It is a beautiful place, but lacks the look-out and the river of the Water-works location.

There are pleasant grounds in the suburbs of the city, on the Preston street road, which could be easily turned into an elegant park. Cedar Hill would make another delightful place as would the grounds south of Portland avenue taking in the old cemetery there and running back to Main street absorbing the square of gardens and residences.

In these remarks we have regarded only those places where trees and shrubbery are already growing to some extent. That is to say, in a degree park-like already. To take one of our flat and barren commons and make a park of it would require labor and an immense outlay of money.

We think that one grand park with three or more smaller ones would be the proper thing. These smaller parks scattered about the city, render their vicinage exceedingly attractive to the best class of people, and the parks themselves are grand things for the children and nurse-maids in the day-time and pleasant resorts for the elders in the quiet evenings to smoke and talk, seated on rustic benches, while younger couples stroll through the leafy lawns and beneath the green arches through which peeps the silver moon, and whisper the sweet words of love and devotion.

And here let us suggest that the old graveyard between Eleventh and Twelfth streets might be made a very charming little park. We understand that the ground, if diverted from cemetery purposes, reverts to the heirs of the original donors. Well, now is a better time than ever to turn the melancholy, deserted graveyard into some useful purpose. It cannot remain a graveyard forever. A compromise with the heirs no doubt could now be made, as well as at some future time, to allow the graves to be removed and the place made a blooming garden where happy young ones could play. Surely their rosy faces and merry laughter would be better than the array of broken grave-stones, half overgrown and hidden by rank grass and weeds. We believe that the spirits of the bodies lying mouldered in that place would sanction the innovation. The trees here are splendid, and the park would need nothing but a few graveled walks and a fountain to render it a lovely resort. This transition "from grave to gay," we hope to see accomplished.[157]

Although the *Journal* admonished: "We trust the interest in this important matter will not flag, and that parties owning appropriate lands for park purposes will readily offer their property to the Committee," Louisville's first real attempt to acquire park property languished. A year later, the Common Council was searching for land on which to build a new workhouse and public park, hardly compatible functions.[158]

The next push for a public park occurred in 1868. After listing Louisville's various public improvements and acknowledging "we have an intelligent, moral, refined and enterprising population, variously

It is unfortunate that we have no regular park, and with little prospect of getting one for some years to come.... While doing so much toward rendering the city itself more comfortable, we should not forget that we are peculiar among all cities of our size in not having a single spot away from our places of business and dwelling-houses, where we may take a stranger with a good grace or without a blush at our want of such a convenient resort.

"Third Street." *The Courier-Journal*, 28 October 1870.

estimated at from one hundred and twenty to one hundred and fifty thousand," *Journal* reader Vedette declared, "we have *no public park*, where all classes may seek healthful pleasure and exercise." He pointed to the vicinity of the Water-works as the most eligible site, claiming "this enterprise cannot be objected to on account of its costliness, for, as I learn from other cities, their parks are a source of revenue and profit instead of expense." The reader suggested that if the city fathers could not unite on the location of the single Water-works park, then another "south of the central portion of the city and one south or southwest of Portland could be developed."[159] Other positive comments followed. The *Journal* suggested: "There are in our community several well-known gentlemen of tried ability and energy who should take hold and put it through with all of the dispatch they have other great enterprises. Nature has done her share in giving a beautiful location and scenery, let us do ours by improving the advantages we have."[160] The Common Council responded in a cursory fashion, introducing an ordinance "authorizing the purchase of ground for a City Park," which was amended to "purchase three parks—one east, one west, and one south of the City, at a cost not exceeding $1,000,000." A committee was formed "to ascertain three suitable points for City parks."[161]

When two years had lapsed without any movement, *Journal* reader Reprover placed the blame on the General Council. "They should have furnished park accommodations twenty-five years ago, and to-day we could boast of a park which we might justly be proud of."[162]

"As cities grow up and teem with human life, parks become, in fact, sanitary necessities. I consider that in the view of the present populousness and continuous growth of our city, public grounds of spacious extent are indeed absolutely necessary for the healthfulness and comfort of our citizens, and that they are of essential importance in attracting capital and labor to our midst.... Public parks, I think, go far toward preventing vice in communities as dense as ours, by serving as places of innocent and pleasant resort to those who, from not having pleasant and comfortable homes of their own, are led to seek their enjoyment and hour of ease in such places as they may find provided, and who would often turn from the haunts of vice and crime to the purer, more agreeable influences of such parks, if there were such to go to." These were not the words of Frederick Law Olmsted, although he held such convictions. They were part of Mayor John G. Baxter's message to the Common Council and Board of Aldermen in *Louisville Municipal Reports* when he was elected in March 1870.[163] "For the end in view," he continued, "an ordinance will be transmitted to you providing for the purchase of four, and not more than six, tracts of land—two to eight hundred acres each, outside the city limits, and the others of not more than ten acres, inside—and authorizing the issue of $800,000, in 30-year, 7 per cent Bonds, to pay for and improve same. I hope that this ordinance will be passed by your Honorable Body, and that when submitted to the voters of the city it will receive their hearty assent."[164]

The initiative to create two large parks was derived from the City Charter adopted in 1870 that in Baxter's view divided the city into "two districts for park purposes." Third Street was determined as the line separating the eastern and western districts.

As promised by Mayor Baxter, a park ordinance was introduced, debated, revised, and passed by the Common Council and Board of Aldermen and set for a vote in the general election on 1 August 1870.[165] "It now remains with the citizens to redeem the neglect of the past, and provide for the increasing population of our city, park privileges similar to those enjoyed by other cities," the *Louisville Commercial* declared.[166] While newspaper editorials and letters to editors seemed to indicate the outcome would be positive, the ordinance was overwhelmingly defeated, 1,899 to 11,394.[167] "We must have parks of some description some time," the Republican-leaning *Commercial* lamented, "and it is a matter of wonder why an intelligent community should display such marked opposition to a measure of so much importance to all classes of our citizens."[168] "The defeat of the parks project is overwhelming. It was procured by a combination of all classes against it," *The Courier-Journal* remarked. "The great body of property owners and the negroes *en masse* voted 'no.'... They were told that if constructed the parks would be restricted to the use of white men."[169] Years would elapse before another park initiative would be undertaken by city government.

An interesting account of the acquisition of land options for a park of some 700 acres in 1871 by the Baxter administration "with the co-operation of Gen. John B. Castleman" was reported decades later in a city directory.[170] Termed "the first effort to establish a park system in Louisville," the designated area was delineated on an "old map in the Board of Park Commissioners." The property's northern boundary was Broadway at the bridge crossing Beargrass Creek and it extended out along the west side of Newburg Road, encompassing both sides of Beargrass Creek. The only improvements on the land at that time were the Hutchings, Cood, and Haggin residences and an old tannery. "This was wonderfully beautiful and adaptable for park purposes," but according to the account, "the various attacks made in certain circles upon Mayor Baxter prevented his taking continued interest in the scheme." The same general area would be considered for park land over a decade later.

This matter deserves the attention of the authorities, and it may be hoped and believed that they will not be backward in attending to it. The park movement of a year or two since was thought worthy of being laid before the people, and it seems somewhat inconsistent that the most should not be made of our present facilities in this direction.

"Of Public Interest," *The Courier-Journal*, 29 May 1871.

12
PLEASURE DRIVES AND CRESCENT AVENUE (1868)

COACH MANUFACTORY.

NO. 483 JEFFERSON STREET, CORNER THIRD.

THOS. ROBINSON

Manufactures and keeps constantly on hand, a large assortment of

Coaches, Cabriolettes, Rockaways Buggies, and Carriages of every desription.

Prompt attention will be paid to all orders. Persons wishing to purchase are respectfully invited to call and examine my stock previous to purchasing elsewhere.
N. B. Repairing done in the neatest style.

Advertisement from the 1848 Louisville directory. The vehicles pulled by plodding teams of a previous generation had given way to sleeker, lighter carriage models drawn by a single, more responsive horse by the 1880s.

Opposite page: Advertisement from *The Louisville Post,* 11 July 1881.

UNDER THE EDITORIAL HEADLINE, "A Great Want in Louisville and Jefferson County," *The Louisville Daily Democrat* on 3 October 1867 complained about the city's lack of a beautiful drive, compared to those around Cincinnati and St. Louis. "We are very sure that there is no town in the United States of half the size of Louisville which is so disgracefully distinguished by the defect we have pointed out." Months later, a letter in the *Louisville Daily Journal* proposed a local park system connected by "a very wide, handsome avenue, superior to anything in this country, in a semi-circular direction, all around the city, from the Water-works across the country to the House of Refuge, thence to the river below Portland."[171] A reader responded in the next day's *Journal*: "And as for the grand 'Crescent Avenue,' a park as it were in itself, all around the city, why the idea seems to commend itself to every mind at once." "We are glad to see that all the city papers have taken up the question of a Park and of the Crescent Avenue with a spirit and earnestness that, if continued, will probably lead to some beneficial action," the *Journal* commented 23 July 1868. Proposing a drive "a hundred feet wide, and properly graded and planted" that would soon become "adorned with handsome villas and cultivated grounds," the *Journal* observed that "the increase of population and of taxable property produced by the improvement would make the outlay remunerative in actual returns to the city treasury."[172]

Only months before the initial local discussion of a parkway, Frederick Law Olmsted and Calvert Vaux had described for the first time their concept of a parkway for the Brooklyn Park Commission.[173]

The Parkway plan which we now propose advances still another step, the mall being again divided into two parts to make room for a central road-way, prepared with express reference to pleasure-riding and driving, the ordinary paved, traffic road-ways, with their flagged sidewalks remaining still on the outside of the public mall for pedestrians, as in the Berlin example. The plan in this way provides for each of the several requirements which we have thus far examined, giving access for the purposes of ordinary traffic to all the houses that front upon it, offering a special road for driving and riding without turning commercial vehicles from the right of way, and furnishing ample public walks, with room for seats, and with borders of turf in which trees may grow of the most stately character. It would contain six rows of trees, and the space from house to house being two hundred and sixty feet, would constitute a perfect barrier to the progress of fire.

"The key innovation of the parkway that Olmsted and Vaux first described in this report, and first saw constructed in Brooklyn, was the separation of ways of transit that it introduced," the editors of *The Papers of Frederick Law Olmsted* pointed out. "By this arrangement, private conveyances could quickly and easily move through the city without the impediment of the carts of commerce or the jolting of cobblestone streets."[174]

Within their 1869 Buffalo, New York, park system proposal, Frederick Law Olmsted and Calvert Vaux had employed a "parkway" connecting the Driving Park, The Parade, and The Park.[175] Only shortly before, they had proposed the idea of separating driving traffic from delivery wagons and carriages for a stretch in Brooklyn called Eastern Parkway.[176]

> Every pleasant afternoon, between four and half-past five, the coupes and bretts, phaetons and skeleton buggies that crowd the drive present a most handsome appearance; the first two, rolling ponderously along with a pair of long-tailed bays, or chestnuts, or blacks, as the case may be, attached, and with fond mamma and papa in the backseat, keeping a proud but at the same time a sharp eye on the black-eyed or blond-haired daughters in front. The phaeton, with a nimble little horse in the shafts, and a grinning contraband in the complementary rumble, seats just two and no more, and those, Mrs. Grundy says, shall be both of the softer sex....
>
> "Third Street." *The Courier-Journal*, 28 October 1870.

In discussing Benjamin Grove's 1860 Southern Park, *The Courier-Journal* pointed out that "the grounds, it is true, do not possess very extended natural advantages, but a judicious laying out of malls, avenues and drives, added to the one course around the Park, would certainly do much to beautify the Park, and make it an attractive place of summer resort."[177] "This park, situated as it is at the end of

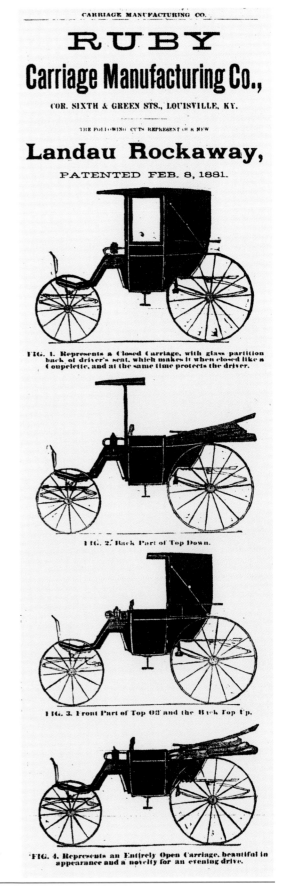

CARRIAGE MANUFACTURING CO.

RUBY
Carriage Manufacturing Co.,
COR. SIXTH & GREEN STS., LOUISVILLE, KY.

THE FOLLOWING CUTS REPRESENT OUR NEW

Landau Rockaway,
PATENTED FEB. 8, 1881.

FIG. 1. Represents a Closed Carriage, with glass partition back of driver's seat, which makes it when closed like a Coupelette, and at the same time protects the driver.

FIG. 2. Back Part of Top Down.

FIG. 3. Front Part of Top Off and the Back Top Up.

FIG. 4. Represents an Entirely Open Carriage, beautiful in appearance and a novelty for an evening drive.

If our citizens can find pleasure in the Third-street drive and in the Central Park, they will surely rejoice in the prospect of having the grounds of the Grand Central Exposition and Villa Park thrown open to their uses at an early day.

"Public Parks and Drives," *The Courier-Journal*, 26 June 1872.

Illustration for the Bradley Carriage Company in *The Industries of Louisville* (1886), 134. The firm had been in business almost 50 years. This sleek, single-seat model was obviously built for speed.

the Third-street road," the paper noted in May 1871, "is the most, if not the only, available drive around the city, and has by common consent been adopted as the fashionable place of afternoon resort."[178] In essence, the park laid out by Grove had been modified into the city's first driving park, where horses and carriages could be driven for pleasure and sport.

In a letter to *The Courier-Journal*, printed 26 June 1872 and headed "Public Parks and Drives," Q characterized the situation. "For a long time all efforts at establishing parks and drives have been resisted by some of our most worthy, influential and best citizens. But in spite of this old fogyism, a short drive has been made out on Third street near the House of Refuge and the street and drive are daily thronged with buggies and carriages."

"The facts are, we have few pretty pleasure drives, and scarcely a place to go on hot summer evenings for rest and recreation," *The Courier-Journal* lamented 22 July 1880. "Louisville does not lack natural advantages, for they are numerous. The river, the knobs on each side of the river, the Brownsboro pike, and, above all, the 'River Road,' are attractive enough, but are comparatively neglected."

> The River road is separated from the city by slaughter houses, paper mills, distilleries, and most horrible of all, by a glue factory. But when you leave behind you the dust and dirt and heat of the city, when, through much tribulation to the finer senses, you have reached what is indeed the River road, there are few pleasures more delightful than to see the sun sink behind you, to pass the slower pleasure-seekers and come upon the river, calm, peaceful and beautiful as a hidden lake. Just beyond the water-works the Ohio is broad and the current slow, and it seems in reality more like a lake than a river. Every year more and more will its beauty be recognized, and not only will the river road, but the river itself, be sought and traversed by the not very unfortunate individuals who are forced to pass the summer months within reach of those places.[179]

"Among the Blue-Grass Trotters," an article which appeared in *Harper's New Monthly Magazine* in 1883, brought national attention to the sudden popularity of horses with a trotting gait, and the fact they were being bred for speed in Kentucky. "The growth into favor of the trotting gait in the last thirty years may be somewhat connected with the improvement of the roads of the country," William Henry Bishop wrote. "Whereas traveling in the saddle was formerly a necessity, wheeling is now everywhere easy. Driving as a diversion is more easily learned and carried on than riding." The breeding of trotting stock was begun in Kentucky by R. A. Alexander at Woodburn in Woodford County before the Civil War.

James C. McFerran began the process of developing his Glenview property into a successful trotting farm in 1867. At the first Glenview stock sale in 1875, *The Daily Louisville Commercial* pointed out that "the reputation of the State, her material worth, and the prosperity of Jefferson county particularly, are all directly involved in the success of enterprises similar to this."[180] "Nothing more notable in connection with the trotting interests of Kentucky has happened in many a long day," was the characterization in 1881 of McFerran's purchase of the great Alexander-bred trotting sire Nutwood for $15,000.[181] The popularity of driving one's conveyance for pleasure or sport put increasing pressure on communities to provide more open roadways with better surfaces. Driving parks became destination points. When Churchill Downs was established in 1874, it was operated by the Louisville Jockey Club and Driving Park Association. Before Churchill Downs, the Oakland and Woodlawn tracks also accommodated thoroughbreds as well as trotters.

An interesting use of the term boulevard occurred in an 1869 proposal to create such an avenue diagonally from the southwest corner of First and Main streets to the northeast corner of Third and Jefferson streets. The idea was to connect the new Galt House with the emerging downtown. The boulevard was to have a width of 50 to 60 feet in Nicholson pavement or cobblestone or plank or gravel, not for horse traffic but "for pedestrians only" as a "grand promenade." Handsome stores were to be erected along the sides of the boulevard, and the new street was "to be roofed over, arcade fashion." "A boulevard so opened through that portion of the city augurs relief from the monotony of plain squares," *The Courier-Journal* pointed out in support of the anonymous "innovator." "He would help Louisville to aspire to Parisian grandeur in the matter of groundwork and its good results to commerce and society. In this boulevard theory he has struck the key-note of true cityhood. The owners of our soil, brick and mortar hold the destiny of the boulevard, and they alone can decide whether it shall come in vogue or not."[182] The boulevard idea failed to catch on.

This great estate [Woodburn] is well known as the home, and one of the earliest breeding places, of some of the very best American running stock. Of late it is becoming equally famous for trotting stock, into which, like others of the breeding establishments, it inclines to merge its activities in preference to the first.

"Among The Blue-Grass Trotters," *Harper's New Monthly Magazine* 67 (1883): 729.

13

MAYOR BAXTER'S SKELETON PARK
(1870-1881)

THE TOWN'S ORIGINAL CEMETERY DATING TO 1786 on the south side of Jefferson Street between Eleventh and Twelfth streets was replaced in 1832 by one several blocks to the west. "The old City Cemetery…is no longer a place of interment," the 1844-1845 city directory noted. "Some attention was paid to ornamenting this relic of the olden time, by the late city authorities, and quite a number of sycamore trees were planted within and outside the palings, which, in a little time, will render this square quite agreeable to the residents in that vicinity." In 1870, the placement of an iron fence and pavement around the cemetery led Mayor John G. Baxter to claim that he "would be glad for our citizens to have access to this place as it is," but with "the graves so thickly covering the ground, they are apt to be desecrated by being trampled upon…unadvisable to throw it open to the public."[183] Baxter proposed to the Common Council later in 1870 that a large monument be erected with the names of the citizens buried in the cemetery and that the remains of those buried be reinterred around the monument, surrounded by a suitable enclosure. "If this be done, the city could lay out the balance of the grounds in pleasant walks, and make other improvements."[184] The Mayor hoped families would reinter their ancestors in Cave Hill Cemetery, but in the meantime, according to the 10 July *Commercial*, "work of improving the ground…will commence this week."

By the summer of 1872, a temperance lecture was given at the Jefferson Street park.[185] A year later, the *Louisville Daily Ledger* described "Graveyard Park" as "just now a verdant oasis in the midst of a brick and mortar waste."

> If it was properly laid out and a fountain or two placed in it no lovelier spot could be found. We understand that there is nothing in thus improving it, which would conflict with the rights of the friends of the deceased who are buried there. The graves need not be disturbed, and the expenditure of a little money would give pleasure and health to thousands of our citizens.[186]

Toward the end of Baxter's second term as mayor, the old graveyard was formally transformed into Baxter Square, a public park, described as presenting "a neat appearance."[187] In a sense, the site remained a cemetery as "all those remains not removed by parties interested, still rest undisturbed under the beautiful sward with which the ground of the square is now covered."[188]"Messrs. Nanz & Neuner, the popular florists, have just filled their contract for decorating it," *The Courier-Journal* reported 1 May 1881.

> The ornamentation consists of one hundred rustic iron and wooden settees, two handsome and unique rockeries with grotto and spring fountains. A miniature lake, with rustic bridge, invites the youthful natator to try its waters, and two large iron fountains throw their spray and cool the air. The music stand, twenty feet in diameter, holds the center of the grounds. The walks are made of broken stone and gravel, covered with sand. The entire park is well set in bluegrass…. Among the trees are some fine sugar and silver maples, European lindens, horse chestnuts, evergreens and magnolias.[189]

The Louisville Commercial observed that "Baxter Square is now lovely, the fountains being in good working order and the entire grounds in the finest condition. Dr. Geo. N. Griffiths is on hand daily at the park to see that the work which is continually going on is properly executed, and many of the most attractive features are the result of his taste and attention. The squirrels and other little animals now in the park, which add no little to the amusement of the children, have all been placed there by him."[190]

"The new park even more popular than was expected," a *Louisville Commercial* headline pointed out about Baxter Square in May 1881. "More are likely to be wanted."[191] The *Commercial*'s reporter asked Mayor Baxter "how it would do to buy and turn into a pleasure ground the square bounded by Brook and Floyd and Green and Jefferson streets?" This block had just become available when the terminal of the Louisville, Cincinnati & Lexington Railroad and its depot along the south side of Jefferson moved to the riverfront. While Mayor Baxter thought the time had come when the city should provide three squares, not just the one honoring him, he did not favor the railroad terminal site for a park. "This would be an admirable location, but the improvements on that square and the cost of it considered, make it greatly preferable to turn that into a market space for hay and feed generally and wood, charcoal and other country products. The building is suitable and large enough for a general market, and the grounds fine

> The only trouble with this park is that it is too small for the ambitious city of Louisville. We need one of several hundred acres to accommodate the growth of the population, and that will let us all raise our heads high as any other town that boasts of extensive pleasure grounds.
>
> "The New Park," *The Courier-Journal*, 1 May 1881.

Trustee Lucien Alexander's Baxter Square owl is no more. The owl was sent to Mr. Alexander as a contribution to the extensive menagerie he has been collecting in the park, and which will next year be taken out as an adjunct to a circus. The owl was named Jeff in honor of Jefferson county, and because it was a non-committal name as to sex, a mystery which has not been solved yet. Yesterday the owl flew out and sat gloomily on the plank in the basin upon which Martha, the alligator, suns herself when taking her usual nap. When Martha woke up and found Jeff on the plank she gave a sly flip of the tail, yanked Jeff into the water, and drowned it.

"Death Of The City Owl." *The Courier-Journal*, 30 August 1881.

for wagon teams." Instead of a public breathing space, the site would become crowded with vendors and known as the Haymarket.

The idea of transforming the old railroad depot into a marketplace was discussed in *The Courier-Journal* in detail by "an old-timer, who has the interest of the city at heart, and who has traveled extensively, and from him obtained the following novel and sensible views concerning the development of certain parts of the city."[192] The "old-timer" presented various reasons for converting the depot into a market. "It can be made one of the finest market places in the world, and also one of the most profitable. One thing that has long been wanted in Louisville is a general market."

Converting the depot on the east side into a park matching Baxter Park on the west side did not gather support. The depot was removed, and in 1890 the block was leased to the Farmers, Gardeners and Fruit Growers Market Co. On the 1892 Sanborn maps, sheds have been added and the space labeled "Hay Market."[193] The Haymarket was for more than half a century a bustling, viable area.[194]

Johnston family residence overlooks the south side of Jefferson Street, site of the original Haymarket east of Brook Street. T. Edgar Harvey, *Commercial History of the State of Kentucky* (Louisville, 1899), 19.

In 1881, in response to the reporter about "Skeleton Park," the "old-timer" pointed out that although Baxter Park "seems to be a popular place of resort, it is not large enough for the people." A *Courier-Journal* editorial reiterated: "Baxter Park is a happy idea, and is bright and satisfactory enough as far as it goes, but it doesn't go far enough and it can not be stretched…. During the last ten years there has been a good deal of talk about parks, but the only result has been the conversion of the Twelfth street graveyard into a very pretty little *mélange* of bright flowers, laughing waters, green grass, forest trees, glints of sunshine, filled with taffy-tolu-chewing people and babies. But Baxter Park is but a hint as to what ought to be done on a larger scale."[195]

The city's most devastating tornado occurred on 27 March 1890. After flattening Baxter Square, it damaged buildings on West Main Street and then toppled the Water Company standpipe on River Road.[196]

More than a year after the tornado, "Baxter Square is beginning to look like itself again," *The Courier-Journal* reported, and the park commissioners "approved all the contracts for the complete restoration of the square."[197] This work was authorized before the Olmsted firm had been retained. The park was converted into a children's playground in 1901 by the Recreation League.[198] The playground was substantially upgraded in 1956.[199]

27 March 1890 tornado destruction of Baxter Square pictured on the cover of *Scientific American*, 12 April 1890.

Devastation view published by W. Stuber & Bro. Both, The Filson Historical Society.

14
FAIR GROUNDS PARK IN CRESCENT HILL (1871)

A JULY 1871 LETTER TO *THE COURIER-JOURNAL* mentioned there had been talk of converting the Fair Grounds in Crescent Hill into "one of the most tasteful and beautiful little public parks in the Union," as a "more expressive and suitable" honor to Mayor Baxter than the Jefferson Street park.[200] The writer suggested that in addition a broad avenue be created "through a highly cultivated and beautiful region, already adorned by numerous fine old country seats and modern villas, to the present Fair Grounds." This would have connected the park on Jefferson Street with Baxter Avenue and the proposed avenue to Crescent Hill.

Promoting the upcoming fair, additional features of the Fairgrounds were described in the *Louisville Daily Ledger*, 31 August 1871.

The time track is exactly half of a mile in length, and elliptical in shape. It sweeps around the amphitheater nearly to the front line of the grounds, and to the brink of the hill in the rear…. There will be trots against time every day of the fair.

The grounds embrace forty-three acres, well adapted for the purpose. Nature, which has done a great deal to beautify them, has been improved by art. Beautiful walks and drives, eighteen feet wide, meandering through the grounds, have been laid out and covered with tan-bark. Over six hundred deciduous trees, some of them twenty-two feet high, and evergreens have been set out in ornamental clumps, and numerous shrubs and flowers have been planted. The whole has been arranged by Mr. Joseph Serb, an excellent landscape gardener, according to a beautiful design, and with a view to artistic effect.

In the northern portion of the grounds next to the Brownsboro road, the lake has been deepened by the removal of 15,000 cubic feet of earth, which has been utilized elsewhere on the grounds. In the center there is a beautiful artificial island, and the embankment has been so constructed as to admit of a carriage over it, leading from the Brownsboro pike….

Louisville has no park, and these public spirited gentlemen propose to supply this great need as far as lies in their power.

The grounds are to be further beautified, and next spring will be thrown open to the public. It is contemplated to run a street railway to the Fair Grounds, thus affording a cheap and ready means of access. Season tickets will be sold to families at a nominal sum, and our people can escape from the heat and dust of the city, and spend a day in the cool shades for a trifle.

Louisville and Jefferson County Association stockholders issued bonds in 1871 to pay for the Fair Grounds' improvements. Their intentions were curtailed by the panic of 1873 when interest payments could not be made. A court-ordered sale of the property resulted in an auction sale of lots. Eventually, Lewis Lentz purchased the entire tract for $24,136, and sales of sizeable "suburban building lots" were made along what became Crescent and Field avenues.[201]

"Fair View," at Auction, 15 May 1875. Samuel W. Thomas files. The spring feeding the lake (not shown) runs under Crescent Avenue and into Brownsboro Road.

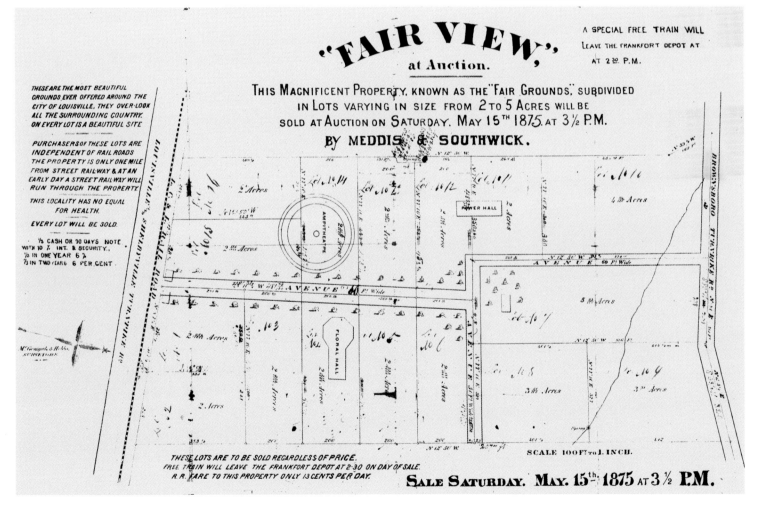

15

DU PONT FAMILY'S
CENTRAL PARK (1872)

CENTRAL PARK.

To avoid the Heat and Dust of Town,

GO TO CENTRAL PARK.

The Largest Grounds and Finest Shade Trees in the city.   jy4 1t

Advertisement in the *Daily Louisville Commercial*, 4 July 1872.

IN A LETTER TO *THE COURIER-JOURNAL*, printed 26 June 1872 and headed "Public Parks and Drives," Q contended: "As to parks there seems to be a great change in public sentiment. Witness the great success of the Central Park just established. The thousands of people—men, women and children with which that park was thronged during yesterday and last night, give evidence that Louisville needs and desires a park upon a larger scale." The 18-acre tract between Fourth and Fifth streets, Weissinger (now Park Avenue) and Magnolia Street had recently been purchased from Stuart Robinson by Alfred Victor du Pont, who, with his brother, Bidermann, had recently purchased controlling interest in the Central Passenger Railway Company.[202]

The descendants of the Delaware powder-making family had come to Louisville in the 1850s, purchasing the old Cromie paper mill.[203] Their improvement of the Robinson property, aptly named Central Park, created a destination for patrons of their street railway. "It is one of the most beautiful places in or about the city, being covered with large forest trees and all sorts of flowers and shrubbery," the *Louisville Daily Ledger* reported upon its opening in June 1872.[204] Rev. Robinson's old brick house was made into Bidermann du Pont's residence.[205]

Looking toward the Du Pont residence in Central Park. *Louisville Illustrated*, 1889, Part 2.

"Messrs. Dupont have greatly added to the natural beauty of the place by laying out walks and drives, and very cunningly constructed arbors and shady nooks," the *Ledger* observed. "The water-works have been extended to the place, and we understand that fountains and lakes are to be added to the other attractions…. The place has been christened Central Park, and is accessible to all parts of the city by the Fourth and Sixth-street railways…. In the absence of public parks Messrs. Dupont have conferred a public benefit by opening such a delightful place." *The Courier-Journal* remarked, "It is wonderful how

much work has been done in so short a time to get the grounds in order. A cornfield upon one part of the ground has been sodded over and gravel walks extended in every direction…. The price of admission is ten cents, and…the grounds will be open all day."[206]

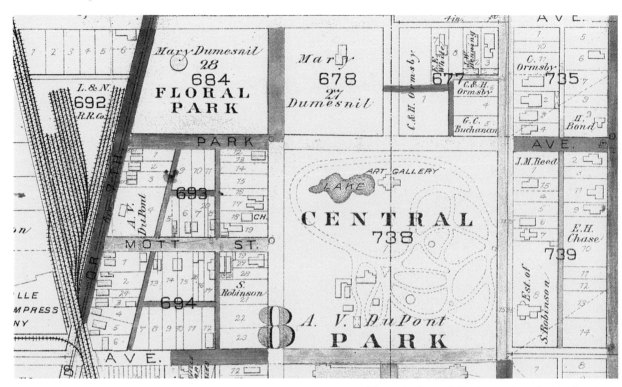

Plan of Central Park north of the Southern Exposition Building. *Atlas of the City of Louisville, Ky.*, 1884, Plate 13.

AT A MEETING IN SARATOGA of the American Social Science Association in 1880, Frederick Law Olmsted differentiated the attributes of local grounds from those of large parks. Interestingly, parts of his address were reprinted in "Mr. Olmsted on Parks," in *The Louisville Commercial*, 14 September 1880.

The objects which are more or less provided for on our parks might at less cost and greater value be provided for in a series of smaller grounds, placed as nearly as practicable at regular distances through and around it. Such scattered smaller grounds would be more accessible; would less embarrass other interests of the town; would less interfere with its natural development; and would involve less contention with local jealousies and consequent wasteful compromises. They would on the whole be less costly.

There is an important element of values in most parks which could not well be provided for in such small local grounds. What is desirable in this respect is a long, unbroken, spacious drive, ride and walk, offering suitable conditions to a large number of people to obtain together moderate exercise in the open air, with such other conditions, favorable to gayety, as can be conveniently associated with them.

The most pleasant amusement afforded the people of this city last summer was the series of concerts in the open air at Central Park…. The announcement that Prof. Eichhorn will give a series of concerts this summer will be hailed with delight. Music never sounded more sweet than it does in the beautiful park, with pretty girls and their beaux as listeners.

"Central Park Concerts." *The Courier-Journal*, 31 May 1880.

16

Maximilian G. Kern's Grand Central Exposition and Villa Park (1872)

It has been jocularly stated that the only drive a Louisville man has for his foreign friends is that to Cave Hill. There are no bewildering, romantic river roads, no sylvan glades penetrated by the inevitable macadam. He must, perforce, take his visitors to the great city of the dead for an evening airing, and descant upon the inevitable end of all the pomp and vanity of life.... Colonel Barret and the Central Exposition Company promise us river drives in the future, and with that we must rest content for the present.

"Cave Hill Cemetery," *Daily Louisville Commercial*, 3 May 1872.

Q's June 1872 letter to *The Courier-Journal*, also described the creation of the Grand Central Exposition and Villa Park on land just west of the Louisville Water Company's Ohio River pumping station. "The grounds we understand, embrace about 130 acres of the most beautiful land in the country, and are now being improved in such a manner as not only to furnish splendid roads and avenues, but at the same time magnificent views of the city and all the surroundings. The grounds commence almost at the city limits and are covered with native forest trees, and are to be ornamented, hill and dale, with lakes, fountains, and every other improvement which can make them pleasing."[207]

In the "incomprehensible siege of cold weather" in early 1872, the *Louisville Commercial* asked its readers to think about summer and Louisville's need of "breathing places" and public parks. "The scheme for improving two or three hundred acres near the Water works is commendable, and we hope the gentlemen who so generously have conceived the plan will succeed."[208] Within months, the Grand Central Exposition and Villa Park project had been expanded to include a racetrack and zoological garden. "What was once a probability is now a fixed fact," *The Courier-Journal* heralded 25 May 1872, "and this enterprise of these public-spirited gentlemen is hereafter to be perhaps the greatest object of interest to be seen about Louisville. The project embraces several purposes, each one distinct in itself, yet all forming part of one magnificent whole." The exposition grounds were to include a large lake for fishing and boating as well as "smaller lakes and drives and walks and beautiful fountains." To the west on 52 acres was Villa Park, "to be laid off with walks and roads, and avenues, of such width and grade and windings as will most adorn and accommodate the whole tract; and at the proper time, it will be subdivided into villa sites of such shape, size and position as will make them suitable for suburban residences.... Villa Park, like the Exposition grounds, is covered with a growth of immense forest trees, poplar, beech, walnut and sugar trees, which, together with the uneven surface of the land, peculiarly adapts it to picturesque ornamentation.… It has not the extent of some public parks in this country or in Europe, yet it is larger than many of them."[209]

"It has been for years a subject of remark that we have had no representative race-course," *The Courier-Journal* pointed out in May 1872. "Oakland went down, Woodlawn followed, and it has been said that Louisville could not sustain a race-course.… The proprietors of Villa Park have donated a hundred and odd acres for this purpose.… It is, in a word, all that is wanted for the National Race-course of America."[210] The Woodlawn Race Course between Westport Road and the railroad had gone out of business and the grounds were being sold.[211] Churchill Downs was a mere idea in the minds of Meriwether Lewis Clark, Jr., and his wife, Mary Martin Anderson Clark, who were embarking for Europe to study horse racing.[212]

Within days the engineer for the Falls City Association had determined that the running and trotting tracks planned by the Association could be accommodated on the 128 acres provided by the proprietors of Villa Park. "Their clubhouse will be erected upon one of the beautiful hills near the place where the grandstand will be located, commanding a view of the running park and the country around for miles."[213]

Making each of these tracts possible was the nearness of the Louisville, Frankfort & Cincinnati Railroad for the transportation of horses.

J. Richard Barret was a native of Green County, Kentucky, who after attending Centre College moved to St. Louis and graduated from St. Louis University in 1843. He practiced law and was a congressman before the Civil War. His congressional biography also noted that he organized exhibitions for the St. Louis Agricultural Society.[214] In this regard he must have been acquainted with St. Louis landscape architect M. G. Kern, whom he enlisted in the mammoth Louisville project.

Maximilian G. Kern, a native of Stuttgart, Germany, studied and traveled in Europe before coming to New York City in 1848. He soon moved to Cincinnati, learned English, and published *Practical Landscape Gardening* in 1853 under the name G. M. Kern. Mariana Griswold Van Rensselaer, who later wrote glowingly about Frederick Law Olmsted, acknowledged the significance of Kern's book in her series on landscape gardening in *The American Architect and Building News*.[215] Kern taught at Farmers' College near Cincinnati before moving to Alton, Illinois, in 1857, and then to St. Louis, where he was in charge of Lafayette Park. He was made superintendent of parks, reportedly designing Benton Park, Laclede Park, Washington Square, Missouri Park, St. Louis Place, and Hyde Park.[216]

After his work in Louisville came to naught, he laid out Forest Park

In describing Frederick Law Olmsted's New York home and office in a brownstone at 209 West 46th Street in 1873, biographer Justin Martin pointed out in *Genius of Place* (Cambridge, 2011), 314:

Everywhere, all over the house, there were books. The office had reference works such as Augustus Mongredien's *Trees and Shrubs for English Plantations*, G. M. Kern's *Practical Landscape Gardening*, and *Gardening for Ladies* by Jane Loudon. Elsewhere, books simply overflowed their cases; stacks grew on every available surface, and tottering piles were arrayed on the floor. According to a rough inventory, he owned about 2,000 books.

in St. Louis, which was dedicated in June 1876.[217] Born in 1825, he was still working in St. Louis into his eighties, and died about 1915.

In a short piece headed "Grand Central Exposition and Villa Park," *The Courier-Journal* noted 28 June 1872: "Mr. M. G. Kern, the landscape gardener, is now engaged in laying off these grounds, and will, in a short time, introduce water for fountains and lakes, construct roads, avenues, &c. The Louisville, Westport and Harrod's Creek railroad is in a rapid state of completion. It will, when finished, furnish a very important means of access to the Exposition grounds. But by river and also horse-railroad there will be ample accommodation for visitors during exhibitions and at all other times."[218] The newspaper then suggested the improvement of Reservoir Avenue, now called Mellwood Avenue. "This is 100 feet wide, and can easily be made a splendid drive of itself, and at the same time ample means of access to Villa Park and the Exposition grounds. The sooner this broad avenue is improved the better. Let the board of directors of the Water Company take notice accordingly."

> The Ohio river presents a water avenue of never failing reliability to the very confines of the grounds, that by steamers and ferryboats can be cheapened to a fare of five cents. Next, the Louisville, Harrods Creek and Westport railroad, passing through the river bottom along the road to the water-works engine-house, and being a steam railway, presents the most abundant facility for transportation of stock, forage and the heavier materials and supplies necessary for the successful issue of race meetings. The horse railway of the same company, authorized by its charter and now in process of construction along the Reservoir avenue at the foot of the Highlands, gives the most abundant means of approach, at the ordinary street-railway prices, to the grounds of the Falls City Association, with the additional advantages of being brought to the gates and entrances of "Grand Central Exposition and Villa Park." Besides all these ways of approach, Barbour's street railroad out the Brownsboro turnpike, now fully organized, will bring passengers within a few hundred yards.
>
> "Racing Ground." *The Courier-Journal*, 29 June 1872.

> Mr. M. G. Kern, the landscape gardener, has been engaged for several days in laying out plans for further improvements upon the Exposition Grounds and Villa Park, and the work thereon will be prosecuted under his supervision.
>
> We are fortunate in having the benefit of the great science and good taste of Mr. Kern in this great undertaking.
>
> "Grand Central Exposition and Villa Park." *Daily Louisville Commercial*, 17 November 1872.

The layout of the grounds of the Grand Central Industrial Exposition and Villa Park were delineated on the 1873 Map of the City of Louisville, Kentucky, on the heights overlooking Reservoir (Mellwood) Avenue. Between Mellwood and River Road was the oval track for the 128-acre Falls City Running Park. Between River Road and the

Ohio River, 91 acres were set aside for a trotting track. The Louisville, Westport and Harrods Creek Railway was shown skirting the south side of River Road and then curving south along the Muddy Fork of Beargrass Creek.

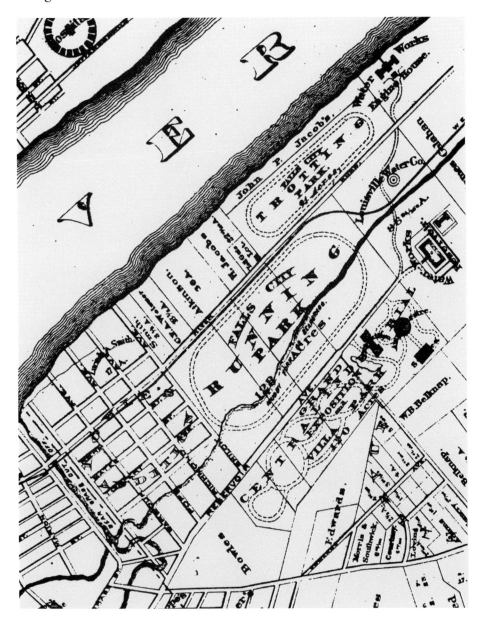

Section from *Map of the City of Louisville, Kentucky*, 1873. When this map accompanied the publication of the 1876 *Atlas of the City of Louisville*, the outline of the exposition and park grounds and racetracks had been obliterated.

The entire enterprise was dashed by the financial panic of 1873. Max Kern may have used some of the ideas generated in Louisville in his plan for the huge 1,326-acre Forest Park in St. Louis that was established in 1874 and opened in 1876. According to the history of Forest Park, Kern produced a layout in collaboration with other local German engineers, "designed as a driving park for carriages, with winding roads, disclosing a new view around each curve. At frequent intervals, the roads provided openings, called concourses, 'as congregating and resting places from

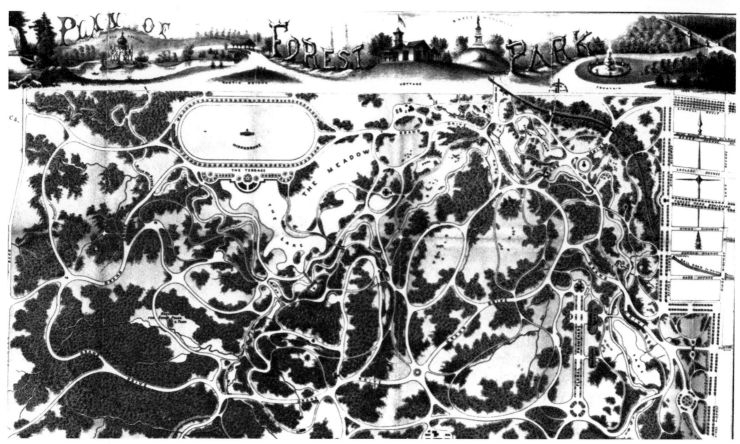

"Plan of Forest Park," St. Louis, 1875. Missouri Historical Society.

which the most attractive views can be enjoyed.'"[219] Besides space for buildings housing conservatories, museums, and a zoo, a major feature of Forest Park was the Hippodrome, a one-mile track where men could test and race their horse-drawn vehicles.

Postcard of Louisville Golf Club about 1900. University of Louisville Photographic Archives.

The Villa Park tract was sold in 1880.[220] However, much of the Villa Park land south of River Road west of Zorn Avenue has remained in recreational use, and is currently being developed as Champions Park.[221] The now-defunct River Road Country Club began leasing the 44-acre property that included a nine-hole golf course from the Louisville Water Company in 1952.[222] It had previously been the Standard Club, and before that the Louisville Golf Club. The land to the west had a mixture of residential and commercial uses until the area was cleared after the 1937 and 1945 floods. In 1955

Harland Bartholomew and Associates prepared a comprehensive plan for various recreational uses, titled "A New Riverfront Park." Included was a landfill. This plan evaporated quickly, but was given one last boost by Grady Clay in a 1959 address to the Louisville River Area Foundation, now known as Riverfields. With the expectation of the Riverside Expressway, Clay noted the importance of planning waterfront recreational projects with the highway. He referred to the area for boaters and tourists as Holiday Town.[223] Mayor Bruce Hoblitzell thought the area was needed for commercial barge and terminal purposes and immediately quashed the idea. A crucial section of the riverfront was given over to commercial development.

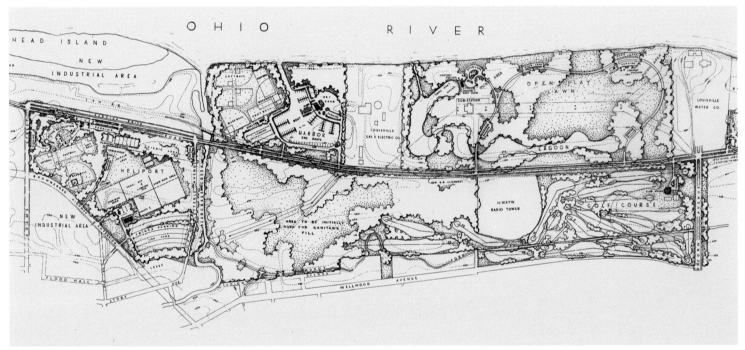

Section of Plan for the Development of a New Riverfront Park, 1955, by Harland Bartholomew and Associates.

17
THE LOUISVILLE PARK ASSOCIATION: A JOSEPH PAXTON PARK PROPOSAL (1874)

THE GRAND CENTRAL INDUSTRIAL EXPOSITION appears to have been one of the local failures brought on by the financial panic of 1873. The adjacent running and trotting horse tracks of the Falls City Association, although depicted on the 1873 map of Louisville, were not constructed either. In the spring of 1874, a proposal for a jockey club and running park on the old Churchill family property was announced. J. Richard Barret, who had headed the exposition and tracks projects along the Ohio River, responded in *The Courier-Journal*.

> I feel glad that a "pleasant club-house, with adjoining grounds," will make a delightful resting place at the end of the extended drive out Third street, and that a "grove at the spot" set apart for this purpose will shelter the house and the grounds from the heat and the glare of the sun. Oh, most delightful grove! But what will shelter the faces of the people from the heat and glare of the sun in the evening?[224]

Another *Courier-Journal* reader critical of the formation of the organization that would be named the Louisville Jockey Club and Driving Park Association pointed out that the Churchill property was too far away from Louisville and that it lacked water for sprinkling the track and access streets.[225]

In *The Daily Louisville Commercial*, another unidentified letter-writer lamented that racetracks were only viable two weeks out of the year. He also pointed out that Louisville had no pleasure drive or resort where the horse owners could enjoy riding or driving. The writer proposed creating an alternative "park association" to undertake the project.

> The formation of a park of this kind may be eventually one of the most important features for the health and interests of Louisville. The richer classes may inaugurate the movement, and after its success is undoubted some arrangement may be made hereafter for the city to purchase the grounds and improvements, throwing it open for public use, and reserving to the stockholders such privileges as they might wish to retain,

with the privacy of their club-house.

To make an ornament to Louisville should be one of the objects in view by each subscriber in such an enterprise, and that the possession of money should enable him to do something in the future for his poorer neighbor. It has been a misfortune that the earlier officials of the city did not see the utility and necessity of parks, and that they did not purchase, thirty or forty years ago, a hundred acres of land in a central locality, accessible to all. It is not too late to retrieve that error. And who is there more fitting to do this than those who have been blessed by prosperity? There are five hundred men in Louisville amply able to contribute liberally to such an undertaking. It is perfectly feasible to lease for ten years a tract of land accessible from all parts of the city to street railroads. The privileges can be retained by purchasing at a fixed value at any time and canceling the lease. With proper management, under directors and president of good taste and judgment, this tract of land could be made, at small cost, an ornament of which the city might well be proud; and in three or four years its usefulness would be so demonstrated that all classes would ask the city to buy it and make it the public resort of Louisville…. The main object in view should simply be the establishment of a park by the rich men of Louisville, which in the future, either by their own action or by that of the city, might be made a source of health and pleasure to the poor man who has no carriage and horses to insure needed and beneficial exercise in the fresh country atmosphere.

Some of the most charming spots visited by the writer in Europe have been small parks of thirty to fifty acres in extent, beautifully and tastefully embellished with flowers and groves, lakes, and walks, wherein 5,000 or more persons daily congregate, and for several hours thoroughly enjoy themselves.

The writer then described in detail the makeup and mechanics of the corporation—called the Louisville Park Association—that would undertake such an enterprise. "The cost of such a park must not be underrated. To make it in every respect a success $40,000 should be raised for the improvement, and annual dues of at least $10,000 to keep it in repair and perfect order. The club-house should be commodious and tasteful, combing a first-class restaurant, with first-class wines, together with a perfectly satisfactory department for the ladies to obtain their ices, fruits, &c."

At the end of his letter to the *Commercial*, the writer pointed out that the famous English architect and landscape designer Joseph Paxton received large amounts for his designs, "sometimes $10,000 or $15,000." Paxton was the successor of Humphry Repton, who had followed Lancelot "Capability" Brown in the triumvirate of noted English landscape designers. The writer related that one of Paxton's designs had been presented to him, "and has been laid away for several years waiting for an opportunity to use it." He concluded that "with an ultimate view of benefiting their fellow citizens who toil from morn till eve without hope of obtaining aught but moderate enjoyment, here is a field for philanthropy at little cost, and one which is to be hoped will soon be crowded with eager co-laborers. Such persons as N. Bloom, Frank Guthrie, John M. Martin, M. Lewis Clark, J. Watts Kearney, John T. Gray, Henry Duncan, E. H. Chase, James Bridgeford, S. Ullman, Julius Barkhouse, Mayor Jacob, Isaac Caldwell, Louis Rehm, Sr., B. W. Jenkins, Judge Ballard, General Murray, and scores of others could easily be induced to inaugurate this movement."[226]

Who was the letter-writer? Mayor Charles D. Jacob would come to mind. He had been in Europe in 1857 and 1858, but surely he would have signed the letter. Perhaps it was Major John R. Throckmorton who had been in Liverpool and other parts of Europe before the Civil War and who owned much of the land planned for Villa Park and the Grand Central Industrial Exposition along the Ohio River.[227] Another possibility was the longtime superintendent of Cave Hill Cemetery, Robert Ross, who had worked at Chatsworth before coming to America.[228] Yet another was Benjamin Grove, who certainly would have known about Paxton and would have prized one of his park plans and would have been able to adapt it to a Louisville site.

Joseph Paxton had been superintendent of the gardens at Chatsworth before becoming internationally recognized for designing London's Crystal Palace. His Birkenhead Park served as the inspiration for Vaux and Olmsted's Central Park. According to Olmsted's biographer, Laura Wood Roper, while visiting England in 1850 his experience of Birkenhead "broke on him like a revelation." The park near Liverpool was the first Olmsted had ever seen.[229] He was most impressed that it was essentially man-made, a 120-acre creation designed to appear as formed by the hand of nature.

Also visiting England in the summer of 1850, landscape gardener-turned-architect Andrew Jackson Downing met architect Calvert Vaux and persuaded him to return to America as an architectural assistant. Downing requested Olmsted to write about Paxton's public park in the May 1851 issue of his magazine, *The Horticulturalist, and Journal of Rural Art and Rural Taste*.[230]

Joseph Paxton by Henry Perronet Briggs, 1836.

Walking a short distance up an avenue, we passed through another light iron gate into a thick, luxuriant, and diversified garden. Five minutes of admiration, and a few more spent in studying the manner in which art had been employed to obtain from nature so much beauty, and I was ready to admit that in democratic America, there was nothing to be thought of as comparable with this People's Garden. Indeed, I was satisfied that gardening had here reached a perfection that I had never before dreamed of. I cannot attempt to describe the effect of so much taste and skill as had evidently been employed; I will only tell you, that we passed through winding paths, over acres and acres, with a constant varying surface, where on all sides were growing every variety of shrubs and flowers, with more than natural grace, all set in borders of greenest, closest turf, and all kept with most consummate neatness. At a distance of a quarter of a mile from the gate, we came to an open field of clean, bright, green-sward, closely mown, on which a large tent was pitched, and a party of boys in one part and a party of gentlemen in another, were playing cricket. Beyond this was a large meadow with rich groups of trees, under which a flock of sheep were reposing, and girls and women with children, were playing…. I was glad to observe that the privileges of the garden were enjoyed about equally by all classes.

Entrance to Birkenhead Park.

Lawn in Birkenhead Park. Both by Samuel W. Thomas, 2010.

Besides describing how the park had been created, Olmsted pointed out that the town of Birkenhead had paid for the project, partly by selling lots for villas around the park's perimeter.[231] The idea that money could be raised by making land adjacent to a park more desirable, would be a point that helped Olmsted sell Louisville's power structure on its own plan 40 years later. Olmsted in his 1875 entry, "Park," for *American Cyclopedia*, in which he described parks in Europe and America, referred to Birkenhead Park as "one of the most instructive to study in Europe, having been laid out and the trees planted under the direction of the late Sir Joseph Paxton, over 30 years ago."

Olmsted's article, "The People's Park at Birkenhead, Near Liverpool," prompted A. J. Downing to begin calling for a similar park in New York City. After he died in 1852, Calvert Vaux took over the firm, later moving from Newburgh, New York, to New York City. In 1857 he persuaded Olmsted, whom he had first met at Downing's home, to join him in entering the design competition for Central Park.[232]

Joseph Paxton died in 1865, so his plan that *The Courier-Journal* letter-writer referred to and evidently possessed must have pre-dated the

President Drexler had a consultation with President M. Lewis Clark yesterday. The base-ball magnate and the thoroughbred judge consulted about an offer of the base-ball club for the use of the race-course for grounds.... Secretary Price said that negotiations had been going on for some time, but that President Clark and the directors are opposed to the scheme and that it is almost certain that the offers of the base-ball people will be rejected.

"Base Ball At The Track." *The Courier-Journal,* 11 January 1893.

Civil War. That document has never surfaced. Had it been implemented, Louisville could have claimed the distinction of the only American city with a park designed by Joseph Paxton, the innovator of urban parks.

The letter did not resonate as the writer had hoped. Probably the jockey club and driving park concept was too far along to be reconsidered.[233] Many of the gentlemen singled out by the writer as potential supporters of the park association concept became directors of the Louisville Jockey Club and Driving Park Association several weeks later. Included was young Meriwether Lewis Clark, Jr., who had devised the plan for the organization and would soon become its president.[234] The Louisville Jockey Club and Driving Park Association got underway in June 1874 with plans for a trotting track within a one-mile running course. The tracks were completed in November, well in time to plan for the inaugural Kentucky Derby on 17 May 1875. The driving park aspect of the track that became known internationally as Churchill Downs was short-lived.[235]

The Louisville Jockey Club and Driving Park Association's original grandstand and clubhouse (at left). *Louisville Illustrated* (1889), Part 7.

Baseball Parks (1874-1922)

"Now that the Louisville Eagle base ball club have their grounds inclosed back of Central Park, the members will commence practice immediately and the 'nine' will be chosen by the directors on next Wednesday," *The Courier-Journal* reported 4 June 1874. "The grounds will present a handsome appearance when completed, and all lovers of the popular game may rest assured that their anticipations of a good club will be fully realized." But the playing field must have become the groundskeeper's nightmare in late 1874 when "several enterprising members" of the club undertook to develop "probably the finest skating rink in the West." The "monster pond" was some 400 feet square, "situated directly on the baseball grounds…. A red lantern suspended on the corner of Fourth and Walnut will be a signal announcing that the ice is safe and that the rink will be open to visitors."[236]

Before a real interest in baseball could manifest itself, the potential participants did battle on both sides of the Civil War. The Louisville Base-ball Club was reorganized in the spring of 1865, and "will begin their games during the coming week, near the grounds of the old Phoenix Club, on the Park Barracks road."[237] When the newly organized Olympic Base-ball Club, whose president, Thomas H. Sherley, would become the first president of the Louisville Board of Park Commissioners 25 years later, challenged the Louisville Base-ball Club in July 1865, the latter's grounds were then at Eighteenth Street and the old Portland Railroad.[238] The Olympic Base-ball Club would later lease Elliott Park. The square bounded by Twenty-eighth and Twenty-ninth streets, Magazine and Elliott streets had been part of a large farm that Dr. Theodore Elliott subdivided in 1868. In doing so, he agreed to set aside the square as a city park which the contiguous owners would first fence off and ornament. After Dr. Elliott died and the venture collapsed in the 1873 panic, the square was rented by J. H. Lewis, who leased it to the Olympic Base-ball Club. At the expiration of that lease, the Elliott heirs rented it to the Eclipse Base-ball Club, which played there for many years until the grandstand burned down.[239] After a decade of legal wrangling, the Board of Park Commissioners took over the square as a public park.[240]

We also learn that the corresponding secretary has been authorized by the board of directors to communicate with some professional clubs East, and the probability is we will see some good playing in Louisville this season.

"Base Ball." *The Courier-Journal*, 4 June 1874.

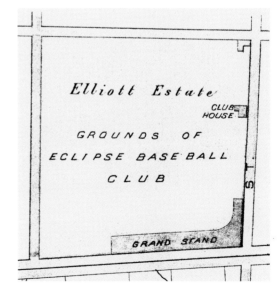

Eclipse Base-ball Club grounds. *Atlas of the City of Louisville, Ky.*, 1884, Plate 24.

How do the Base-ball clubs seem to look upon lacrosse? Is there a rivalry between you?

No, sir, none in the least. Last year we were treated in the kindest manner by the Louisville Base Ball Club; they gave us their grounds for practice and matches and did all they could to help us along. If that is a rivalry, it agrees with lacrosse.

"The Louisville Lacrosse Club." *The Courier-Journal*, 12 February 1882.

Pete Browning is perhaps holding a Louisville Slugger bat. *The Courier-Journal*, 29 January 1890.[250]

Baseball flourished in Louisville, at some expense to cricket. The Eagle Base-ball Club was organized in 1867. Although "acknowledged to be the best junior club in the country," by 1870 its performance level diminished until 1874 when its players had matured and were "probably better fitted now to cope with the senior nines than ever before."[241] The Eagles played in a park "said to be the handsomest in the country," accessible on the Fourth-Street line. The Eagles' field was on the southwest corner of Fourth and Magnolia streets, which in 1883 became the site of the Southern Exposition and then St. James Court.[242]

In December 1875, W. N. Haldeman, Charles E. Chase, and Thomas H. Sherley met in the Louisville Hotel with their counterparts from Chicago, St. Louis, and Cincinnati to organize the western clubs of the National League.[243] New York, Boston, Philadelphia, and Hartford would become the eastern clubs in February 1876. The National League season opened in Louisville on 25 April of that year at the Eagle grounds with the Chicago White Stockings shutting out the local Grays. Although the home team lost, *The Courier-Journal* characterized it as "the finest game of base ball ever witnessed in Louisville."

It was estimated that six thousand persons were present.... The arrangements for accommodating the spectators have been admirably conceived. The stands converging at the entrance gate enable the people to see one another, as well as everything occurring in the field. Of these stands there are two sheltered, one being devoted to stockholders, with a splendid site for the reporters, while the other is divided into two large compartments, that nearest the home-plate being for the ladies.... It is probable that our ball park is one of the very best in the United States.[244]

The next year, "Louisville gathered together the strongest and best club the country had ever produced." But at the end of the season, "they shamelessly sold out. The best and most trusted players were discovered to be rascals." It was the first stain on baseball's reputation, as the four players involved were blacklisted and the Louisville Grays never again suited up. "Base ball in Louisville is one of the lost arts," *The Courier-Journal* regretted.[245] Amateur baseball teams, including the Falls City Club of the National Colored League, continued to play at the grounds south of Central Park until the development of St. James Court.[246] The Eclipse Club returned to Elliott Park and became a charter member of the major-league-status American Association in 1882.

"'Line 'em out Petey,' will no longer be heard at Eclipse Park," *The Courier-Journal* lamented in early 1890. But Louisville won the pennant

"A Crowd at the Park," *The Courier-Journal*, 1 May 1892. The Louisville Colonels were members of the revamped National League.

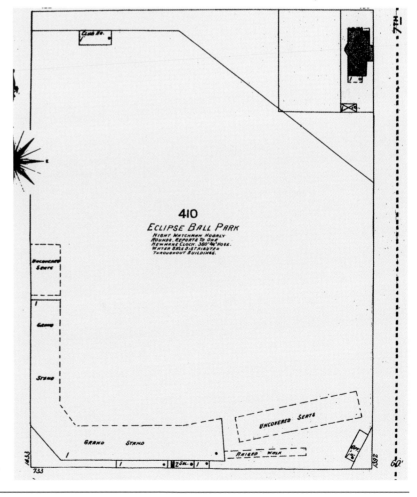

Below: Eclipse Ball Park, at corner of Seventh and Kentucky streets. 1892 Sanborn map.

in 1890 without its star hitter, The Gladiator, Pete Browning, who had left for Cleveland, taking with him his Louisville Slugger bats made especially for him. The American Association folded the next year.[247] Louisville became part of the revamped National League in 1892, playing again in Eclipse Park at Twenty-eighth street and Elliott Avenue. The next year, the team tried to play at Churchill Downs, but was unable to schedule its games around the racing calendar.[248] Finally, early in 1900, according to *The Courier-Journal*: "Louisville is off the baseball map. The local National League franchise, players, and all that goes with the Louisville Club have been disposed of."[249]

As the University of Louisville neared an agreement to acquire the old Industrial School's site, the deal was complicated in late 1922 by the suggestion that the Louisville Baseball Club build a new facility on the southern edge of the campus. The team's grandstand at Eclipse Park had recently burned.[251] "The baseball club is a municipal asset," Mayor Huston Quin declared, "and it is to

Old and new routes of Eastern Parkway and proposed baseball field for the Louisville Baseball Club. *The Louisville Times*, 27 December 1922.

1928 bird's-eye view showing Eastern Parkway has been re-routed to allow construction of Parkway Field on the University of Louisville's campus. Caufield and Shook Collection, University of Louisville Photographic Archives.

the interest of the city to see that the Colonels obtain a suitable site for the proposed concrete grandstand."[252] The site, however, was bisected by Eastern Parkway, which terminated at Third Street. Under the crafted agreement, the University of Louisville obtained the bulk of the Industrial School grounds; the Louisville Baseball Club got land for its new grandstand; and the city and the parks board agreed to straighten out the terminus of Eastern Parkway, diverting it north of the new field and converting it, between Third and Brook streets, from a parkway into a "heavy traffic street."[253] In the fall of 1924, Olmsted Brothers (project 7084) configured the campus for the University of Louisville, which took up residency in the fall of 1925.[254] Parkway Field was designed by local architect Leslie Abbott and used until the Fairgrounds stadium opened in 1956.[255]

The game of base ball has done more than anything else to break up the gang spirit; the game in which boys meet and match individual prowess and acquire fame and championships without throwing rocks at each other.

Recollection of R. J. Meaney about 1895. The Filson Historical Society.

Babe Ruth warming up for an exhibition game that the Colonels won at Parkway Field, 2 June 1924. By Charles Betz, *The Courier-Journal* archives.

Even after major league baseball departed Louisville for Pittsburgh in 1899, the sport grew so much in popularity among young males at the amateur level that the Board of Park Commissioners was obliged to provide level open ground for baseball diamonds. By 1915 there were ten diamonds in the park system: five at Shawnee, three in Cherokee, and two at Iroquois. Before the start of the amateur baseball season, the local chapter of the Amateur Baseball Federation petitioned the Board for additional diamonds in the various parks, particularly two more in Shawnee. The Board requested the Olmsted firm to recommend where additional diamonds could be constructed.

An improvised baseball diamond between Fifth and Sixth streets on the old site of the Louisville Horse Show Association auditorium overlooking the Falls of the Ohio. By R. C. Ballard Thruston, 11 October 1914. The Filson Historical Society.

I played baseball. I operated a club—Brown Taxi. We played all over the state. Every town around here had a salaried team. They had ballparks. Back then, we tried to get a game over as fast as we could.... We were professionals, you know what I mean. We didn't care who won or lost. We went out there and played baseball. If we could get away earlier by losing a game we would.... We didn't care what they did. We were out there for the money.

Leo Wackenthaler in Samuel W. Thomas, "Time And A River Of Memories," *The Courier-Journal*, 5 August 1984.

19
SAND ISLAND PARK PROPOSAL (1881)

"IN YOUR WANDERINGS ABOUT THE CITY have you ever discovered a suitable place for a park which everybody could reach?" a *Courier-Journal* reporter asked "an old-timer" looking for a novel project that might move Louisville forward. In a considered, comprehensive, and coherent response, printed in the 10 July 1881 *Courier-Journal*, the old-timer made the following suggestion. "Louisville has the chance of making for herself one of the finest parks on the face of the globe at the least expense, which in time would not cost the city a cent, and might be profitable, and would advertise Louisville all over the country."[256]

The island between the canal and the river, called "Sand Island" and other names, which is an eyesore to Louisville, the steamboat men and the citizens in general, is gradually being washed away by the currents. The dam that was erected on it some years ago by Gen. [Godfrey] Weitzel, and is gradually decaying and going the same way, could be rebuilt of stone twelve or fifteen feet high and connected with the wall of the canal on the one side and on the outer side parallel with the Kentucky channel on the falls, and down past the bridge till it struck the wide part of the island. With the dredgings of the canal and boats they could get sand gravel and raise the island above the high water marks. Then they could take the whole island and change it into a park at but little expense. There could be three hotels put on it—one at the Shippingport end, one in the

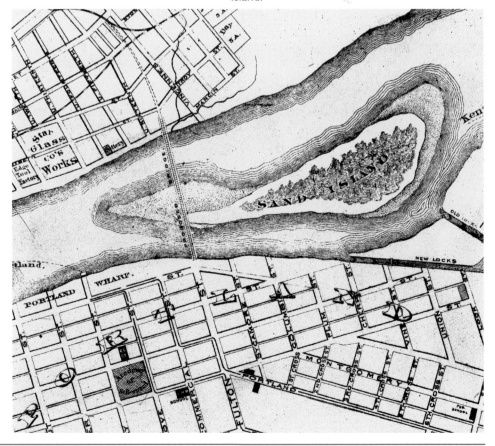

Section of Beers & Lanagan, *Atlas of Jefferson & Oldham Counties Kentucky* (1879), depicting Sand Island.

Pencil sketch of Portland from Sand Island by Benjamin Grove, 1853. The Filson Historical Society.

center and one at the Louisville end—and leased out for the year at such terms as would almost pay the interest on the bonds.... Also there could be baths and bath-houses erected either by the sanitary force of the city or private individuals, both for male and female, keeping a good steam and shower bath run by water power which could be made to pay by charging a small price, thus preventing disease, saving life and affording a swimming place for women.

Also, to make the place more profitable, the city of Louisville and State of Kentucky could give building sites to Eastern capitalists that would bring thousands to the city. The expense would be light in comparison with other places, the cement being manufactured right across the river within sight of the island, the clay for making the brick being obtainable in the city, the lime being a few miles from Louisville on the Narrow-gauge road, and for mixing the mortar down under your feet; the lumber coming over the bridge from Indiana and Michigan could be slid down from the bridge easily. The slate to cover the roof is found within five or ten miles from the river, and, to top it all, the cotton coming from the South over the bridge could be let down upon the island, manufactured and sent East, thus giving employment to thousands of people and adding tens of thousands to the population of the city.

The park will suppress crime; men who now go to beer gardens will go to this place, where no liquor is sold. If he wants to fish, he can fish; if he wants to boat, he can boat; if he wants to bathe, he can bathe.

And, to correspond with the park, High avenue which is now for the biggest part an eyesore, would then be made the fashionable avenue in Louisville. By removing a few obstructions on the north side of High street, a fence could be put on the outer side of the pavement all along, sloping down to the canal, and on the lawn seats. On the south side of High street would be erected the fashionable residences of Louisville, and with the boats passing up and down the canal and the rail cars crossing over the bridge; ferries, etc., up and down the harbor; the breezes of the river; above and away from the dust of the city, it would be the fashionable drive of the city.

Then what would be the impression of a stranger looking down upon the park? The stranger passing up and down the canal on a boat, crossing the river on the bridge, if he stopped at Louisville and made a visit to the place he would advertise Louisville all over creation. With electric lights, the hotels, the mills, the fishing and boating, it would equal anything on the face of the earth. I defy any place in the United States to equal it.

The bridge that the "Old-timer" made several references to had not yet been built, but there had been talk on the street about the project for some time. "No project has attracted more attention among the people around the falls than the new bridge," *The Courier-Journal* pointed out 20 September 1881, when the letting of the contract for the stone work was reported. "Bridge tolls here are so high as to be an embargo on business, and mechanics on both sides of the river have taken special interest in that enterprise which promises to secure a new bridge in the shortest possible time."[257] A month later, the cornerstone was laid for the Kentucky and Indiana Railroad. "This will be the only bridge west of Cincinnati on the Ohio River, across which wagons and other local traffic can pass. With the many advantages in favor of the erection of such a work, it is surprisingly strange that it has not long ago been successfully carried out. That it will be mutually beneficial and advantageous to both Louisville and New Albany, no wise and fair-minded man can doubt."[258]

The K&I Bridge opened in 1886 along with a railway connecting Louisville and New Albany, called the Daisy.[259] Its completion was delayed by the huge Ohio River floods of 1882, 1883, and 1884, each a record. Any thought of creating a park and other developments on Sand Island was dashed.

In the afternoon I went over to "gravel island." It lays immediately in front of the vilage and it is so called in concequence of the extencive beds of gravel which projects above and below it; and only appears when the water is low. The island itself is made up of sand and mud supporting in summer a great number of herbaceous plants which are now begining to make their appearance above the sand. It was all overflowed this spring at the time when the water was the highest. The trees are verry tall cotton wood & elm the sycamore, willow, and the *Acer rubrum* and *A negundo* are common the latter are now in flower. Among the herbaceous plants only three are in flower viz. the *Viola cucullata* where here grows larger than on the commons, *Rannuncules abortivus* and the [blank].

Increase Allen Lapham, 10 April 1828.[260]

View from Kentucky side of the Kentucky & Indiana Bridge soon after it opened in 1886. Sand Island can be seen behind piers. Railroad train is seen crossing on tracks under the main superstructure. A Daisy car is seen at right on a track cantilevered at the side of the bridge. *The City of Louisville and a Glimpse of Kentucky* (1887), 15. Inset shows how Daisy railway cut under the railroad track, creating city's first spaghetti junction.

20
LOUISVILLE PARK INITIATIVES (1880S)

"IN THE ABSENCE OF PUBLIC PARKS the people will go to these public gardens to refresh their lungs with an atmosphere devoid of dust, and yield themselves up to the enjoyment of an hour or two of care-ignoring pleasure," *The Courier-Journal* observed in the summer of 1875.[261]

In his "Centenary of Louisville" paper delivered to the Southern Historical Association 1 May 1880, Reuben T. Durrett challenged the city's power structure: "We have no park now except the House of Refuge grounds, used for other purposes, and are not likely to have one until wiser and better men get control of our city affairs." He noted: "This was the nearest our city fathers ever came to giving the people a public park, and it was certainly far enough from any thing of the public park kind."[262]

In Mayor John Baxter's last annual message to the General Council in 1881, he wrote: "For many years past I have been a strong advocate for a public park, to be located some where near the city limits, where it would be most accessible to a majority of our people.... Now our city has grown so large that the vacant grounds have been built on, and for children there are no places to play but on the streets. A park would contribute more to the health, wealth, and moral purity of this community than any thing I can imagine.... There is not a city in the United States of even half our size which does not possess a public park. We have no place either for a drive for our own citizens, or where we can show strangers and visitors.... The park should contain from 500 to 1,000 acres of land."[263] Early in Charles D. Jacob's new term as mayor, his call for action and appropriation of funds stimulated a bevy of suggestions of possible sites. The modern park movement had begun. In his 3 August 1882 message to the General Council, Mayor Jacob recognized that the city charter specified that the city provide two parks, one east and the other west of Third Street. He suggested that the city divest itself of Gas Company stock and "public parks be purchased and beautified in the two districts."[264]

"There is not in all this region such sites for public parks as may be found on the banks of the river," *The Courier-Journal* pointed out in

Central Park
CONCERTS

COMMENCING Friday, July 2, and continue every Tuesday and Friday, weather permitting, at 8 o'clock P. M. Admission 35c. Season tickets, admitting gentleman and lady, $3. Tickets for sale at Warner & Bro's., Fourth st.   je30 d3&Tu&Fr2m

Who Wants to be a Bachelor?
THE OLD BACHELORS

OF this city take pleasure in announcing to their very numerous friends, and the ladies in particular, their first grand

Picnic at Woodland Garden

Next Thursday, the 15th inst. They will do their utmost to secure enjoyment to all who may be present. Cards of admission 25c. Ladies free.

Shooting Park

THIS beautiful Grove, just above the Water-works is newly improved, and just the place for Families to spend a nice afternoon.
Every Sunday afternoon a Sacred Concert.
The Narrow-gauge railroad runs a train to the Park every hour in the afternoon.
The best of refreshments will be furnished and the strictest order kept by   FRED. HESER.
my21 FSu&Tu3m

Floral Garden

TYROLER CONCERT every night. Go and see the Tyrolers, No. 27 Jefferson st., bet. First and Second.   jy10 SaTu&ThIm

PICNIC.

THE best picnic of the season will be given by the St. Patrick's Benevolent Society, at Floral Park, on Monday, July 26. All preparations are made, and those who attend will have ample opportunity to enjoy themselves. Tickets 25c.

Advertisements, *The Courier-Journal*, 8 June 1875.

July 1882. "This would be of incalculable benefit to young children especially, to say nothing of their parents."

This land can be purchased at cheap rates, and should be promptly secured. The old farm of Ormsby Hite, fronting the road and river, containing some forty acres, can be bought at very reasonable rates, and a more suitable place for a city park we do not know. It is very well stocked with shade trees and fruit trees, and very little outlay will be required for putting it in order for immediate use of the public.[265]

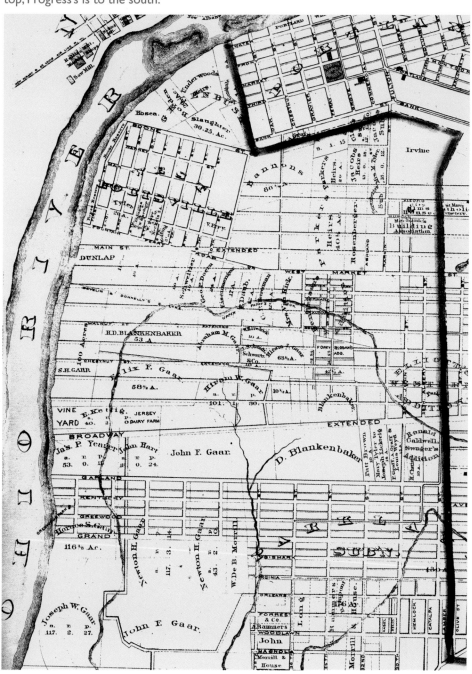

Section of city map, *Atlas of Jefferson & Oldham Counties Kentucky* (1879). W's proposed site is at top; Progress's is to the south.

"Are suggestions in order in regard to eligible locations for a new 500-acre park?" W. wrote *The Courier Journal* in August 1882. "If so, the very first consideration is access; second consideration, cost to the city; third consideration, adaptability; fourth consideration, beautiful scenery."

All these can be found combined in the following location, viz.: South of Bank street, at Thirtieth or Thirty-third street, westward toward riverside limits, taking in an area of 500 or 600 acres of land, at an approximating cost of $25,000 for the land and as much more for the embellishments…. The West-end, heretofore overlooked, will be sought for; capitalists, having an eye to its future, will invest. No more beautiful location can be found in the city—(we don't want a park in the country, to be reached only by the wealthy few, in comparison with their poorer citizens dependent upon a line of street cars at only five cents fare from Cave Hill Cemetery to the Portland ferry.) This is a great item. By all means locate the new park at the city limits, not two or three miles in the country. When all the facts are considered pro and con, I believe the above location will be decided upon. The Indiana hills in the distance will be a beautiful background to this landscape picture.[266]

A writer signing himself as "Progress" responded, "I am glad to see the interest in a public park on the increase," acknowledging "that a public park is a necessity." He thought a better site than the one suggested by W. would be between Broadway and Virginia Avenue, from Thirty-fifth or Thirty-sixth streets to the river." In any case, Progress hoped "the subject may be agitated till we get a park."[267]

The Courier-Journal editorial page soon weighed in, suggesting locations for two new parks and the purchase of Central Park by the city and its expansion to the south (where the Southern Exposition would soon be located). The two new park locations were both on the Ohio River. "We ought to have a river park of two or three hundred acres between Broadway and Market streets. We should have another one along the river just above the cut off, where is now a corn field."[268] In its conclusion, the editorial admonished: "The park making should be attended to certainly within the next five years. The longer the delay the more difficult of accomplishment will be the work, the costlier will be the ground; the farther off we will have to go to get parks."

> The making of public parks we have characterized as a necessity. Aside from the aesthetic view of the subject, the rendering of the city more attractive, etc., the sanitary reason comes before us very forcibly. The people who are packed in the crowded portions of the city, the little children who are wasting away and pining for the sweet fresh smell of grass and flowers and for pure air—these need the parks, which are medicines for soul and body. Everybody needs them. They will draw the young from the multitudinous haunts of sin and shame. They will purify the physical and moral atmosphere. They will be blessings, not in disguise, but blessings palpable, substantial, spirit-refreshing.

"It occurs to me that the most eligible locality for a park of large dimensions, with every advantage of accessibility, has been strangely overlooked," X Y Z informed *The Courier-Journal* later in August 1882. "The property to which I refer is a tract of about 450 acres, owned by Messrs. Howard and Madison Miller."

> Its northern boundary is within one and a half miles of

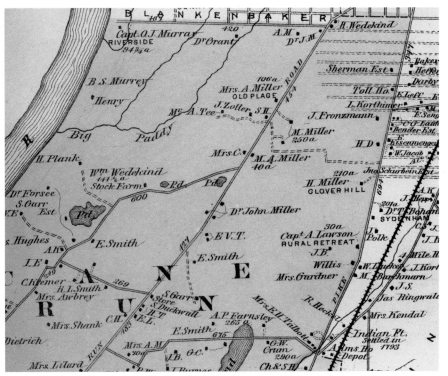

Section of Cane Run and Shiveleys, *Atlas of Jefferson & Oldham Counties Kentucky* (1879).

the city limits. It is approached by the Seventh, Eighteenth street and Cane run turnpikes, and an avenue a few yards in length connects it with the Chesapeake and Ohio railroad at a nearer point from the city than the race-course or Exposition Grounds. There are upon this property about eighty acres of original forest trees, being the only large body of timber within that distance of the city, and if not soon utilized for park purposes must necessarily be removed to subject this land to tillage. Its surface is undulating, and under the direction of a proper management it could be made as beautiful and attractive in all the attributes of a park as could be desired.[269]

"One of these many park schemes, which I happened to know about, has this point of interest, it contemplated the purchase of the 'Morton & Griswold Woods,' which became the nucleus of Cherokee Park," attorney and historian Temple Bodley later recalled. "About 1881, Judge Joshua F. Bullitt suggested to me a movement for its purchase as a park by the city and prepared a legislative bill giving the necessary authority. We went to some trouble in sounding out leading men and city officials with a view to pressing the scheme, but meeting little encouragement, abandoned it. Not very long afterwards, Mr. Wm. Clark laid before a meeting of gentlemen a plan for the purchase by the city of a large park extending from Broadway up Beargrass Creek to the south including the rolling country afterward embraced within Camp Taylor."[270] The proposal described in some detail in several articles in the fall of 1882 in *The Courier-Journal* was signed simply C. L. F. The land for the park was situated between Newburg and Poplar Level roads south of the South Fork of Beargrass Creek, principally property held by descendants of John and Ann Clark, parents of the founder of Louisville, George Rogers Clark, and the explorer, William Clark. "The selection of proper grounds in the right location formed for parks by nature, and requiring but little and inexpensive improvements, is of the utmost importance for all cities, and more particularly so for cities with limited means like Louisville," C. L. F. argued.[271] But, as Temple Bodley remarked, "nothing came of this scheme either." In fact, Andrew Cowan did investigate that section as he put together the tracts for the eastern park before its purchase in 1891. "Owners of some property out on Poplar level road were desirous to sell their land to the Board," Cowan remembered. "A number of real estate agents were actively at work to accomplish the sale. I went over the land with one of them, to show a seeming interest in that section, but as some of the land was badly washed, and access to the property from the City was out Shelby Street to the unattractive Poplar level road, I did not feel any uneasiness about its being purchased."[272]

"The grounds at Crescent Hill Reservoir are being beautified and improved in a practical manner, and will soon become a most pleasant and attractive place for our citizens and strangers to visit," Louisville Water Company president Charles R. Long noted in his annual report for 1882. "It is the purpose of the company to erect a suitable building and gate-ways at the entrance of Crescent Hill grounds on the Shelbyville and Brownsboro pikes during the year for the protection of the premises and comfort of visitors, and we hope to have the work completed by the opening of the great Southern Exposition to be held in this city the coming summer and fall."[273] The Water Company had constructed a new reservoir on higher ground between 1876 and 1879, and in doing so had created a nearby lake out of the borrow pit. The first announcement of a formal agreement for Reservoir Park's public use appeared in *The Courier-Journal*, 9 June 1907.

Creation of the new reservoir grounds and the city's preparation for the Southern Exposition distracted attention from the quest for park

Steps to Reservoir gatehouse. *Frank Leslie's Popular Monthly* 20 (November 1885): 525.

lands for several years. The subject of public parks for Louisville was raised by Capt. Thomas Speed at an 1887 meeting of the Salmagundi Club, a discussion group of leading citizens. A committee was appointed "to collate the argument, and present it with additional suggestions in the form of a report at a future meeting."[274] Col. Andrew Cowan was asked to prepare the report, and Charles Hermany was requested to prepare the map of the proposed park locations. The report and map were published in *The Courier-Journal* on Sunday 5 June 1887. "In its salient features it was the system the city has today," Temple Bodley recounted. "A boulevard connecting the three large parks was publicly suggested at the time, but it was objected that the distance between them was too great for horse-drawn vehicles. Until the advent of the fast and untiring automobiles, such a boulevard would probably have been little used and of little benefit except to owners of property along the line."[275]

Charles Hermany's "Plan of Proposed Parks." *The Courier-Journal*, 5 June 1887.

1. East of Mockingbird Valley Road (a continuation of Chenoweth Lane north).
2. Frankfort Avenue.
3. On 1884 atlas shows as head of Lake Avenue.
4. Proposed square, Preston and Kentucky streets.
5. Central Park.
6. Floral Park.
7. House of Refuge/U of L Belknap Campus.
8. Greenland Race Course.
9. Churchill Downs.
10. Baxter Square (city's first cemetery).
11. Western Cemetery.
12. National Park.
13. Twenty-eighth Street.

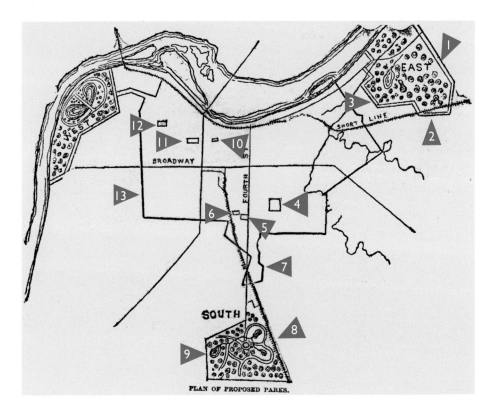

PLAN OF PROPOSED PARKS.

Hermany's map shows the major parks were to be established outside the city boundaries. Inside the city limits, he showed several existing private parks that were open to the public—Central and Floral parks along Fourth Street; the first and second cemeteries on either side of Fourteenth Street; what seems to be National Park (a beer garden between Main and Rowan streets, east of Twenty-fourth Street), and a large square east of Fourth Street.

At first glance, Hermany's map appears to delineate Louisville's major parks much as they came to be, but only his West Park fits into the present scheme as Shawnee Park. East Park incorporated the old Villa Park grounds, the Louisville Water Company's Ohio River Pumping Station grounds and those surrounding the Crescent Hill Reservoir, as well as a significant amount of land to the east including Mockingbird Valley and parts of Rolling Fields. East Park also encompassed much of Crescent Hill north of Frankfort Avenue, particularly the old fair grounds along Crescent Avenue which were being developed as a subdivision called Fair View.[276]

Andrew Cowan's report described the East Park part of the plan as follows.

> On the east side is the present water-works ground, comprising about two hundred and fifty acres in three tracts partially improved and extending from the river to the Shelbyville turnpike, which, with the addition of about six hundred acres, will make a magnificent park. On both sides of the water-works property, the land is beautifully situated and adorned with groves of fine forest trees. Beginning at the new reservoir grounds and widening to the east, and also to the west side, until the river is reached, affording a water front of suitable width, there is presented a varied landscape of hill, vale and bottom land of surprising beauty. The park could be easily reached by several lines of street-cars, by Story avenue, Reservoir avenue, the Brownsboro and the River road and the Shelbyville pike, also by the Narrow-gauge railroad running along the base of its bluffs, by the Short line railroad to its western front, and from the city wharf by boats, landing the passengers at the park dock.
>
> A Grand Avenue to the park can be run by way of East Broadway and the "Daisy" road [Grinstead Drive] through Forest Hill, a handsome tract of land belonging to the city; thence by a bridge across the workhouse road and the creek, to a beautiful plateau stretching across the Shelbyville road. By reserving a strip on both sides of this avenue of suitable width to accommodate summer villas, the entire cost of the avenue might be returned within a few years.

Cherokee Park would be located considerably south of the proposed East Park. Hermany's location of South Park is very strange, considering that it appears to encompass Churchill Downs west of Fourth Street and the Greenland Race Course to the east across Fourth Street. At the

A syndicate of capitalists own about a square mile of land two miles south of the city limits, which they propose to sell the city for a park. The price asked is $400,000, and the plan is to issue bonds to that account and to purchase the ground at once....

Even if the ground were worth every cent of the money asked for it, it is believed that it would be bad policy to spend so much on one park, as it would practically defeat any other plan for the building of other parks. This would be something of a misfortune, as the city, spreading as it does over so much territory, certainly needs more than one park. It should certainly have, at least, three, one being located near each suburb.

"The Highland Park Scheme." *The Courier-Journal*, 6 July 1887.

Confronted with unexpected popular opposition and anticipating a veto from the Mayor, the gentlemen who wanted to sell Highland Park to the city asked leave last night to withdraw the ordinance discussed during the past week, and thus ends the plan for a South Park.

"The Park Question." *The Courier-Journal*, 8 July 1887.

time, both tracks were struggling, but there was no discussion in the press about converting them into parks.

Western Cemetery was already derelict, its high brick wall collapsed or torn down, its tombstones fallen down and rotting, according to "The Village Graveyard." *The Courier-Journal*, 10 June 1883.

In early July 1887, H. A. Dumesnil offered the city the use of Floral Park free for five years. With every elected official in favor of parks, it was difficult to walk away from the gift or as *The Courier-Journal* put it: "Mr. Dumesnil's loan." The newspaper provided a rare description of the five-acre park.[277]

> Floral Park is conveniently situated in one of the most beautiful parts of the city, between Ormsby and Weissinger [Park] avenues, and Sixth and Seventh streets. In former years it was the only fashionable resort of the kind accessible, and was one of the most comfortably arranged parks in the country. The grounds were always kept in faultless condition, the trees and hedges neatly trimmed, the lake supplied with pure, fresh water, while an abundance of rare and fragrant flowers made a most attractive spot.
>
> The school picnics were then all given in the park, and numbers of men and women, now grown up, will recall with pleasure many happy days spent within its bounds.
>
> About seven years ago, for some reason or other, the park was closed, and has since been used but little. The swings and benches have long been torn away, and the buildings are in sore need of repair; but it would take very little to restore the place to its same old self and make Floral Park second in point of comfort and beauty to none of the resorts.

At a subsequent meeting of the Commercial Club, the matter of public parks was discussed. Morton Casseday advocated a park commission to make choices of land for parks. He suggested that John Mason Brown "be intrusted with the preparation of a bill to that end, to be submitted to the next Legislature."[278] Brown agreed on the spot to prepare a draft of such a bill. "He thought it highly important that something of this character should be done. They must have parks and be a city or go on without parks and be a village."[279] At a special meeting of the Commercial Club a week later, Brown read his bill to provide for the establishment of public parks adjacent to the city of Louisville and for their improvement and management. Interestingly, the bill called for the election of Park Commissioners first and then for a vote upon the act itself, "the object being to give the people a chance

---

The current discussion of the subject will doubtless result in some measure which will obtain parks for our city at little cost. The managers of the House of Refuge propose to care without cost for a park of 100 acres if the city will purchase it contiguous to the 130 acres surrounding that institution. It may be that with the expenditure of a small sum of money we may secure a park in the location, extending it to the east and opening Third street.

At any rate our people are interested. Numberless plans will be suggested; all should be considered calmly and deliberately. What is done should be done with due regard to economy, as well as for the future necessities of a growing city.

"The Park Question." *The Courier-Journal*, 8 July 1887.

to defeat it if the Park Commissioners were chosen in the interest of any land scheme."[280]

Brown suggested the arrangement be voted on at the December municipal elections.[281] Instead, according to Andrew Cowan, the act's author used his "persuasive power and influence…to gain a tardy approval by Mayor Jacob and members of the City Council for his park act."[282] Temple Bodley later explained the delay local politics would cause.

> But just when Colonel Cowan's park plan seemed fairly sure of adoption, it was imperiled and long delayed over a proposed extension of the Louisville Gas Company's charter. That company demanded the exclusive privilege for fifty years to make and sell gas, then a necessity for everyone, and without any real protection for consumers.
>
> Mr. Jacob, who had been elected Mayor and dominated the city government, had been led to favor the gas company's demand. The General Council, which was henceforth completely subservient to him, had already approved the charter extension of the monopoly for thirty years, and the State Legislature seemed ready to do so.
>
> Colonel Cowan was very loath to arouse Mayor Jacob's opposition to his cherished park plan by opposing the gas charter, but felt it his duty to fight it and he did. He led the public opposition to it resolutely, ably and successfully. The result was the elimination of nearly all the objectionable features in the charter, but also Mayor Jacob's coolness toward the park plan. He could not be induced to approve the bill establishing it until it was too late to present it to the Legislature then in session, nor until material changes were made in the park bill. Two more years were to pass before Cowan's park system could be established by law.[283]

"Mr. Jacob had not the remotest connection with the conception of the plan that has given us a system of parks, nor did it have his cordial support," Andrew Cowan would declare during the 1893 mayoral campaign when Jacob was being credited as the father of the Louisville park system.[284]

Despite such criticism of Mayor Jacob, *The Courier-Journal* in eulogizing him stated: "He is the father of the parks. It was mainly through his efforts during his last term in office that the Legislature adopted a measure creating a Park Commission, and the park bond issue was voted during his administration. In 1889 Mr. Jacob himself

The history of the park system is this: When public-spirited citizens were organized to oppose the encroachment of the Gas Company, a good deal was said about parks. There was a mayoralty race on hand, and the question of parks was discussed, it being considered a good time to take steps in that direction. Among the foremost advocates of the proposed purchase of parks was Colonel Andrew Cowan. The act was drawn and the initial steps were taken while Mr. Reed was Mayor.

"Some Park History." *The Critic*, 16 August 1891.

I have the honor to acknowledge...the receipt of a resolution passed by your Board on Sept 20th 1898, in which you informed me that not with standing the Board of Park Commissioners on Aug 13th 1891 had changed the name of the Park situated south of Louisville Ky, theretofore known and called "Jacob Park in honor of Chas. D. Jacob former mayor of said city to "Iroquois Park." The present Board because said Park is still commonly known and called Jacob Park and is seldom known or called Iroquois Park have resolved that said Park shall no longer be named or called Iroquois Park and is now named Jacob Park by which latter name it shall be hereafter known and called....

I beg to express my deep sense of gratitude at the honor that has been shown me by the Board of Commissioners for Parks.... I have the honor to be gentlemen your obt [obedient] servant, Chas. D. Jacob.

Board of Park Commissioners meeting 4 October 1898. Minute Book 6, pp. 333-334.

The Third-avenue boulevard, said to be the finest in the South, was Mr. Jacob's pet project. The work of extending it from the end of Third avenue to Jacob Park was done principally by means of private donations, which Mr. Jacob and his friends tried so hard to secure.

"Charles D. Jacob Dead." *The Courier-Journal*, 26 December 1898.

purchased all the property now known as Jacob Park, but which was then called 'Burnt Knob.' The price paid was $9,000. Despite the fact that a syndicate offered Mr. Jacob $23,000 for the property, he refused to sell, preferring to dispose of it to the city."[285] The son of John I. Jacob, considered the richest man in Louisville, had been sent to Cambridge to prepare for Harvard before becoming successful in banking and insurance. He served four terms as mayor while taking five extended trips abroad.

Charles Donald Jacob (1838-1898). "Charles D. Jacob Dead." *The Courier-Journal*, 26 December 1898.

21
MAYOR JACOB'S PARK AND GRAND BOULEVARD (1889)

LESS THAN A YEAR AFTER THE PUBLIC PARKS BILL had been drafted but left to languish, Mayor Charles Jacob and City Engineer Ransom Scowden began "prospecting" for suitable park land in the "picturesque hill country that lies above the eastern limits of the city." They focused on the site surrounding the abandoned reservoir above the River Road pumping station that had been the focus of earlier plans. "City Engineer Scowden considers the plan the most desirable as well as the most practicable that has ever been offered," The *Louisville Commercial* pointed out.[286] "There is really, he says, no other suitable location for a park about the city. The natural advantages of this spot are even superior to those of the celebrated Fairmount Park, of Philadelphia."

Ransom T. Scowden certainly knew the reservoir location. Born in 1837 in Cincinnati where his father was an engineer, he followed him to the Cleveland waterworks and then to Louisville where Theodore R. Scowden took over the engineering department of the fledgling water company. Although the younger Scowden worked on the Louisville and Portland Canal, he would have been well aware of the pumping station and reservoir his father was building on the Ohio River on land he had selected above the Beargrass Creek cutoff. He next worked in Cincinnati, Parkersburg, and Cleveland, before returning to Louisville after the panic of 1873. Before being selected city engineer of Louisville in 1876, he was in charge of Atlanta's waterworks.[287]

Soon after making his glowing assessment of the reservoir site for a park, Scowden, along with Mayor Jacob, had a change of mind. According to Cowan, "certain owners of part of a hill known as Burnt Knob, situated six miles in an air line south from the Court House, got Mayor Jacob to go out and see what a fine place it would be for a park.... The lunch, provided in a log cabin on the hill, was fine; the view towards the city was beautiful that day, so Mayor Jacob promised to buy the north end of Burnt Knob on time and take the deed in his own name. He absolutely controlled the General Council of the City. So when he proposed to sell Burnt Knob to the City for City purposes, at what he had agreed to pay for it, plus the interest, the Council bought it."[288]

The name [Burnt Knob] is derived from the fact that the charcoal burners inhabited the knob before the Civil War. They burned the hill bare, and then decamped to other pastures. The magnificent beeches, oaks, sweet gums and diverse other trees are all of second growth.

"The Beauty of Louisville's Southern Parkway," *The Courier-Journal*, 10 August 1902.

At the same time, the Commercial Club began to influence property owners to remove their fences as a way to beautify the city. "As an example to the citizens the Mayor has had the hospital fence removed, and will take the handsome iron fence from Baxter Square early in the spring," *The Louisville Commercial* reported 10 December 1888.[289] He was robbing Peter to pay Paul. While making Baxter Square more accessible, Mayor Jacob intended to use the fencing to enclose "the new park on the side approached by the boulevard." He expected to soon "secure two more public squares, one in the East End and one in the West End." This, The *Commercial* commented, "will fully solve the park question."

> Then, as it appeared to the interested friends of Brown's Park Act, his many flatterers persuaded the Mayor to go ahead "improving" the property for a Park, and get ahead of the fellows who might claim the glory of establishing "Parks for the People." They easily had their way. The Council voted money for the Mayor, with the City's Engineer, Mr. Scowden, to improve the land that Jacob bought. Land companies sprang up like mushrooms, to get the benefit of an expected boom in the neighborhood of the Park, and along a broad Avenue called the "Grand Boulevard," which the Mayor began to grade without any legal right or title to the land. Mr. M. Lewis Clark was appointed Chief of Parks with a salary of three thousand dollars a year, and Manlius Taylor, Assistant, at fifteen hundred.[290]

However, *The Critic* claimed on 15 September 1889 that "Colonel M. Lewis Clark was appointed a park commissioner by the mayor, and took charge of the work about the middle of July. The *Commercial* states that Colonel Clark is paid a salary of $6,000 a year, but *The Critic*'s information is that the Colonel is doing the work out of pure love for his native land, an example of patriotism worthy of general emulation."

Meriwether Lewis Clark and Charles D. Jacob had long been associates. Clark, the grandson of explorer William Clark, was the long-time president of the Louisville Jockey Club, the organization that owned and managed Churchill Downs, which he had established in 1874, when both were named to the initial board of directors. Clark knew that a park located south of the House of Refuge would require a major thoroughfare that would skirt Churchill Downs and benefit it. Jacob surely was aware of it, too. His sister, Lucy, was the mother of Darwin Ward Johnson, Jr., secretary of the Louisville Jockey Club. *The Critic* later claimed that the suggestion of Burnt Knob "for park purposes was made by Col. Clark to the Mayor."[291] Manlius Taylor was the great-grandson of Hancock Taylor, brother of President Zachary Taylor. Several months after the purchase of the Burnt Knob land, "the wilderness of woods and hills and valleys has been wonderfully changed," *The Courier-Journal* remarked. "Mayor Jacob and Park Superintendent Taylor have done excellent and artistic work."[292] "Mr. Taylor has cut about four miles of roads, with any number of footways and bridle paths," *The Courier-Journal* described 9 May 1889. "On the top of the main hill is a plateau of eighty-four acres covered with bluegrass, and here it is intended that most of the improvements shall be located. An immense lake is to cover twenty acres, and around this a mile track will be built. Between the lake and the track will be walks and drives attractively laid out with bordering shrubbery and flower-beds. The club-house and pavilion will be under a clump of trees on the loftiest point of the grounds."[293] The park, named in honor of Mayor Jacob, opened 1 June 1889.

"Map of Jacob Park and Adjacent Property, Louisville, Ky., Nov. 20, 1890." Louisville Title Insurance Company collection, The Filson Historical Society.

Ransom Scowden's design for Jacob Park's roadways is delineated on an oversize map dated 20 November 1890.[294] Andrew Cowan described the entranceway from the Grand Boulevard as "a loop the loop road" that crossed William Stewart's land four or five times, without obtaining

I've been at work in it for forty-three years straight running. I began clearing up the woods one September forty-three years ago…. It was called Jacob's Folly at that time. You see, Mayor Jacob bought it for a big city park; but most of the people laughed at him because it was so far out in the country.

Interview of John Lowery in James Speed, "Louisville's Park System Grows Into Large Business," *The Herald-Post*, 18 November 1932.

Graded roadway on Iroquois hill. *The Courier-Journal* files.

his permission. Mr. Stewart demanded one thousand dollars an acre for his part of Burnt Knob on which Scowden had built part of his loop the loop road. "At last, after we had threatened to abandon the whole property, the owners were brought to reason and we obtained deeds to the property."[295] Cowan noted that after a large tract was purchased from Rose DeMarsh on the north side of Burnt Knob, it "gave Mr. Codman, the Park Landscape Architect, room to lay out the beautiful roadway which now encircles the hill."[296] The Olmsted firm's 1 December 1897 General Map for Iroquois Park shows the layout of the lower circuit road as well as the improvements at the entrance.[297] Only minor changes had been made to the upper circuit road designed by Scowden.

The Critic was vehemently opposed to the park and Jacob. "Putting aside the fact that it is a long distance from the city, it is nothing but a lot of gulches," and "it would take a million or more dollars to make the ravines that comprise the area fit for a pleasure ground."[298]

Turning into the dirt road after passing the House of Refuge, the heights of the new park can be plainly seen in the distance. With an average horse the park is reached in forty minutes after leaving Third street and Broadway. Inside the park boundaries two roads leading off from the boulevard, which has already been cut, can be seen winding up the hills and to the top at an altitude of 394 feet above the level of the surrounding country. From the five points of the star shaped hill the views and the scenery cannot be equaled in this part of the State….

About the hills roadways have been cut, and bridle paths and footways have been made winding in and out of the groves and forests and down into the valleys. The only offset to the natural advantages offered by the site is the absence of running water. This defect will be remedied shortly, when a main will be extended by the Louisville Water Company. A pumping machine will be put up at a cost of $5,000, and the lakes and ravines and creeks which City Engineer Scowden has laid out will be kept full of fresh running water at a depth varying from two to fifteen feet. Every path and road will be intersected by water, and across the ravines nothing but rustic bridges will be made. The lake will cover an area of forty-five acres on the plateau at the top of the hill and will be a half mile long and about 500 yards wide, which will give plenty of room for safe and not overcrowded boating and aquatic sports. The lake will be heavily stocked with game fish, and there will be plenty to tempt the angler.[299]

When the Board of Managers of the Louisville Industrial School of Reform (House of Refuge) would not allow Third Street to be extended through its property, Mayor Jacob arranged for the election of a new board, which dissolved an injunction preventing the boulevard's construction.[300]

According to Louisville civil engineer Joseph Peyton Claybrook's obituary, he "surveyed and superintended the construction of the roads and the boulevard in and leading to Iroquois Park."[301] His name appears on payroll lists in 1891. Claybrook graduated from the US Naval Academy,

Section of *New Map of Louisville* (1891) showing Grand Boulevard from Churchill Downs to Jacob Park.

Next came the drive to Jacob Park. The boulevard was in perfect condition for driving, and as the ascent of the hill was made, the air was so fresh and invigorating that the visitors declared it equal to a ride through the mountains. When the top of the hill was reached all got out and took a look at the surrounding country…. After a drive over the plateau on top of the hill the party drove half way down to a shady grove, where lunch was spread.

"Rich Men Of The East." *Louisville Commercial*, 25 May 1890. The Commercial Club entertained "visiting capitalists from New England."

took part in the Civil War in both the Confederate navy and army, became a civil engineer working on railroad projects including the building of the Louisville Southern Railroad, was a graduate physician, and served during the first Cleveland administration as superintendent of the Louisville and Portland Canal.[302]

"Ten years ago this summer, August 4, 1890, the decisive vote of the people of Louisville gave them their first park system," *The Courier-Journal* pointed out 6 May 1900. "They have to-day a boulevard and speedway which rivals the largest cities of the country and three large parks which the diversity, beauty and natural advantages are unrivaled…. Strangers who visit Louisville are most enthusiastic in regard to the southernmost park, rightfully called Jacob Park. It possesses not only a topography, but an individuality of its own…. It is not a park in the usual sense of the word and might, as long ago suggested by the architect, have had its name changed to 'Jacob Woods' or 'Jacob Forest' as more fitting."[303] The article signed by E. C. W. also praised Grand Boulevard.

The grand boulevard or approach to Jacob Park is one of those improvements in which Louisville is ahead of far more boastful cities. Its popularity as a driveway is shown by the Sunday afternoon pageant which is one of the greatest summer attractions of the city. The speedway has been the means of bringing many fine horses to Churchill Downs to train as well as a delight to local horsemen, who were so active in bringing it about. Other cities, such as Detroit, Cleveland, Providence, Brooklyn and even advanced Boston are now at work building speedways, but none will out do Louisville's boulevard.

William Marshall Bullitt working his horse on Grand Boulevard. The Bullitt Papers, The Filson Historical Society.

THE FINCASTLE CLUB, NITTA YUMA, AND SOUTH PARK (1887-1890)

"ABOUT A DOZEN YEARS AGO LOUISVILLE REJOICED in the possession, actual or in prospect, of a number of country clubhouses," *The Courier-Journal* observed in 1900. "Among the first and best of these was the beautiful structure on the Glenview heights above the Ohio river, known as the 'Fincastle Club.' The enterprise was fathered and fostered by Mr. John E. Green, who at the time lived on the Glenview estate."[304] Interest in public parks spilled over into the private sector. The Glenview Stock Farm provided the club 13.5 acres conveniently located on the Louisville, Harrods Creek & Westport narrow-gauge railway. A year after its organization in 1887 based upon Tuxedo Park above New York City, the Fincastle Club completed its clubhouse which featured 14 large sleeping apartments and a well-appointed restaurant for its members who were expected "to build themselves nice cottages about the hills and hollows of the club." The Fincastle Club was characterized as "a genuine country club—a retreat surrounded by tall woodland trees and filled with pure air, where careworn business

Shingled cottage of Charles R. Peaslee about 1895. Courtesy of the Charles Peaslee Farnsley family.

men can take their families at a moment's notice and enjoy a few days in almost rural precincts…. The position is elevated and commands a splendid view for miles of the grand Ohio…. During the long summer days the tired business man who has taken refuge in this sylvan spot may stroll among the beautiful trees…dense forests of majestic beech and oak."[305]

A number of summer residences built by 1896, including the cottages of George Avery, C. T. Ballard, A. C. Semple, Paul Cain, W. Meade Robinson, S. Thruston Ballard, and Owen Tyler, were published in *The Courier-Journal*.[306] One place not shown had been built by Charles R. Peaslee about 1889.

While the smaller houses continued to be occupied, the clubhouse went vacant until in 1900 Judge and Mrs. A. P. Humphrey converted it into a single family dwelling.[307] The Humphreys and Charles T. Ballard bought up the summer residences including the Peaslee place, and in 1910-1911 the Ballards erected a Georgian brick house that Judge Robert Worth Bingham bought in 1919. Charles R. Peaslee's summer place had occupied the site. After Judge Humphrey died in 1928, Judge Bingham purchased the old Fincastle clubhouse and replaced it with an amphitheater designed by Thomas Hastings of New York.

❧   ❧   ❧

FARTHER OUT RIVER ROAD, the enclave called Nitta Yuma (high ground) was created in 1890 with the purchase of 100 acres from the estate of James Todd by George Garvin Brown, Charles R. Peaslee, and William Frederick Booker. The development's roads were planned and executed by Booker's brother-in-law, civil engineer Joseph Peyton Claybrook.[308] He and his wife, Mary Booker Claybrook, lived in the old Todd farmhouse at Nitta Yuma year around.

❧   ❧   ❧

Summer residence of George Garvin Brown at Nitta Yuma. *Art Work of Louisville, Ky.* (Chicago, 1893), Part 4.

THE CREATION OF JACOB PARK immediately stimulated commercial housing interest south of the city with direct access via the L&N Railroad. A number of prominent citizens purchased several hundred acres two miles beyond Burnt Knob and formed the South Park Residence Company.[309] "There have been practically no attempts to build any distinctive residential suburb, although there are here and there some very handsome seats outside the city," *The Courier-Journal* observed in its 12 May 1889 article announcing the creation of the "new fashionable residence town and summer retreat." The papers reported that "skilled engineers will lay it out to avoid rectangular streets and lots. The thoroughfares will be curved and magnificent pine forest, varied here and there, with splendid growths of a variety of forest trees, will serve all the purposes of parks, and will be preserved to a great extent for that object. There will be no fences, and the whole town will be inclosed to prevent the intrusion of stock."[310] The extensive development over some 390 acres was surveyed and platted by civil engineers Emil Mahlo and B. W. Fenton. South Park was recorded 9 April 1890.[311] It was

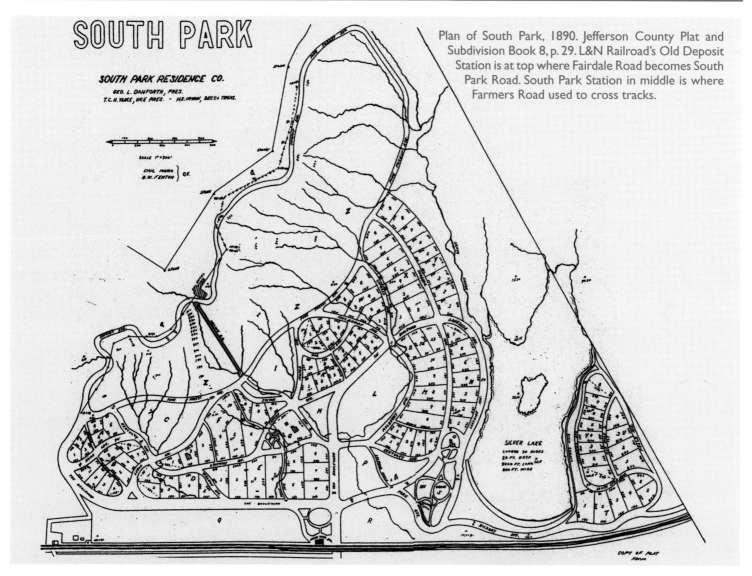

Plan of South Park, 1890. Jefferson County Plat and Subdivision Book 8, p. 29. L&N Railroad's Old Deposit Station is at top where Fairdale Road becomes South Park Road. South Park Station in middle is where Farmers Road used to cross tracks.

the first large-scale subdivision in Jefferson County designed to take advantage of the topography. Along the ridge on the north side, the South Park Hotel opened 9 July 1890.[312] Nearby, an incline railroad was planned to connect the hotel with the town lots. Some tracts were sold, but the venture did not materialize as planned, so the residence company conveyed 329 acres, less 21 lots already transferred to the South Park Land Company. The South Park Fishing and Boating Club continued to utilize Silver Lake. Eventually, the South Park Country Club took over the property.[313]

South Park Hotel opened in July 1890. *The Critic*, 29 June 1890. "Its location in the midst of a dense pine forest, 400 feet above the city, presents a landscape from ten to thirty miles in extent, of surpassing beauty. During the night it is from ten to fifteen degrees cooler than in Louisville."

BOARD OF PARK COMMISSIONERS (1890)

I gave such constant attention, in day light, to the construction work proceeding on all of our Parks, during the whole three years of my term that I had to work at night to keep in touch with my business. I wore out a standard bred horse that cost me $350, and then paid $950 for a wonderful brown horse that served me and the public well, while wearing out two good buggies, which was going some for those days. I left the distribution of places and patronage to the members who demanded and loved that sort of thing.

Reminiscences of Andrew Cowan. The Filson Historical Society.

THE ELECTION OF SIX BOARD OF PARK COMMISSIONERS was held 1 July 1890. "It is generally believed that the vote will be light, and yet a great deal of interest is being taken owing to the action of the Republicans in endeavoring to obtain representation on the board." Two tickets were offered. The "citizens" ticket was made up of all Democrats; "calico" consisted of three Democrats and three Republicans.[314] In promoting his candidacy, Democrat R. T. Durrett prepared a lengthy piece for *The Critic* pointing out the lost opportunities and present prospects of parks in Louisville.[315] He was defeated. "General Apathy was in command of the voting forces, and that is how two Republicans managed to be elected Park Commissioners of this Democratic city," *The Courier-Journal* acknowledged.[316] Democrat John Finzer was the largest vote-getter, although he had been out of the city for two months. His tobacco-producing brother and "Jailer Bailey made an invincible organization for him…. The whisky men and the Liquor Dealers' Protective Association were for Mr. Sherley…. Gen. Castleman's personal popularity carried him through and his vote is a very handsome one." The Republicans elected were Andrew Cowan and E. C. Bohne. Gottleib Layer barely beat out E. J. McDermott. Bohne indicated he wanted a Democrat to head the Board and suggested Thomas H. Sherley, who was elected president in July 1890.[317] Later, due to the whiskey distributor's travel demands, the position of vice president was created, to which Castleman was named.

The referendum on the Parks bill was finally put to the voters 4 August 1890. "Returns from most of the precincts indicate an interest in the park question that will be a surprise even to its most sanguine friends," *The Courier-Journal* reported the next day. Ten thousand votes were cast for the park bond, and only 3,000 against the issue. "This is an admirable showing, and it in effect orders the old fogies to the rear. It is a victory won in the face of a determined opposition as unaccountable as it was discreditable. For nearly four years this agitation has gone on, and at last intelligence triumphs, and Louisville takes a long step forward."[318] The Board of Park Commissioners wasted no time in meeting to "discuss the ways and means of disposing of the $600,000 of municipal bonds for parks, of which the people yesterday authorized the issue."[319]

> Mayor [pro tem William Lee] Lyons was informed by resolution that the Commissioners were ready to receive all the park property in charge of the city as soon as it was practicable for the city to turn over the property. This includes Jacob Park and the small squares in the city—Baxter Square and Floral Park. The Commissioners then adjourned.
>
> No action was taken in regard to the election of a permanent Secretary and in Park Superintendent, as there is yet no money for salaries.… Col. Lewis Clark is the only person mentioned for Superintendent, the compensation of which post will probably be fixed at $3,500. Col. Clark's great services in constructing the boulevards and in the work of beautifying Jacob Park are appreciated, and these with his high reputation as a business and public-spirited man, make it unlikely he will have opposition.[320]

The Commissioners moved swiftly to develop the system that had long been contemplated and hoped for.[321]

> The Board of Park Commissioners are authorized to establish at least one park in the western portion of the city, one in the easterly and one park in the southerly portion of the city, and to acquire land for the purpose by purchase, condemnation or acceptance of gift. In establishing said parks full discretion is given to the Board as to the location, the suitability of the ground and the cost thereof. The Board now solicits proposals for land suitable for park purposes within or beyond the boundaries of the city. Proposals must be in writing, addressed to the President. The Board reserves the right to reject any or all proposals. By order of the Board, T. H. Sherley, president.[322]

While a number of proposals were received from newspaper advertisements, they were deemed "so indefinite, uncertain and unsatisfactory" that the Board decided to pursue the selection of parks directly. After the Burnt Knob property was turned over to the Board for the southern park, property was subsequently purchased for the eastern and western parks.

Jacob Park was increased substantially from 320 acres to 616 acres through purchases negotiated primarily by Board president Sherley. A map of the land acquisition around Burnt Knob, published in *The*

"The understanding is that the commissioners will pay back every cent advanced, and, of course, the law requires that every cent expended before the Park bill passed will be paid back to the city." Thomas Sherley, president Board of Park Commissioners, in "That Jacob Park Money."

The Courier-Journal, 13 December 1890.

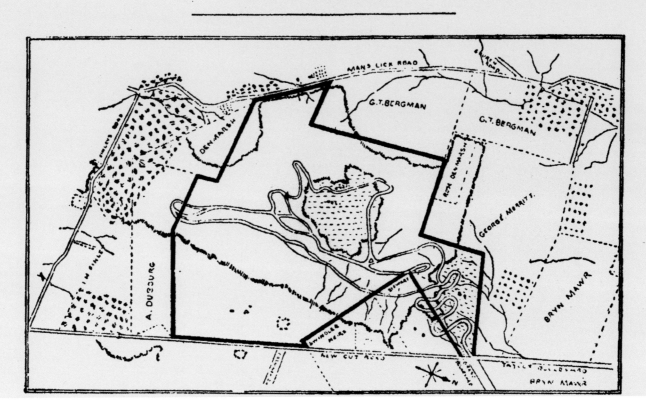

THE COURIER-JOURNAL: LOUISVILLE, SUNDAY MORNING, JUNE 14, 1891.

JACOB PARK IMPROVEMENTS.

Cheap Purchases of Adjoining Lands—Its Ragged Outlines To Be Straightened and Beautiful Drives Provided.

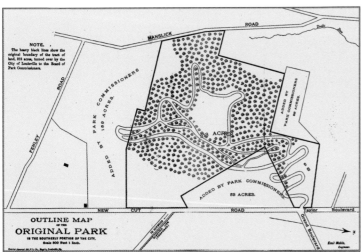

Emil Mahlo, "Outline Map of the Original Park," *First Annual Report of the Board of Park Commissioners*, dated 21 July 1891.

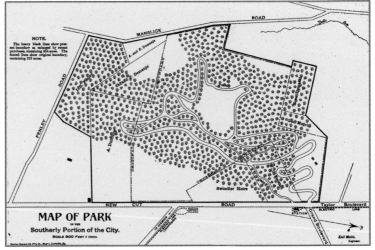

Iroquois Park plat showing original zigzag entrance, undated. Louisville Olmsted Parks Conservancy.

Courier-Journal, 14 June 1891, shows the layout of the roadways, reportedly designed by Ransom Scowden, but his proposed lake and other water features were not included.[323] The newspaper's map was derived from one prepared by the new park engineer, Emil Mahlo, for publication in the *First Annual Report of the Board of Park Commissioners,* dated 21 July 1891. About that time, without any prospect of being city engineer in a new administration or park engineer with the Board of Park Commissioners, Scowden moved to Chicago.

"In Jacob Park we have the raw material for one of the most beautiful parks in the world," The *Louisville Commercial* observed 6 May 1891. "Properly utilizing these natural features in laying out a park is an art which has its recognized masters. Such material as we have in Jacob Park should only be intrusted to a master. No journeyman or bungling apprentice or uninstructed amateur should be allowed to meddle with its magnificent possibilities. Our suggestion is that some master of the art of park development, like Frederick Law Olmsted, be employed to come here, examine the ground and furnish plans and specifications for its improvement on the truest principles, then have all the work done in the park conform to them…. After years perhaps, we will have a park to challenge the admiration of the most competent critics of the world." Obviously unknown to The Commercial, five months before, Park Commissioner Andrew Cowan had acted upon the same sentiment.

"A large force of men have been set at work improving and beautifying the grounds of Jacob Park," *The Louisville Times* reported 12 May 1891. "The washes are being filled up, the drives improved and flowers planted. The Eastern Park has one decided advantage over Jacob Park, in that it is abundantly supplied with water. There is no water whatever in the latter, and the Water Company wants $6,300 a mile for laying the pipes to it, and will do nothing till a right of way is secured. The intended improvements of the boulevard will be withheld till the suits for right of way are settled."

In its August 1891 report, the Olmsted firm pointed out that Jacob Park even lacked "an adequate supply of drinking water." Except

Grand Boulevard in background leading to zigzag entrance of Iroquois Park. *Second Annual Report of the Board of Park Commissioners* (July 1892).

for areas at the top of the hill, Jacob Park lacked the broad clearings that the firm liked to emphasize in a park such as Cherokee. "In this respect," the report noted, "a thousand dollars of outlay will give you at once more of what you want than the outlay of a million would come near giving you in fifty years on the Iroquois hill." The firm suggested enhancing "the beauty of the present forest," but "to attempt to apply what we are accustomed to distinguish as a 'park-like' treatment to ground of this character would be…foolish."[324] The report also observed that Jacob Park was far distant from the "dwellings and working places of the mass of people." The firm may not have realized that with the numerous floods of the 1880s, Louisville was moving south, and that Churchill Downs provided an impetus to build a major road in the direction of the park.

In a painful irony, Charles Jacob was injured in the park that bore his name. "Four or five years ago he was driving through Jacob Park, the great, wild breathing place which he gave to the city," *The Courier-Journal* recalled.

> He was driving along a new embankment, when it gave way and the trap was overturned…. Mr. Jacob was caught between the wheels, and still holding the lines, was dragged about fifty yards in his perilous position. The horses were very gentle, and had been accustomed to being fed with sugar from a woman's hand. It was while the horses were running that they spied two women in a buggy. The horses stopped running and, trotting up to the buggy, poked their noses in, expecting to receive their allowance of sugar. It was this circumstance that probably saved Mr. Jacob's life, although it did not save him from many severe bruises and a violent shaking up.[325]

The Board of Park Commissioners operated through a number of standing committees whose memberships were appointed by the president. One committee had oversight of "shade trees" along public streets, as enumerated in the Park bill.[326]

"In reply to the question put by a stranger: 'What is there worth seeing in Louisville?' the reply has been more than once, 'the streets,'" *The Courier-Journal* pointed out in May 1896. "The streets in the southern part of the city are, indeed, so picturesquely and so gracefully shaded as to make them a happy wheeling ground for the roving wheelman. The trees which give them their charm, even more than their many picturesque residences, are under the supervision and care of the city Board of Park Commissioners, a body whose importance to the public welfare is far greater than the over-practical or superficial observer

Trees line Second Street north of Jacob Street about 1893. Frederick H. Verhoeff Collection, The Filson Historical Society.

may suppose. The inclusion of these hundreds of sidewalk trees in the jurisdiction of a department of the municipal government with such a title is in itself a sign that the aesthetic and hygienic importance of street-shading is officially recognized."[327]

Our shade trees are far more valuable than our electric lights. Various influences are destroying them. The dirt of the city, its smoke and dust-laden atmosphere are harmful to the trees. The asphalt pavements deprive them of their water supply. The cement sidewalks are as injurious as the asphalt pavements. Leaking gas-pipes poison the soil; neglect shortens their lives and ignorant pruning shortens their years.

But perhaps their greatest enemy is the electric light linemen who attack our trees with spikes and hatchets, and make of them ladders and poles in order to save a little money for the company.... A lineman has no more right to hack up a tree than any other fool with an ax, and an example should be made of the men who thus wage war against our shade trees.

"The Shade Trees." *The Louisville Post*, 22 July 1893.

BOONE PARK DOWNGRADED TO A SQUARE (1891)

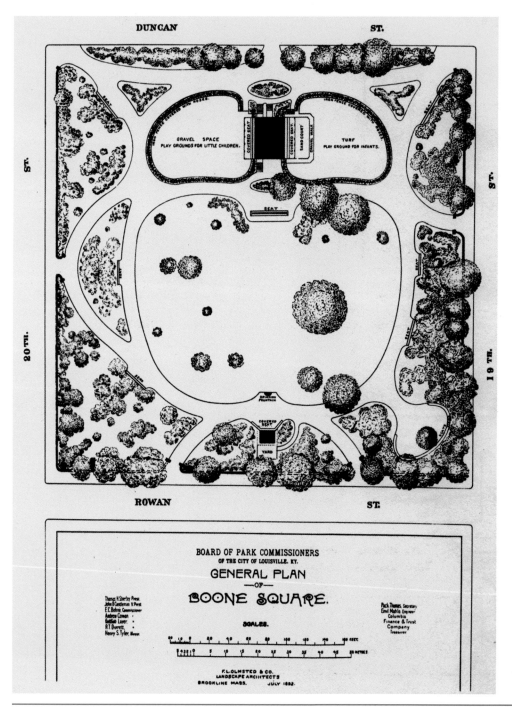

DUNCAN **ST.**

GRAVEL SPACE
PLAY GROUNDS FOR LITTLE CHILDREN.

COVERED SEAT

COVERED SEAT
SAND COURT

TURF
PLAY GROUND FOR INFANTS.

SEAT

20TH. **ST.**

19 TH. **ST.**

ROWAN **ST.**

BOARD OF PARK COMMISSIONERS
OF THE CITY OF LOUISVILLE. KY.

GENERAL PLAN
—OF—

BOONE SQUARE.

SCALES.

F.L. OLMSTED & CO.
LANDSCAPE ARCHITECTS
BROOKLINE MASS.   JULY 1892.

"THE CITY IS TO HAVE A PARK in the West End and soon," *The Courier-Journal* reported after the 12 May 1891 meeting of park commissioners. The purchase price of $23,000 was considered a "reasonable sum" for the block between Nineteenth and Twentieth, Rowan and Duncan streets, the former home of John Rowan's granddaughter, Eliza Harney Boone, and her late husband Col. William P. Boone.[328] He was a native of Corydon, Indiana, and had practiced law in Louisville since 1836.[329] The property was deeded to her on the occasion of her marriage in 1842, when their two-story, brick house on a raised basement, facing Duncan Street, was erected and the "beautiful forest trees" were planted. "The sycamores and maples…are said to be the handsomest in Jefferson county."[330] The Board had considered the acquisition of the beer garden called National Park nearby, but its site was open on only three sides and its

Plan of Boone Square dated July 1892. *Second Annual Report of the Board of Park Commissioners* (July 1892). While credited to F.L. Olmsted & Co., it probably represents the work of Henry S. Codman and Park Engineer Emil Mahlo.

cost was $2,000 more.[331] The grounds of National Park were between Main and Rowan streets, east of Twenty-fourth Street, first listed in the 1882 city directory.

Frederick Law Olmsted and Henry S. Codman inspected the Boone property on 20 May 1891 and evidently gave their seal of approval to the Board of Park Commissioners' recent purchase of the site.[332] The "engineering force" under Engineer Emil Mahlo was put to work in Boone Square in early June 1891, and their survey was soon completed and sent to Olmsted & Co. On 11 August, the plans for the improvement of Boone Square presented by Henry Codman were adopted by the Board.[333] By the end of 1891, work on Boone Square (the Olmsted firm did not consider the property large enough to be termed a park) was well underway. According to *The Critic*:

> The walks have been laid out and graded, and are now being paved. Grass will be sown and fine shrubbery planted at once, so that next spring this square will present a fine aspect. The contract for building a rustic stone wall around it has been let, and work on it begun.[334] The remodeling of the old Boone residence into a café and house for comfort will be commenced at once.[335]

Boone Square, *Second Annual Report of the Board of Park Commissioners* (July 1892). View shows entrance on Rowan Street, which intersects Twentieth Street at left.

In 1982, a derelict Boone Square was taken under the wing of The Olmsted Festival, a multi-purpose project masterminded by Eleanor Bingham Miller, C. J. Pressma, and Nancy Comstock. Money was raised to support the redesign of Boone Square by Miller, Wihry & Lee in keeping with the original plan. Boone Square Park opened in May 1986.

25
RETAINING FREDERICK LAW OLMSTED (1891)

Louisville has unquestionably the most unique and beautiful park sites of any city in America. This is the expressed opinion of Frederick Law Olmsted, than whom no greater authority lives.

Report of the Park Commissioners, 23 November 1897. *Annual Reports City of Louisville…1897*, 485.

The oldest inhabitants of that neighborhood look back to the time when it was always thrown open to the public, and the recent purchase which renews to them and their families the privilege of loitering under its shade trees is a matter of general rejoicing. Of late years, since its original owners have moved elsewhere, the gates have been closed to the public, and signs warning people not to trespass have kept all from its precincts.

"Boone Park." *The Courier-Journal*, 24 May 1891.

ANDREW COWAN WOULD CLAIM LATE IN LIFE that his most valuable service as a park commissioner, "aside from the location of Cherokee Park, was through the employment of Mr. Frederick Law Olmsted, the great landscape architect."[336] Political friends of a well-connected local engineer, Clarence Weaver Parsons, pressured the commissioners to hire him, threatening that they would have to answer to the public if an out-of-state landscape architect was selected over a competent local engineer. A Louisville native, Parsons had worked in various engineering capacities in other places, later serving as City Engineer in the administration of his uncle, Charles Parsons Weaver, who was mayor from 1897 to 1901.[337]

Park Commissioner Cowan's initial correspondence to Olmsted, dated 8 January 1891, was written on his company letterhead.[338]

Dear Sir:

By an act of the Legislature, passed last year, the City of Louisville is authorized to provide a system of public parks, and I have sent you today, by mail, a copy of the park act.[339] The Board of Park Commissioners is now fully organized, and the bonds are in their possession ready for sale at the first favorable opportunity. I take the liberty of writing to you for the purpose of obtaining suggestions as to the course which should be pursued by the Board in the selection of lands, and the best way for improving them for park purposes. We have already turned over to us, by the City, about 300 Acres situated four miles from the City, together with the Boulevard leading thereto. This property was purchased two years ago, by the Mayor, and about $70,000.00 has been expended upon it for improvement without, in my opinion, any real advantage, because no study of the ground had been made, and the work is, therefore, largely of a temporary character, and much of it valueless. As one of the Board of Park Commissioners, I am very anxious that the work now in our charge shall be started right and conducted in the best manner. Hon. S. H. Wales[340] of New York City, suggested to me, in a letter of recent date, that you would doubtless be willing to give me some suggestions, and I will, therefore, ask you to write me a letter setting forth your views, as to the course which the Board should pursue. If you can do this so that I may have the letter before the next meeting of the Board, which occurs January 22nd, it will be of great value. I insist that the first step to be taken is the selection of a thoroughly competent landscape architect. If you are of that opinion, I shall be glad to have you emphasize it in your letter, as there is very considerable pressure on the Commissioners to appoint an ordinary civil engineer, with several assistants to take charge of the work.

Yours truly

The Louisville Commercial observed it its 14 September 1880 issue: "F. L. Olmsted read, at the Social Science Association [at Saratoga, New York], an interesting paper on Parks. Subjoined are some of the views expressed in it." The long column that followed without any further introduction was recognition of Olmsted's far-flung reputation.

If I were asked what is chiefly to be guarded against in undertaking a park, I would soberly answer that it is "practical business tact"—this being the common term, for a habit of mind cultivated in commercial life of knowing nothing of value which is not apparent in the market rates of the day....

Twenty-five years ago we had no parks, park-like or otherwise, which might not better have been called something else. Since then a class of works so-called has been undertaken, which, to begin with, are at least spacious, and which hold possibilities of all park-like qualities....

In the short history of one of our parks changes involving changes of organization and policy with regard to its plantations have occurred not less than six times, and twice, at least, the changes have involved serious change of the general design. Upon another, for which I am supposed to have some responsibility, the resident professional officer, who received my instructions for the work, was changed five times in three years, and always against my advice....

There is an important element of value in most parks which could not well be provided for in such small local grounds. What is desirable in this respect is a long, unbroken, spacious drive, ride and walk, offering suitable conditions to a large

I was the only member of the Board who knew about the great reputation of Frederick Law Olmsted, whose first work was on Central Park, New York City.... The Board would not invite him to come here, with a view of being employed. I then wrote him a personal letter, describing what had been done to secure Park sites, and expressing my personal anxiety that the land might be skillfully treated. I invited him to come to Louisville as my guest, to be present at a dinner in his honor to which I would invite some twenty of our leading men.

Reminiscences of Andrew Cowan. The Filson Historical Society.

number of people to obtain together moderate exercise in the open air, with such other conditions favorable to gayety, as can be conveniently associated with them.

When the art first emancipated itself from the trammels of conventionality in England and began to try to reproduce more nearly the effects of nature when at her best, its professors thought needful to apologize for their seeming conceit in calling themselves "landscape-gardeners." To-day, this term has become so degraded, they think, by popular misconception, that they prefer to call themselves "landscape-architects," getting the title from the French title *architecte paysagiste*.

M. G. Van Rensselaer, "Landscape Gardening," *The American Architect and Building News* 22 (1 October 1887): 158.

"We have not heard of more than a half dozen skilled professional gardeners," Mariana Griswold Van Rensselaer observed in her landmark series on landscape gardening in *The American Architect and Building News* in the late 1880s.[341] "Even these men, with few exceptions, are little known outside the wealthy circles of the great cities, and not half appreciated where they are known." Of these few, including Andrew Jackson Downing, Van Rensselaer pointed out Frederick Law Olmsted as being the most exceptional, supported in her praise by the "foremost of the living French landscape-gardeners," M. Edouard André. "There is no living European artist whom he [André] praises so greatly. There is none in whom he recognizes so high a degree of that power to design broad and beautiful landscape pictures, and at the same time comfortably accommodate vast concourses of people."[342]

While pointing out that Olmsted's Prospect Park in Brooklyn was the most beautiful in America because of its advantageous site, Mariana Van Rensselaer noted that Central Park was the "most interesting and instructive." Olmsted was 35 years old when in 1857 he was elected Central Park's first superintendent, reporting to the engineer-in-chief, who had prepared a topographical map of the recently acquired site. While Olmsted had some early training as a civil engineer and had farmed on Staten Island, it was only out of necessity after a stint in journalism failed that he undertook park work. On the day in September 1857 when Olmsted was chosen superintendent, the park commissioners decided to set aside the engineer-in-chief's plan and to conduct a design competition for Central Park. Olmsted was barely aware of the lay of the land when he was approached by Calvert Vaux to enter the competition together. The London-born architect had been a partner of renowned American landscape gardener Andrew Jackson Downing, an advocate of Central Park before his death.[343] Olmsted and Vaux's Greensward plan was selected, and Olmsted was named architect-in-chief. "Central Park was to be the actual and symbolic beginning of Frederick Law Olmsted as a landscape architect and the infancy of the park movement in America," biographer Lee Hall asserts. "Urban land—subjected to art, engineering, and management— would be transformed into rural experience, a sanctuary of spiritually uplifting aesthetic pleasure."[344] Elaborating, Hall quoted from Vaux and Olmsted's description of their Greensward design, which would differentiate it from many future park plans (Louisville's included) that provided roadways for testing trotting horses.

It will be perceived that no long straight drive has been provided on the plan: this feature has been studiously avoided, because it would offer opportunities for trotting matches. The popular idea of the park is a beautiful open green space, in which quiet drives, rides, and strolls may be had. This cannot be preserved if a race-course, or a road that can be readily used as a race-course, is made one of its leading attractions.

Like New York's Central Park, Prospect Park in the nearby and then-separate city of Brooklyn was first under the design control of Egbert L. Viele. But following the Civil War moratorium, the project was placed in Calvert Vaux's hands, and in 1866, after the return of Olmsted from California, their plan for Prospect Park was produced and accepted. Like Central Park, it incorporated a water reservoir. Vaux and Olmsted were appointed landscape architects for the project, which met with acclaim from Mariana Van Rensselaer, the most prominent critic of the day.

Olmsted, Vaux & Co., Landscape Architects, was formed in the spring of 1866. Vaux's old partner, Frederick Clarke Withers, who would design the Church of the Advent in Louisville, rounded out the company.[345] In the summer of 1866, Olmsted stopped in Buffalo to consult with a civic group about forming a public park.[346] What transpired would be repeated a quarter-century later in Louisville. Olmsted was asked to make a presentation to civic leaders that turned out to be a public meeting chaired by former President Millard Fillmore. During Olmsted's hour-long talk, he proposed that Buffalo not single out one of the three potential sites for a park, but instead utilize all three, tied together by parkways, as part of an overall park system. According to Witold Rybczynski: "In two hectic days, he had conceived this extraordinary tour de force—the outlines not of a park, but of an ambitious park *system*," a master plan that "would govern the growth of Buffalo for years to come."[347] As Francis R. Kowsky described in his study of the Buffalo parks and parkway system, the additional tax revenues the city would realize from the new development that would take place around the parks and along the parkways would offset the cost of the system.[348] Based upon his successes in Buffalo, Boston, and elsewhere, Olmsted would make the same claim for Louisville.

Vaux and Olmsted severed their partnership in the fall of 1872, and a decade later Olmsted would center his work and residence at Fairstead on Warren Street in Brookline, Mass. In the meantime (1878), and until he retired in 1895, Olmsted worked on a number of major projects including the Boston park system, known as the "emerald necklace," and the World's Columbian Exposition in Chicago, as well as many country estates, including Biltmore.[349]

Frederick Law Olmsted first inspected the property George W. Vanderbilt was amassing at Asheville, North Carolina, in 1888. Vanderbilt's prominent New York architect, Richard Morris Hunt, soon began working on concepts, and when he first visited the site in 1890, construction was underway. Much of the supervision was undertaken by Hunt's son, Richard Howland Hunt, who had studied at MIT and the École des Beaux-Arts before joining his father in 1887. In September 1885, Dick Hunt had married Pearl Carley of Louisville. The daughter of Frank D. Carley probably provided insight about Louisville society to Olmsted, his step-son John C. Olmsted, and Henry S. Codman, who were at Biltmore at various times.[350]

WHILE COWAN WAS SIMPLY REQUESTING ADVICE from Olmsted for the park commissioners in early January 1891, Olmsted responded on 19 January as though he had been invited to Louisville, replying that he was unable to leave Chicago. Cowan pointed out by return mail the necessity for the commissioners to acquire "a good deal of land in the immediate vicinity or adjoining" Jacob Park "to make it accessible without crossing private property, and to fix proper park boundaries. It may be that to an experienced Landscape Engineer it might seem better to abandon the site altogether, and at any rate the park commissioners, in my opinion, ought not to acquire the additional land until they have the advice of an experienced Landscape Engineer." He informed Olmsted he had corresponded with John Y. Culyer of Brooklyn the previous fall, but he would not pursue it further until he had "fully presented the question to you and ascertained that we may not be able to wait to secure your services."[351] Culyer was well known to Olmsted, having served as chief engineer on Olmsted, Vaux & Company's 1871 "Design for Prospect Park."[352] Cowan requested Olmsted to reply when he could come, and if he could not do so soon, he asked him to suggest another landscape architect "we might at once apply to for advice."[353] The possibility of his firm missing out on a project got Olmsted's attention.

His talented junior partner, Henry Sargent Codman, was able to break away from his landscape responsibilities at the World's Columbian Exposition in Chicago to make "a cursory examination of the ground" the commissioners had identified for the three parks.[354] He was accompanied on 18 February 1891 to Jacob Park, the Water Works, and along the Ohio River between West Market Street and Broadway by commissioners Sherley, Cowan, Durrett, and Castleman.[355] They requested a proposal from the firm. On 26 February 1891, F. L. Olmsted & Co. wrote Thomas Sherley, president of the Board, offering to "make a thorough study of the premises" and to provide preliminary advice for $250, and if that was satisfactory to proceed to prepare "general plans for laying out the several works that you may determine to be desirable…to be of such character that a competent resident expert with a suitable staff may be able, by reference to them, to carry on the work necessary to realize their intention."

> It may be presumed that full preparation of these general plans would occupy us from one to three years…. While engaged in the study of them, we should repeatedly visit the premises and confer with your Board and with its superintending officer, advise as to the methods of work to be pursued and as to the preparation of detailed working plans, and be at all times open to consultation by correspondence. We should require to be furnished by you with adequate topographical maps of the sites to be improved and with all desirable information, and also that our necessary travelling expenses and any expenses to which we may be put for their draughting of working details, shall be refunded. Our charge for preparing the general plans and for such incidental service as we may be able to give you in carrying them out while they are under study and in preparation, will be computed at a rate of twelve dollars and a half for each acre included in these plans.[356]

Cowan responded to the firm that he thought "your proposal will not be accepted in its present shape, but if you can see your way to modify it, so far as to make it ten dollars an acre instead of twelve and a half, I believe that it will go through when presented to the Board."[357] At the subsequent meeting, the Board declined to invite Olmsted to Louisville, and decided to "await further developments."[358] However, ten days later, president Sherley wrote the firm: "We now have elegant weather and the people are urging us to select the grounds and improve those we have, and I trust that your Mr. Olmsted will be able to come at once."[359] The agreement Sherley included applied only to the consulting phase of the work for $250. No mention was made of the planning phase.

"For some time past," *The Courier-Journal* commented 20 May 1891 in regard to a previous night's meeting of the Board of Park Commissioners, "they have been corresponding with Frederick Law

Olmstead and H. S. Codman, of Boston, two of the best landscape artists in the country. As the result of this correspondence the two gentlemen arrived in the city yesterday afternoon, and are stopping at the Galt. Mr. Codman called on the park commissioners last night to let them know that Mr. Olmstead and himself were in the city. To-day the two gentlemen will be taken out to the new East End park…and the experts will go over the grounds carefully and tell the Commissioners what should be done. If satisfactory terms can be arranged, the two gentlemen will stay here for some time looking after the improvements of the parks. They will also go out to Jacob Park, where the work of improvement has already commenced."[360]

After a full day inspecting Eastern, Jacob, and Boone parks, the two landscape architects were entertained by Andrew Cowan at a Pendennis Club dinner of some 20 civic leaders and Park Commissioners.[361]

> In spite of the rain Messrs. Olmstead & Codman visited the new park purchase on Beargrass and the other parks now in the hands of the Commissioners. The high praise which Mr. Olmsted bestowed upon the new purchase should be very satisfactory to the people of Louisville. He said without hesitation that he had never seen a piece of property more entirely endowed by nature with the advantages for a beautiful park. The growth of trees, the luxuriant grass and the beautiful rolling conformation of the land were all especially adapted to park purposes. He unhesitatingly declares that Louisville has secured a prize.[362]

Surely, Olmsted called upon his memory of a similar meeting in Buffalo a quarter-century before when he outlined for civic leaders a three-park system connected by parkways that would stimulate residential growth while improving the city's quality of life. One of the Pendennis Club dinner guests who had "the privilege of hearing Olmsted talk about the origin of parks and their evolution from village commons or greens to the delightful pleasure grounds of to-day," recorded his definition of a suburban park as: "a public pleasure ground whose object should be to cultivate and gratify the taste for sylvan scenery, to give town people seeking recreation a glimpse of the hills and vales and woods, and to rest the mind. This is done by imitating the most beautiful aspects of nature as far as possible, in nature's own way."[363]

On the morning of 22 May, Olmsted and Codman examined potential land for a western park with Commissioners Sherley and Cowan before preparing a report to the Board.[364] "Mr. Olmsted entertained the Board in an extended verbal report of his visit here, and

I never saw a park in my life which has as many natural advantages as the property just purchased. The trees are of a splendid quality and beautifully grouped; there is a magnificent supply of fine spring water, the rocks and shrubs are perfect and all in all it is a lovely place naturally.

Frederick Law Olmsted, *The Louisville Times*, 21 May 1891.

investigation of our Parks, and proposed Park and Boulevard system," Board minutes of 22 May 1891 recorded. "President authorized to enter into contract."[365] Under the headline "The Park Commissioners Employ F. L. Olmsted & Co. to Take Charge of the Park Work," *The Louisville Times* stated the firm would be paid $12.50 an acre to plan and supervise the execution of the work.[366] The *Times* clarified this report: "This firm will furnish the plans and exercise only that general supervision necessary to secure their proper execution. All the physical labor will be performed by our home people, under the immediate supervision and direction of local architects and engineers." Olmsted returned to Boston the following day; Codman resumed work on the World's Fair in Chicago. When board members later voted on the contract on 9 June, Sherley and Castleman were against it, but Durrett, Bohne, and Cowan prevailed.[367]

The contract with Frederick Law Olmsted & Co., executed 17 June 1891, directed the firm "to furnish us with working plans for the improvements of all the parks under the control of this Board. These working plans and instructions are furnished after a complete and careful topographical survey is made by local engineers, who are in charge of Mr. Emil Mahlo, an engineer having had large experience in this line, being at one time the resident engineer of Fairmount Park, Philadelphia."[368] The contractual agreement did not mention a parkway system connecting the three major parks.

While some newspapers had been critical of Mayor Jacob's dealings in the creation of Jacob Park, Frederick Law Olmsted must have expressed his own reservations to local leaders and others before his firm was hired. Board president Sherley thought it incumbent to have Andrew Cowan write Olmsted a confidential letter requesting "another and different report on Jacob Park" that would "secure one more vote on the board" for his proposal to buy more land for the park. Cowan believed Sherley was being pressured by "numerous and influential land owners out that way" to increase the value of their holdings. Cowan also pointed out to Olmsted that Park Avenue from East Broadway to Daisy Road was "sure to be made" and that it was important to have it on park property that could be controlled. "Whether you make the entrance to the Park at Willow St. or elsewhere, this Park Avenue is desirable and necessary for many reasons."[369] Olmsted's subsequent written report to the Board seems to have complied with Cowan's request.

On the other hand, if you want a treasure of sylvan scenery, alternative and supplementary to the treasures which you will have on your other properties, the grandeur or forest depths in the dim seclusion of which you will wander musingly for

As was to be expected, the employment by the Commissioners of an outside firm of landscape engineers to plan and supervise the work of perfecting Louisville's system of parks has given rise to some local jealousy and complaint. As a matter of fact, however, there is no home talent with sufficient experience to satisfactorily execute the work, as has already been demonstrated by the so-called improvement of Jacob Park.

The Louisville Times, 23 May 1891.

hours, this you may find ready to your hand on the Iroquois Hill, and the beauty of the present forest there may be extended and increased and given diversity and made more interesting by processes which, judiciously organized and patiently pursued, will not be difficult or unreasonably costly.[370]

In August 1891, the Olmsted firm prepared a written report of its May inspections, reiterating the "impromptu advice" that had been presented to the Board "drawn from our knowledge of the experience of Park Commissions in other cities."[371] The report, which was published in the 20 September *Courier-Journal*, did not mention connecting parkways, as the May Board minutes suggest Olmsted had addressed.[372]

The firm's initial point dealt with the selection of park sites that meet the "real requirements of the community" and not designations intended "to make real estate in their vicinity more valuable." The firm was highly critical of the city's intention to create parks in three different geographical areas. "Nothing can well be more undesirable for the community as a whole" than to create parks "for the benefit of a particular division of the community." That advice would have been applicable if the local park movement was just getting underway, but the creation of three regional parks had been in the community's sights for several decades. The southern park was already open, tracts comprising the eastern park had been purchased, and negotiations for a western park site were ongoing.

> The only policy that you can adopt, with the slightest prospect of a respectable success, will, in our judgment, be based upon the purpose: First, to develop within each one of your three properties a treasure of rural and sylvan scenery of a character distinct from that which you will develop within either of the other two, the distinction being determined in each case by regard for the existing topographical peculiarities of the particular site; second, to make provisions on neither site for any form of recreation, means for which will be in a marked degree discordant with, or subversive of, the natural character of that site; third, to supply suitable means for making the enjoyment of the scenery of each park available to those escaping from the city, in the form of walks, roads, and places to rest, shelter and refreshment, such means being regarded not at all as the substance of your parks, but as the wholly subordinate implements and tools by which the substance is to be made use of.

We advise you also to be prepared to strenuously disappoint all notions that any may have formed that you are to spend the public money intrusted to you upon objects of curiosity or decoration; your business is to form parks, not museums or collections of ornaments. If gifts are offered you of objects simply ornamental, by all means decline them. Admit nothing to your parks that is not fitting and helpful to their distinguishing purpose.

The Olmsted firm noted that the large public properties in the country could provide "something radically different" from city gardens. "What is it? Simply the healthful soothing and refreshing effect which experience proves is exercised upon people escaping from the splendor and bustle, the confinement and disturbance of towns, into the midst of spacious natural scenery. Not into a succession of scenes, but into scenery in a comprehensive sense."

Pretty bits of decoration in garden plants and architectural objects are not helpful to such scenery as is thus required; they are destructive of it. They are admirable in their place, but in association with elements of scenery such as make a park another thing from a garden, they put nature out of countenance.

The firm cautioned the Board to "Take Time!," counseling "the principal work that you have to do is a work of preparation whereby nature will be invited to produce, by growth, in the course of years, that which is to be desired in a park." The result of adequate planning and design was scenery. "The best effect of scenery will be to promote a restful, contemplative and musing disposition of mind. It grows in value as it gives less gratification to curiosity, and as its effect is less sensational. It grows in value as it grows in age."

If you want the refreshment that is to be had in the contemplation of superb umbrageous trees, standing singly and in open groups, distributed naturally upon a gracefully undulating greensward, to procure such scenery in higher perfection than, with large outlays to obtain it, is yet to be found in any public park in America, all that is needed is the removal of fences and a little judicious use of the axe on your Cherokee Park site.

Report of F. L. Olmsted & Co., 26 August 1891. Folder 1260, Olmsted firm papers, Library of Congress.

26

LOUISVILLE PARK ENGINEER EMIL MAHLO (1891)

TO PREVENT THE WASTE BROUGHT ON by the political and management vagaries that Olmsted had witnessed in his long career, the firm's report advised the Board to guard against "a wavering purpose and unsteady aims…. All that can now be done in the way of precaution against it lies in the carefully provident study of the plans which it is the first business of the present Board of Park Commissioners to prepare and hand down to its successors." The crucial first step in producing such plans was the creation of topographical surveys, "which you now have in progress…. The closer, more accurate and finer they are, the better your plans will be fitted to the ground; the less costly they will be to carry out."[373]

"Mr. E. Mahlo was employed as an engineer to prepare maps of all the parks," *The Courier-Journal* announced 27 May 1891, "so that they can be sent to Mr. Olmsted, who will look over the maps and send back his plans for the laying out and adornment of each park." According to the newspaper, Emil Mahlo had been employed for two years in Philadelphia's Fairmount Park "assisting in laying out the grounds, and was for eight years a United States Government Engineer."[374] Monthly reports during 1870 for the Commissioners of Fairmount Park from the Engineering Department, signed by Sub Assistant Engineer Mahlo, are extant. During this period the first topographical map of Fairmount Park was produced.[375] Early in 1871, the Philadelphia park commission requested Frederick Law Olmsted and his then-partner Calvert Vaux to submit a proposal to complete Fairmount Park. Olmsted had been asked in late 1867 to review the existing park work. Very likely he suggested a topographical map be prepared to guide future layout as he would later request in Louisville. Although Olmsted anticipated being named architect for Fairmount Park, he was passed over, but he quite possibly saw some of Mahlo's survey work.[376] Mahlo had also published a detailed map in 1879 of the Black Hills of Dakota for the Department of Interior, US Geographical and Geological Survey. Most recently, Mahlo and his partner had platted the 390-acre development two miles beyond Jacob Park called South Park, the first large subdivision in Jefferson County.

Emil Mahlo was acknowledged as the Olmsted firm's choice for the position.[377] Olmsted himself reiterated the firm's recommendation in a note to Andrew Cowan.

> When just before leaving Louisville, I gave Mr. Sherley our report recommending the employment of Mr. Mahlo. He told me, what I had not known before, that Mr. Mahlo is not a citizen of Louisville, and that, consequently, there will be strong opposition to his employment. He also said that he was committed in favor of one of the other candidates. This is to be regretted. But there can be no question that Mr. Mahlo promises to be much the better man for the place. It has invariably occurred, in our experience, that an engineer who has been engaged only in the ordinary run of engineer's work, such as that of railroad, sewers and streets, finds it very difficult to disembarrass his mind of the customs of such work and to give due consideration to, and find means of realizing, the requirements of grace, beauty and naturalness, that are made upon him in the work of parks…. It appeared to me that Mr. Mahlo had an unusual aptitude for the business, and that the other gentlemen, even if his superiors in general engineering, of where was no evidence, would find it very much more difficult to enter into the spirit of the required operations.[378]

"Mr. Olmsted, the park architect who has the work of beautifying the park in charge, has sent on some of his instructions, and Monday another corps of engineers will be put to work on the East-end Park," *The Courier-Journal* noted 7 June 1891.

Mahlo appointed A. J. Casseday, assistant engineer; F. D. Hamilton, leveler; O. P. Schmidt, leveler, first corps; R. T. Jacob, rodman, second corps; A. C. Bohne, rodman, first corps; Robert Tevis, chainman; H. Ormsby, chainman; M. A. Bruns, flagman; William Grove, axeman. "The Commissioners have given Mr. Mahlo authority to purchase all the needed instruments and the camping outfit for parties in the field, and also to use one of the Jacob Park horses in riding around to look over the work."[379] *The Critic* outlined the work undertaken by the surveying parties in November 1891. The topographical survey of Cherokee Park had been completed and the maps sent to Olmsted & Co. Survey work in Iroquois Park was underway.

> Two corps of engineers are engaged in making topographical surveys. Each corps is in charge of an assistant engineer, who acts under orders of Park Engineer Emil Mahlo. They are camping on the ground in tents, and number about seventeen

We desire to inform your Board of the excellence for our purpose, of the different topographical surveys which have been made under the direction of your Engineer. They have so far admirably served their purpose for making the designs of the parks, and their thoroughness and accuracy have been of the greatest assistance to us in our part of the work. They are better surveys than we are often able to obtain.[381]

F. L. Olmsted & Co., dated World's Columbian Exposition, Jackson Park, Chicago, to John B. Castleman, 17 October 1892. *Louisville Municipal Reports for the Year Ending August 31, 1893* (Louisville, 1884), 192.

men, including the cooks. These topographical surveys are made very thoroughly, in order to procure elaborate records of measurements and data of the ground. The closer, more accurate and finer they are, the better the plans which are prepared and furnished to the Board of Park Commissioners by the consulting landscape architects and engineers, F. L. Olmsted & Co. of Boston, will be fitted to the ground, and the less costly they will be to carry out…. All topographical features of the ground are shown; all important trees and other objects are carefully located and mapped, and contours three feet apart vertically are run, showing the depressions and elevations of the ground.[380]

By the time Mahlo undertook the survey of Cherokee Park, it included an additional 27.4-acre tract the heirs of Frederick M. Baringer had conveyed to the Board of Park Commissioners. The property included the site of the family homestead and graveyard on the prominent hill, as well as the nearby walled-off spring, which recently has been rediscovered and restored.[382] Mahlo completed the topographical map of Cherokee Park in November 1891 and sent a tracing to the Olmsted firm. Surveys were made in December depicting the "available approaches to the park."[383]

There was an old Baringer graveyard out there on the hill opposite where the clubhouse is on the golf course, when I was a kid. There was a bunch of stones in there crumbling down with some iron pieces in them, a gateway and all. The graves were moved to Cave Hill Cemetery.[384]

Recollection of Carl Baringer Yager, 2001.

Stone steps leading to the Baringer spring. University of Louisville Photographic Archives.

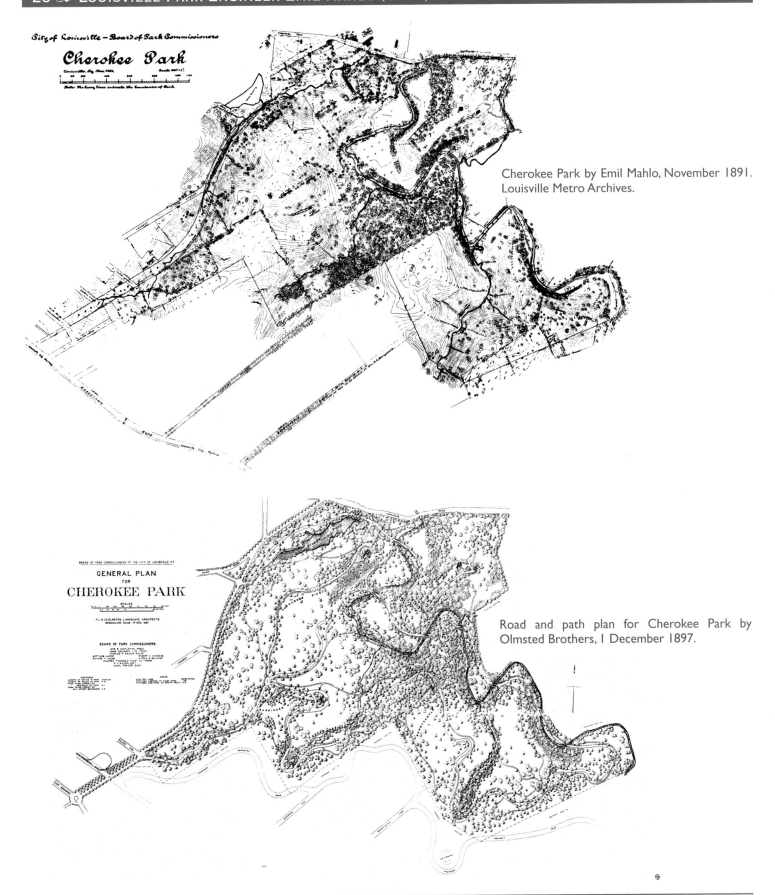

Cherokee Park by Emil Mahlo, November 1891. Louisville Metro Archives.

Road and path plan for Cherokee Park by Olmsted Brothers, 1 December 1897.

EASTERN PARK (1891)

Castleman statue at intersection of Cherokee Road and Cherokee Parkway, 1920. Caufield and Shook Collection, University of Louisville Photographic Archives.

The Equestrian Statue of General Castleman, looks out over a splendid Park and Parkway, which he did nothing to secure for the people, but nearly succeeded in depriving them of, by his efforts to have the Eastern Park located on a tract of about sixty acres, then known as the Schwartz Woods, and several years later christened Castlewood.

Andrew Cowan to Wm. Marshall Bullitt, 23 January 1914. Bullitt family papers, The Filson Historical Society.

Section of Beers & Langan, *Atlas of Jefferson & Oldham Counties Kentucky* (1879).

AT THEIR 5 MAY 1891 MEETING, the commissioners were tight-lipped about the potential location of the parks. "The question as to what control the Water Company will give over its property has not yet been settled," *The Courier-Journal* reported. "But the Commissioners hope to have a park in this neighborhood."[385] However, by then, Andrew Cowan had switched attention from the Water Company property for the east-end park to the Morton and Griswold tract along Beargrass Creek that had been suggested to him by Morton Casseday.[386] Cowan negotiated with owners and representatives of adjacent properties and obtained options on all the lands for the eastern park "before any other member of the board knew of his design," Temple Bodley would later point out.

He then confided that he had gone to Mr. Bohne alone and asked his support; but Mr. Bohne said he was committed to vote to buy the Swartz [Schwartz] Woods, of which General Castleman owned about ten or twelve acres, now known as Castlewood.[387] Mr. Bohne also said he thought the price asked by the owners of the Cherokee lands was more than the board should expend for the eastern park; and furthermore, that General Castleman already had two others of the commissioners pledged to vote for the Swartz Woods. Thus, with Bohne's vote, he had a majority of the board with him.

Finally, Mr. Bohne agreed that before he would vote for the Swartz Woods Colonel Cowan should have time to see if he could get the price of the Cherokee tracts reduced, and meantime pledged secrecy. Thereupon Colonel Cowan got $16,000 in private contributions toward the purchase, and Mr. Bohne was satisfied to vote for the Cherokee purchase.[388]

The Board of Park Commissioners announced the purchase of 250 acres "magnificently adapted, both by nature and art, for a park unsurpassed in beauty," for less than $140,000 on 8 May 1891.[389] "Beautiful drives will be made through the land," *The Courier-Journal* reported. "Rustic bridges will be built over the Beargrass. In a very short time a fine landscape gardener can make the new park most attractive. The land is very rich and is probably the finest farming ground about the city. The name for the park has not yet been chosen. The Park Commissioners have been too busy getting hold of the property to think of names." Views sketched in the park appeared in the next Sunday's *Courier-Journal*, along with colorful descriptions of the various points of interest. For the time being, it was referred to as Eastern Park.

Prompting completion of the eastern park land purchase was the threat of intrusion through the core of the park by a railway beltline being developed by the Louisville Terminal Railway, recently authorized by the Kentucky legislature.[390] Realizing that once the land was publicly owned, it then could not be condemned for railway purposes, the railway's attorneys brought suit against the landowners individually, trying to block their sales to the Board of Park Commissioners. The legislature had authorized the beltline from the Ohio River at Adams Street southeast to beyond Cave Hill Cemetery and then westward to the Ohio River. Within days, public outrage forced the railway to withdraw its suits and seek another route.[391]

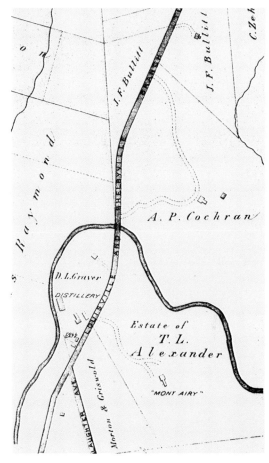

Section of *Atlas of the City of Louisville, Ky.*, 1884.

As early as 1837, Mr. Prentice, in the Louisville Journal, had indicated the site of our Eastern Park, as a suitable place for such purpose, but it took no practical shape.

"The Parks of Louisville." *The Courier-Journal*, 5 June 1904.

Louisville and Shelbyville Branch Turnpike (now Lexington Road) Bridge over Beargrass Creek, 1907. Detroit Publishing Company, Library of Congress.

Of the five different bodies of land which go to form the proposed Park, the country seat of the late A. P. Cochran is, if anything, the most beautiful. Upon it there stands, ready built, an elegant brick residence of twenty rooms. A fine stable and carriage house complete the improvements. Beautiful shade trees are scattered over the place. There is also a fine orchard. Over fifty varieties of trees grow on this splendid country place.

First Annual Report of the Board of Park Commissioners (July 1891), 14.

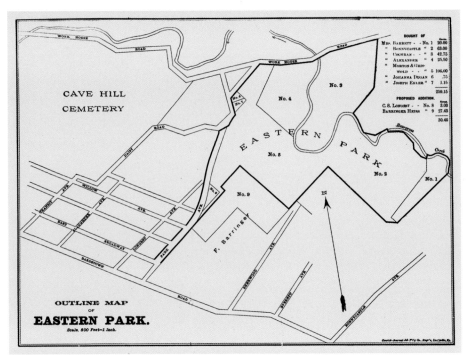

"Outline Map of Eastern Park," *First Annual Report of the Board of Park Commissioners* (July 1891).

F. L. Olmsted Senior's personal involvement with the Cherokee Park development was limited. His firm was engaged by the City of Louisville in 1891—four years before his retirement from practice at the age of 73. During those four years most of the firm's representation in Louisville was by his step-son John (a leader in the Cherokee Park design for twenty-four years), by Warren Manning and by James Frederick Dawson.

Olmsted Associates, Inc., *Journal of the Development of Cherokee Park, Louisville, Kentucky 1891-1974*, 4.

According to biographer Laura Wood Roper, Olmsted visited Louisville, "where the firm was laying out Cherokee Park" in September 1891 on his way from Chicago to Biltmore.[392] Unfortunately, there is no account or report of his observations. At the time, a survey crew was preparing a topographical map of Cherokee Park. The final product was sent off to Fairstead in November as the basis for the park's layout. Although Olmsted was traveling extensively during the next several months and experiencing insomnia, he would have had opportunities at home to work on the overall design of Cherokee Park. "In March, 1892, the first plans for drives in the park and for Park avenue were received from Messrs. Olmsted & Co., and the preliminary work of construction commenced," Mahlo later noted in his annual report.[393] Olmsted was expected in Louisville at that time and the firm promised to forward the revised Cherokee Park plan so Mahlo could "get as much of this staked out as possible before Mr. Olmsted comes to Louisville.... We would suggest that that portion of the road be staked first which leads from the entrance of Willow Street up over the hill and then down through the valley along the creek. It would also be well to get that portion staked which is in thick woods, because that is less easily seen than the part in open country."[394]

Apparently, Olmsted bypassed Louisville on his western excursion, and in late March the firm wrote Mahlo of his plans not to mark the park entrance with a circle. "To procure the necessary importance to the

Guard house at trestle bridge at main entrance to Cherokee Park about 1895. The Filson Historical Society.

Trestle bridge spanning ravine at Willow Avenue entrance. R. G. Potter Collection, University of Louisville Photographic Archives.

entrance, it is our intention at some time in the future to recommend the erection of a lodge or some other suitable structure which would form a part of the necessary bridge across the ravine and be directly connected with it. We had not before proposed this because we did not think the commission ought to undertake a large expenditure for architectural construction before they began the more important work on the Park."[395] A temporary wooden trestle bridge, 210 feet long, was erected to span the ravine at the Willow Street entrance. Park Avenue (now Cherokee Parkway) from the circle (Castleman statue) to the bridge was then graded, as was a 30-foot drive in the park to the "forks" and beyond to the Alexander house as well as through the Baringer woods. Cecil Fraser was in charge of this construction of a mile of roads that were opened to the public.[396] One of Fraser's lasting changes was replacement of the trestle bridge that formed the main entrance to Cherokee Park with fill from nearby roadwork. Henry Bickel was authorized to fill in the ravine entrance to the park at a meeting on 13 November 1899.[397] While "the park gives every sign of great care and attention to detail," officials were concerned that "Eastern Park does not draw the thousands and thousands of people that go to Jacob Park every Sunday." (*The Courier-Journal* continued to use the parks' old names.) Improved public transportation would help along with "refreshment houses."[398]

In early April 1892, Olmsted set sail with his son Rick and Harry Codman's younger brother, Phil, on a six-month excursion to England and France to see parks and landed estates, including Birkenhead Park

We would recommend painting the railing of the temporary bridge at the entrance of Cherokee Park a light brownstone color, or a warm grey, the bark of most trees.

F. L. Olmsted & Co. to Pack Thomas, 22 August 1892.

Without invitation from the Board and on my own account I visited Cherokee Park with [Cecil] Fraser.... In the grading of Bardstown Road there was a surplus of some 5000 cu. Yds. of earth and Fraser got the Park Board to secure it to fill across the valley at the entrance.... It is now just finished and is a vast improvement over the wooden trestle bridge.

Minutes of John C. Olmsted, 11 November 1900. Olmsted firm papers, Library of Congress.

Henry Sargent Codman about 1891. Courtesy of Ryerson and Burnham Libraries, The Art Institute of Chicago.

The deceased endeared himself to the Commissioners by his gentle manners and courteous bearing while in the discharge of duties in which he showed singular skill.

Board of Park Commissioners' resolution at a special meeting, 17 January 1893, on the death of Henry Sargent Codman.

Cherokee Park entrance improvement by Cecil Fraser. *Art Work of Louisville, Ky.* (1903), Part 1.

and Chatsworth. During the remainder of 1892, Harry Codman was left handling both the preparations for the World Columbian Exposition in Chicago and most matters in Louisville. Upon their return, 29-year-old Harry Codman died suddenly, leaving the elder Olmsted without his most trusted colleague.

In response to learning that the Olmsted firm had done nothing "about the design for a temporary bridge at the entrance to Cherokee Park," Board member Andrew Cowan wrote Codman in April 1892 emphatically: "I suppose Mr. Sherley must have written F L O & Co. to hurry up with the plans, for we are all being subjected to a great deal of annoyance & criticism about the delay in doing something for opening Cherokee Park. There is going to be trouble for some of the Board, unless you put us on the way to active work out there, without much more delay…. Please do not put off the work on our plans, for we are losing weeks of the finest weather for what we have to do & the people are restive over the delay."[399]

Apparently, when the firm informed Board president Sherley that it had not designed a bridge because it believed it would detract from the park, Sherley responded:

I must confess I can see no reason for the assertion on your part, that any Park Commissioner who should favor the building of the bridge into the Park, should be considered by you as falling a little short of the breach of trust imposed upon him to preserve the Parks to their legitimate uses. It is quite natural for men who sometimes think for themselves and who have the interest of the Parks under their control, to express their opinions in reference to certain matters, even before they are brought before the Board, but it strikes me as a little queer how you should have received your information as to the opinion of any member of the Park Commission upon any subject which has not been brought before the Board or officially communicated to you…. I frankly confess to you that your reasons for opposing the building of the bridge are, to my mind now, very conclusive that it is not the proper place to make an entrance to the Park.

In the absence of your argument, I had previously expressed my individual opinion that the building of the bridge as proposed would have been best for the people and not detrimental to the beauty of the Park.[400]

The Olmsted firm evidently had heard that Sherley had been asked by property owners adjacent to Cherokee Park and officials of a railway company interested in developing a line along the boulevard approaching the park and in building an iron bridge into the park what he thought of such an idea. He had replied without any knowledge of details, he thought it not objectionable. Sherley backed away from the railway idea, and the Olmsted firm designed a wooden trestle bridge in keeping with the park. Later, the firm got its way, and the bridge was removed and the ravine was filled in to allow a graceful entrance into Cherokee Park.

At the annual meeting of the Park Commissioners in July 1893, "the road from the Cochran hill to the Work-house road was ordered to be graded. This will give a complete circuit of Cherokee Park."[401]

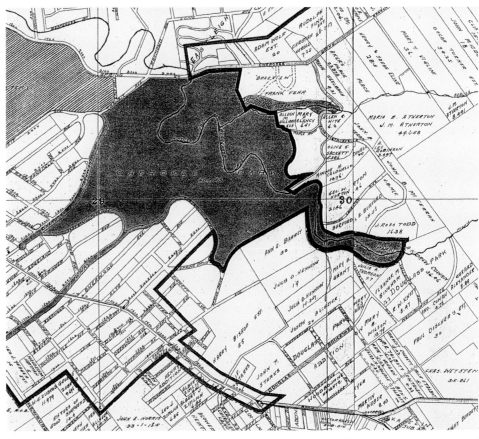

Development around Cherokee Park as depicted on the 1913 *New Map of Louisville and Jefferson County*.

Scene in Cherokee Park along Beargrass Creek. *Art Work of Loiusville, Ky.* (1903), Part 5.

Roadway in Cherokee Park with Norton Hall (razed for Louisville Presbyterian Theological Seminary in 1961) in background. *Art Work of Loiusville, Ky.* (1903), Part 7.

28
WESTERN PARK (1891)

WITH THE SAME DILIGENCE ANDREW COWAN HAD EMPLOYED to select and negotiate the acquisition of land for the eastern park, he began checking suitable and available land along the Ohio River for the western park in May 1891. The Park Commissioners had made it clear they intended to locate a large park in the west end, "so as to put the citizens of the lower half of the city on an equal footing with those of the upper half."[402] After several weeks, he had identified 136 acres with a river view in an area bounded by the north side of Broadway, the south side of Madison Street, and west of Paddy's Run—property owned principally by the Kettig, Gaar, and Blankenbaker families.[403] The problem noted by *The Louisville Times* was that two-thirds of the amount set aside for the acquisition of park property had already been spent, and "no western park has yet been purchased."[404] While the bond issue was intended to provide $1 million, the Sinking Fund Commissioners had reduced it to $600,000. Of that, only $400,000 could be spent on acquisition, while the remainder was authorized for improvements. After purchase of the east-end land and its improvement and the cost of Boone Park, only $122,000 remained for park land purchase.

"The Park Commissioners have been trying to locate the western park for the past year," *The Critic* observed in April 1892. "After a hard battle they have at last decided upon the site."[405] "Mr. F. L. Olmsted, the veteran and highly accomplished landscape artist, said when Col. Cowan was showing him this proposed site: 'I consider this very fine. In securing this bank of the river you will control, for landscape purposes, a thousand acres.'"[406]

> Mrs. Kettig's place is a beautiful country home. It has growing on it many handsome trees and plenty of flowers and shrubbery. There is a roomy two-story dwelling on the place, which can easily be converted into a pleasant resort.[407] Judge Gaar's place has a good residence and some fine beech trees, maples and oaks. The Blankenbaker place has a fine grove in which are many oaks, and the entire place is well shaded. The only part

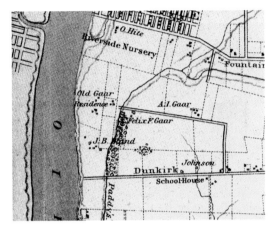

Section from *Louisville and Its Defenses*, 1864-1865. The "Old Gaar Residence" is identified north of the Dunkirk road, which became Broadway when it was extended. The patriarch, Jacob Gaar, was the first to settle in the area about 1831, calling the farm Riverview. The residence was still standing in 1893.[409]

> The place has been beautified for years by Mr. Kettig, who took a great personal pride in the property, and one of the reasons that his widow has offered it to the city is that she and her children may be able to enjoy the pleasures of the old home, and see the work of her husband's hands maintained and further carried out.
>
> "The West End Park." *The Critic*, 14 June 1891.

of the property on the river front that is subject to overflow is about fifty feet in width, and this can be terraced and made a beautiful walk.

The river front has the best facilities for bathing in the city of Louisville. The ground is all located above the outlet of the western outfall sewer and there can be no contamination of the river water. The current is on the Indiana side and there is a big sand bar along the Kentucky shore affording an excellent bathing beach. The entire property is above the average in fertility, and grass grows luxuriantly everywhere.[408]

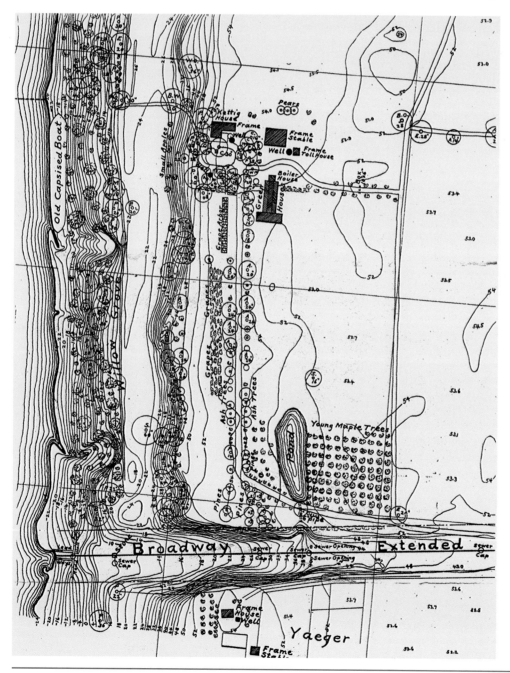

Due to the necessity of acquiring some of the 138 acres (168 acres at low water) for the western park by threat of condemnation, it was not accomplished until the spring of 1892. *The Critic* acknowledged that "Col. Andrew Cowan raised $14,000, and to his great personal energy is largely due the location of Shawnee Park." The cost was $105,000 less $14,000.[410] An engineer corps was dispatched to determine the boundary lines in April 1892 and a topographical survey was undertaken in June and completed and sent to the Olmsted firm in September.[411]

Anticipating possible criticism with its preliminary plan for Shawnee Park, the Olmsted firm spelled out its philosophy in developing multiple city parks, justifying its concept and role for the west-end park. It was to be a park the firm was philosophically ill-suited to design.

Preliminary Map of Shawnee Park, 18 August 1892, by Hugh Wanless, Jr. Frederick Law Olmsted National Historic Site, Brookline, MA. Wanless was a draughtsman for the Board of Park Commissioners.

We deem it an important point that the principal parks of a city should be distinguished one from another somewhat markedly in the way in which they are used and in their landscape treatment…. Having this general principle in mind, we have aimed to so design the three principal parks of Louisville that they would serve somewhat different purposes, each being as complete as possible in itself, and the purpose to which each park is designed being in harmony with the existing topography and natural growths. Having thus selected a principal purpose to be accomplished in each of the parks, we aimed to improve and increase their natural adaptability to those purposes, and to make the necessary artificial constructions, (enabling the people to use the parks in great crowds, with the least possible injury to natural growth), as little inimical as possible to the selected character of landscape.

Iroquois Park is intended to embody so far as possible the character of a great natural forest. In Cherokee Park it is intended to develop to the utmost its present character as a piece of moderately gently-rolling country, with somewhat scattered, broad-spreading trees and a picturesque, small river. In neither of these parks are there extensive meadows suitable for large numbers of boys to play ball upon. In neither would it be appropriate to have any gardening of a formal character, or any considerable number of buildings, or other artificial features, such as would be appropriate in a small city park where the landscape was a minor consideration, and where the need of applying a good many artistic artificial objects might be felt, owing to lack of varied and picturesque natural features.

Shawnee Park differs from the other two in having a considerable proportion of nearly level land almost free from trees, and in commanding views over the great river…. In seeking to determine, therefore, what should be the principal controlling characteristic of this park, it has seemed to us that it would consist in its use as a great public play-ground, leaving all the other advantages of the site to become of subordinate importance…. The case of Shawnee Park, it seems to us that it would not be inappropriate to develop its landscape in the direction of a great public common.[412]

In all cases where public parks are large enough to tempt people to go to them with the conscious or unconscious purpose of enjoying natural scenery, and of escaping from city sights and sounds, it is absolutely essential to prohibit the gathering of large numbers of people in organized bodies, or as spectators of parades, exhibitions, public speaking and the like.

F. L. Olmsted & Co. to John B. Castleman, 17 November 1892.[413]

Near the Superintendent's house is a large cage and aquarium containing a singular grouping of birds and water animals prominent among them being great horned owls and the alligator four and one-half feet long, which was donated by ex-Park Commissioner E. C. Bohne. Stalking in vain, yet lordly fashion, about beds of flowers can be seen pea-fowls whose widespread tails almost put the colors of the flowers to shame.

"Fontaine And Western." *The Courier-Journal*, 5 August 1894.

The park commissioners adopted the Olmsted firm's preliminary plans late in 1892 and ordered that construction of the proposed drives be undertaken.[415] In submitting its finished plan for Shawnee Park in

Below: Plat of Shawnee Terrace adjacent to Shawnee Park. "Grand Auction Sale of Lots," *The Critic*, 9 June 1893. The location of the old Kettig homestead in Shawnee Park at the end of Chestnut Street is depicted as a blank rectangle; however, the residence and outbuildings were not removed until 1896.[414]

Below right: Plan for Shawnee Park, dated July 1893, by Olmsted, Olmsted & Eliot. *Louisville's Olmstedian Legacy: An Interpretive Analysis and Documentary Inventory* (1988), 44.

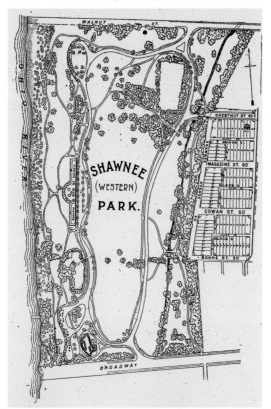

Music Stand, Shawnee Park. *Art Work of Louisville, Ky.* (1903), Part 8.

the fall of 1893, the firm informed board president General Castleman: "The drawing will serve to remind you of our general conception of what this park should be. Entering either of the gates the visitor will find himself upon an undulating prairie, dotted here and there with trees and stretching to the brink of the bluffs of the Ohio River. A driveway makes the circuit of this prairie, and two branches of this driveway lead to points on the verge of the bluff from which the views across and down the river are particularly fine. Upon the bluff and in the course of the circuit drive is a band concert place arranged so that large numbers of people both on foot and in carriages may enjoy the air and the music."[416]

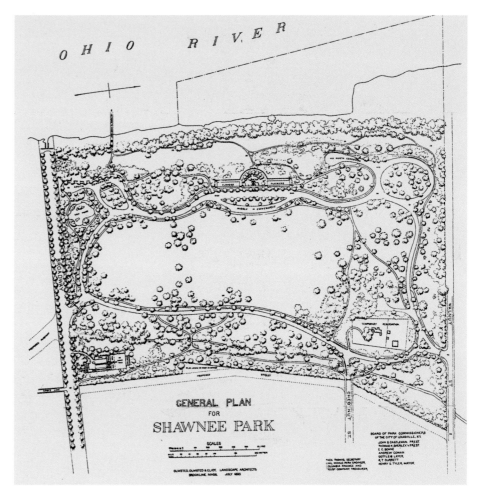

Despite the Olmsted firm's proposal to concentrate the principal parks' athletic fields on the level land in Shawnee Park, by 1900 their intentions in that regard had not been accomplished. In the midst of the park overlooking the Ohio was a music stand set off by a flower bed reportedly containing 10,000 pansies facing a hundred acres of lawn. In the center of that lawn, long-time superintendent of Shawnee Park Ernest Kettig hoped "some day to lay out a big parade ground with tennis courts, baseball and football grounds on the side, where

the citizen soldiery and the younger citizens can disport themselves,"
The Courier-Journal observed 13 May 1900. "Just now the lawn seems
a green velvet carpet waiting to be walked upon."

Pavilion at Shawnee Park near the lily pond. *Art Work of Louisville, Ky.* (1903), Part 8.

Shawnee Park beach. Caufield and Shook Collection, University of Louisville Photographic Archives.

"At the foot of the bank the long hull of the old Atlantic, a wartime transport, 310 feet long, lies hull upward. Where the waves have worn away the oak the huge spikes stand out."

"Beautiful Shawnee," *The Louisville Post,* 7 July 1893.

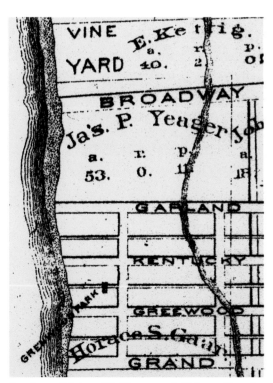

Section of *Atlas of Jefferson and Oldham Counties Kentucky* (Philadelphia, 1879).

Acting as an entrance to Western Park was Fontaine Ferry Park, a summer resort that later became a popular amusement park. The homestead of Aaron Fontaine was Ormsby Hite's Riverside Nursery before Tony Landenwich transformed it into a destination point featuring a bicycle track. "In Fontaine Ferry Park and the Western Park the people of Louisville have a scope of ideal country landscape as beautiful as the sun shines upon, and lacking but the handsome residences and artificially embellished grounds to rival the more pretentious scenery along the Hudson river," *The Courier-Journal* described in 1894. Landenwich added to the nursery's array of mature trees, providing winding walks and drives in tanbark.[417]

Both parks had expanses of fine-sand beaches and the park commissioners had hopes of turning Western Park into a bathing resort, but in the beginning "the sport was chiefly limited to boating and fishing." An imperfection in the beach was an "old capsized Boat," shown on the 1892 Wanless map. "All of her 320 feet of length can be seen now," *The Courier-Journal* reported. "The copper that protected her bottom has been stripped off by many different hands and sold for old metal.... The Old Atlantic was used for transportation during the war and was at one time fitted up to do gunboat service. About four years ago, when lying at New Albany as a wharfboat, she drifted loose in a storm, and turned upside down where she now rests and will rest for years to come."[418] Fontaine Ferry Park, sandwiched between Shawnee Park and the Shawnee Golf Course, became Ghost Town on the River and then River Glen Park before being purchased in 1977 by the city and melded into Shawnee Park.[419]

Between the old Fontaine-Hite property and the west end of Portland was a heavily wooded site long known as Greenbush. During the Civil War, it was a secret assembling place for Confederate troops being shipped down the Ohio River.[420]

The 1879 atlas depicted Greenwood Park on the Ohio River south of Broadway and north of Greenwood, on land owned by the Gaar family. It was the only park shown in that area.

Greenwood Park was made into Riverview Park by John Kessler and Phil Hinkle, and in 1895 it was conveyed to Col. "Lum" Simons, a colorful character well known in political and horseracing circles, who transformed it into "a family resort."[421] "The natural beauty of the park is unrivaled, situated high and dry above the high water mark and overlooking a picturesque bend in the river, where there is good fishing and boating. Thirty-one acres are embraced in the grounds, which are shaded by spreading forest trees and beautified with trailing vines and shrubbery. The park also contains a menagerie which will be enlarged from time to time. A bowling alley, tennis court and other amusements have been provided.… At night the park is illuminated with electric lights, and the tanbark walks and cinder track for bicyclists are always inviting features."[422] In a 1900 picture story, Riverview was described as "Louisville's ideal park, on the banks of the Ohio. How nature and art have combined to produce a magnificent scenic effect."[423]

> It seems almost incredible that only within recent years has this favored locality been brought prominently before the people of Louisville. The only explanation of this apparent neglect of a great opportunity lies in the fact that not until a short time ago was the subject of parks or means of outdoor recreation for our people considered of sufficient importance to enlist the requisite capital and energy for the opening up and development of such places. Louisville has been notoriously behind the times in this particular, and though of late considerable attention has been bestowed on the subject, there are yet very few thoroughly up-to-date resorts where the best classes may go without hesitation for an enjoyable outing.… Nothing else around Louisville even approximates it for scenic effect, or for the quaint and picturesque features with which nature has so liberally endowed the place.

In 1906, Simons conveyed the park property to the White City Company and developed the White City Amusement Park on the site.[424] White City opened in late May 1907. "From a comparative desert the site has been converted into a thing of beauty, a veritable wonderland

Louisville Pictorial Souvenir (ca. 1910). The illustration actually depicts a similar White City Park in Indianapolis.

of interesting sights and pleasant attractions. With a beautiful lagoon in the middle of the grounds and white miniature castles housing all sorts of attractions, all around it, the resort is truly a 'White City,' a place of cleanliness and comfort as well as of pleasures."[425] In less than two years, White City folded under the weight of financial troubles.[426]

Published pictures of White City are deceptive. A 1907 Detroit Publishing Company photograph housed in the Library of Congress and mislabeled Louisville's White City is actually a view of White

Postcard dated 24 April 1909. The Filson Historical Society. This Louisville White City view is confirmed by 20 July 1907 snapshots in the A. W. Terhune album. The Ohio River is behind this scene taken from the Electric Tower.

View taken 20 July 1907. A. W. Terhune album, University of Louisville Photographic Archives.

City Park constructed in 1904 in Broad Ripple, now part of Indianapolis.[427] An illustration of the Indianapolis park was reproduced in *Louisville Pictorial Souvenir* (ca. 1910).

The property was transferred to the Riverside Amusement Company in 1913. The land was eventually acquired by Jefferson County in the mid-1960s.

Immediately to the south, 53 acres of the old Whallen property was purchased in 1921 by the Board of Park Commissioners for Chickasaw Park, which was planned by the Olmsted firm to provide picnic grounds, baseball diamonds and tennis courts "for the use of negroes."[428] Recently, a master plan for the redevelopment of the park area was prepared; its implementation was begun in 2010.[429]

29

BY ANY OTHER NAME (1891)

THE NAMING OF THE THREE SUBURBAN PARKS had been put off as long as possible while suggestions were bandied about, although most citizens as well as the press seemed quite content with compass points—East, West, and South or often Jacob. The names under consideration by the Board of Park Commissioners in August 1891 were outlined in a letter to the editor of *The Courier-Journal*.[430] New Park Commissioner and amateur historian Reuben T. Durrett had weighed in first with esoteric names derived from the languages of the three Indian nations that had claimed ownership and hunted in Kentucky before the arrival of white settlers.[431] Southern Park would be named O-nan-ta, the Iroquois word for mountain. Eastern Park would be called Chen-o-wee, the Cherokee word for the Kentucky River country. Al-wa-me-ke was a Shawnee word Durrett liked for the Western Park. Obviously, for a city already debating Looy-vil or Lewis-vil, Durrett's park nomenclature presented problems. The letter writer suggested naming the parks, Iroquois, Cherokee, and Shawnee. Andrew Cowan thought Beargrass, Forest Hill, and Sunset were preferable.[432] "Probably no names that the park commissioners might have selected would have satisfied everybody," *The Critic* observed following the selection of Cherokee, Iroquois, and Shawnee.[433] "They preserve a unity of idea, just as Chicago has done by naming its parks Lincoln, Jackson, Washington, and Garfield." Boone Square and Baxter Square were not changed.[434]

Two former market spaces in the middle of Market Street, being redeveloped as landscaped strips, were given names recognizing frontiersmen Simon Kenton and Benjamin Logan. The old market spaces were turned over to the Board of Park Commissioners "for Park Purposes" in the fall of 1890.[435] The projects were initiated by Ferdinand F. Lutz, prominent proprietor of the City Malt House, who suggested the improvements to the Board of Park Commissioners in a letter dated 28 February 1891.[436] Two months later, the Board acted to "proceed at once to take charge of and improve the respective Public Squares in Market Street between Sixteenth and Seventeenth streets and Shelby and Campbell streets formerly occupied by Market

We hear that Mr. Cowan suggested the names of "Beargrass" for the Eastern, "Forest Hill" for the Southern, and "Sunset" for the Western park—names in every way preferable to the Indian names selected.

The reason given by the Commissioners for adopting the present names is that it was due the original owners of the soil to be remembered in the naming of the parks.

"Given Indian Names." *The Courier-Journal*, 14 August 1891.

The Park Commissioners... have given deep offense to certain political partisans by bestowing historic names upon the parks, instead of using them to honor officials, for some of whom our city streets, fire engines, etc., are no longer sufficiently important.

The Park System. *The Louisville Post*, 6 July 1893.

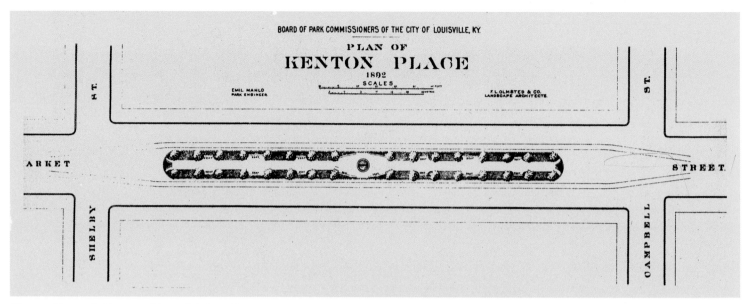

Above: Plan of Kenton Place, Market Street between Shelby and Campbell streets.

Right: Plan of Logan Place, Market Street between Sixteenth and Seventeenth streets.

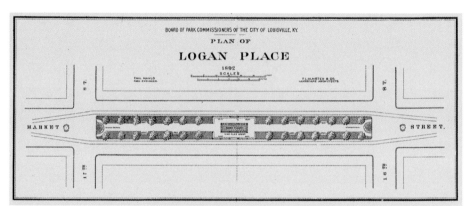

Below: Interior view of Logan Place. All from *Second Annual Report of the Board of Park Commissioners* (July 1892).

Houses."[437] After the Olmsted firm became involved, the site names were changed to Logan Place and Kenton Place, to reflect their size.[438] The city put in stone-flagging crosswalks at each end of Logan Place in the fall of 1891.[439] According to the Board's minutes, work proceeded and contractors were paid during the fall of 1891, but it was not until the December 1st meeting that the Board approved and adopted Olmsted & Co.'s plans for the two spaces.[440] A month later, the Board approved the firm's recommendation to plant sweet gum trees in Kenton Place.[441] The plans for Logan Place were evidently revised, and Olmsted representative Henry Codman made additional changes while meeting with the local architectural firm McDonald & Bro.[442] A rendering of the proposed arbor in Logan Place appeared in *The Courier-Journal*, 7 February 1892. However, it was a plan for a "summer house" at Logan Place by McDonald & Bro. that was finally approved.[443] With some fanfare, Boone Square, Kenton Place, and Logan Place were dedicated 16 August 1892.[444]

Unfortunately, "the experience of several summers has shown that these 'breathing places,' which were intended for the benefit of the poorer classes, have been taken possession of by disreputable characters," *The Courier-Journal* later observed.[445] In 1897, plans were made to replace them with trees, and in 1900 they were removed altogether.[446]

FOR MANY YEARS, *The Courier-Journal* did not acknowledge the park name changes. (The Board of Park Commissioners relented to public usage and changed the name of Iroquois Park back to Jacob Park in 1898.[447]) Neither did its copy editors spell Olmsted correctly, nor, for that matter, did the park commissioners in direct contact with the firm. When board president John B. Castleman wrote 24 March 1893 to acknowledge the firm's name change to Olmsted, Olmsted & Eliot, he referred to it as Olmstead, Olmstead & Elliot.[448] At the time, the Board requested the new firm to extend the "conditions of our contract with you…because of delays incident to the work, growing largely out of the absorption of Mr. Codman's attention at Chicago, making it necessary that we have your advice beyond the period first contemplated."[449]

LACK OF FUNDING;
OLMSTED AND MAHLO WITHDRAW (1895)

Frederick Law Olmsted, Sr., who designed the public parks of Louisville and other American cities…took rank as one of the famous landscape architects of the world. He was a beautifier of cities all over this country and hundreds of pleasure grounds and private estates are monuments to his work.

"He Designed The Parks Of Louisville." *The Courier-Journal*, 29 August 1903.

ANDREW COWAN MADE IT CLEAR EARLY ON that the efforts of the Board of Park Commissioners were underfunded. Initially, the Board anticipated a bond issue of $1 millon, but the Sinking Fund Commissioners were reluctant to take on that much debt, and the issue was reduced to $600,000. Start-up expenses were greater than expected, and revenues from a parks tax were considerably less than they could have been.[450]

At the end of the third annual report to the City of Louisville General Council, dated 6 July 1893, the Board of Park Commissioners requested a $1-million, park bond referendum be placed on the November ballot. The city had been behind in its levies for parks purposes for four years, leaving the parks board without a construction fund. "The building of the parks has just begun," the report declared. "Not one foot of path or roadway has been constructed inside any park, and it is essential that prompt action be taken in this direction."[451] The city's contract with F. L. Olmsted & Co. and subsequently with Olmsted, Olmsted & Eliot was to expire 1 January 1894, and even though the firm had extended the contract, the parks board did not want the prominent park architects to continue rendering service that the board could not carry out for lack of funds.[452]

Harry Codman had died suddenly at the age of 29 in January 1893, leaving the elder Olmsted without his most trusted colleague. The firm took on Charles Eliot as a partner in March, but Olmsted was pressured to pick up the Chicago work that had been entrusted to Codman. In obvious distress, Frederick Law Olmsted wrote John Olmsted from Biltmore in October 1893: "Have you no doubt of the expediency of my going on to Louisville, to Chicago, Detroit, Buffalo, Rochester? It is a long and risky journey for me. I am not quite sure of the plan we had in view when I left. Was it that Manning should go the round with me? Or Eliot, or both? Am I needed in Kansas City? It is so long since I have been at Louisville that I shall be lost there if I go alone. You must send me the names of the people whom I shall need to renew acquaintance with. At this moment I cannot recall one."[453]

He inspected the results of his Louisville planning in mid-March

1894, when on a tour of various cities with Phil Codman, staying at the Galt House for several days while meeting with the Board of Park Commissioners.[454] C. Bonnycastle Robinson wrote Olmsted 14 March about inspecting his place, Bonnycot, in Anchorage. A note on the letter says, "Mr. F. L. O. saw this man next day," but when Olmsted wrote Fairstead on the 15th, claiming to feel "disordered" after not sleeping, he said, "I have put him off till I come again.[455] Manning & Phil have gone out today to Mr. – (the horse breeding place) to stake out for planting. I am confidentially advised that he is not "good pay," but I believe he is not much in debt to us. Phil is to return from here. Manning & I start for Atlanta this afternoon."[456] Olmsted may have been referring to the Glenview Stock Farm, then owned by John E. Green, son of Dr. Norvin Green, one-time president of the Western Union Telegraph Company. Olmsted may have forgotten that two years before the firm had sent Green a preliminary plan for improving his residence, locating his stable, and putting in planting beds.[457]

A year later, Olmsted was even more forgetful and disoriented. He spent the spring at Biltmore with his son Rick, who was there learning the trade, following his graduation from Harvard. It became obvious to Rick that his father was unable to continue working. Vanderbilt had arranged for John Singer Sargent to come to Biltmore to paint separately the estate's landscape architect and the architect of the magnificent mansion, Richard Morris Hunt. Sargent managed to capture Olmsted's head on canvas, and after the old man returned to Brookline with his wife, the painter had Rick pose in his father's clothes to complete the full-length portrait that continues on display in the residence along with Hunt's.[458]

In November 1895, Frederick Law Olmsted, Jr., replaced his father in the firm. When partner Charles Eliot died in 1896, John C. and Frederick Law Olmsted, Jr., became joint owners and partners in the firm of Olmsted Brothers.[459] When the elder Olmsted died at the McLean Asylum in Waverly, Mass., 28 August 1903, at the age of 81, *The Courier-Journal* editorialized that "a disablement of nearly a decade preceded his death, so that the planning of the Chicago Fair was virtually the latest of his works, as the Central Park of New York was the earliest. In that interval of thirty-seven years, all the work in landscape gardening was done by which he is best known and will be longest remembered. It would be difficult to say that any American of his time has a better title to remembrance and gratitude as a public benefactor."[460]

At a meeting of the Board of Park Commissioners on 1 September 1903, president Castleman suggested that "proper notice be taken of

Frederick Law Olmsted, Sr., 1895, by John Singer Sargent. Courtesy of Biltmore.

the death of Architect F. L. Olmsted," and requested a resolution be drafted.

> When one who has filled well his place in life is taken, those who knew him are necessarily filled with regret, but when the recognized leader in any of life's activities is called hence, we can appreciate his great importance and question if there shall be another.
>
> Frederick Law Olmsted, during his long useful life, was preeminently the recognized leader, in this country and abroad, in Outdoor art. To his remarkable skill and taste is due not only the physical development of the most magnificent parks of this Country, but that striving after the beautiful and ornate in nature that now animates the thousands who are giving their life to the work in which he was the pioneer. The impetus which his work and thought have given to the world and especially to this Country, in landscape architecture is ever increasing, and to him above all others in the future will be accorded the credit for the great Park systems that are now so rapidly becoming a part of our civic life.
>
> When we recall that Louisville, starting with his instruction, has, in a little more than a decade, built up a park system which is the admiration of all who know it and which will be more beautiful as his plans are developed, we deem ourselves fortunate that it was our privilege to have him as our guide and teacher.[461]

The continued effects of the economic panic of 1893 forced the park commissioners to curtail all planning and construction work. According to the commissioners' annual report issued late in 1894, the city owed the Board "on appropriations and assessments" for 1892, 1893, and 1894, and at the rate city taxes were coming in, payrolls and other expenditures had to be reduced "to the minimum amount required for the actual care only of the park property." A bank overdraft was arranged to cover the shortfall until the end of the fiscal year, but cutbacks in non-maintenance areas such as engineering were in order.[462] Because of the Board's "depleted state of finances," assistant engineer Cecil Fraser took a leave of absence in the fall of 1894.[463] Engineer Emil Mahlo followed suit in July 1895, indicating he would work "for any compensation the Board may decide upon, or even without compensation at all."[464] When his father-in-law, Fred Leib, died in October 1895, his obituary characterized Mahlo as being "formerly engineer for the Board of Park Commissioners."[465] It appears that

Mahlo was forced out, perhaps because the new members of the Board wanted to introduce more athletic activities in the parks which the Olmsteds had resisted. Mahlo had been the firm's choice in 1891 for park engineer. In the spring of 1896, the new members of the Board of Park Commissioners reassured the firm that in the hiring of a new park engineer, they would "not for a moment consider the application of any one who would not be of the same mind."[466] The firm responded to Board president John B. Castleman that it had been "informed that Mr. Mahlo was not discharged permanently but only temporarily suspended for lack of funds."[467]

> Unless, therefore, there is some better reason than any yet given for Mr. Mahlo's discharge, we are decidedly of the opinion that he had better be retained. It would be both expensive and troublesome to impart to another engineer all the multitude of technical knowledge which we have in the course of years advised Mr. Mahlo upon. In fact, as far as those instructions came from Mr. Fredk. Law Olmsted it will never be possible to repeat them to another engineer or to obtain even the equivalent. In short Mr. Mahlo's intercourse with Mr. Fredk. Law Olmsted makes his services of decidedly greater value to the Board than would be those of an engineer who had not had equal opportunities of receiving ideas from Mr. Olmsted. We trust that no change will be made.[468]

In October 1893, Emil Mahlo had married Katherine Leib, the daughter of wealthy Louisville pork packer Frederick Leib.[469] They subsequently moved to Washington, D.C. He died suddenly 31 August 1904 at the age of 54 at Wiehle, Virginia, a town 18 miles west of Washington that had been planned by Dr. Carl Adolph Max Wiehle. Funeral services for Mahlo were held in the home of Dr. Wiehle's widow.[470] Interment was in Cave Hill Cemetery. Wiehle, formerly a physician in Philadelphia, may have known Mahlo when he worked at Fairmount Park, and Mahlo may have had a professional connection with Wiehle's planned community, part of which would become Reston.

The referendum on the $1,000,000 bond issue finally took place as part of the 6 November 1894 election that produced a Republican sweep. It appeared to pass handily, but the result was challenged.[471] The contest hinged upon whether two-thirds of the people voting on the issue were required to pass the bond issue, or were two-thirds of the all the voters that day needed. The Jefferson Law and Equity Court held the city could issue the bonds, but that ruling was appealed to

The pastoral character of the scenery [at Cherokee Park] would be much enhanced if a flock of sheep was maintained in the park. The sheep should be thoroughbred Southdowns and should be folded at night. The best place for a sheep-fold and sheds would seem to be in the land proposed to be added to the park in the Bonnycastle Run. Any needed buildings could be hidden in the border plantation. The flock must be permanent and composed only of such sheep as can be trained and easily kept out of the shrubberies and off steep hillsides, where they would do the turf more harm than good.

Olmsted, Olmsted & Eliot to John B. Castleman, 6 May 1896. Olmsted firm papers, Library of Congress.

the Kentucky Court of Appeals. In expectation of a favorable decision, John C. Olmsted made an inspection of the parks and submitted a report with suggestions and recommendations to the Board of Park Commissioners in April 1896.[472] One recommendation that presumed a favorable, long-term arrangement with the Louisville Water Company was the elongation of the small pond below the Alexander house. This feature was added to the "General Plan for Cherokee Park" dated 1 December 1897.

In the meantime, in June 1896 the Kentucky Court of Appeals reversed the lower court decision and denied the $1-million bond issue. The Board lamented that "unless some favorable legislation can be had to enable the city government to issue bonds for the future improvement of our parks, the most energetic effort of any Board of Park Commissioners will be greatly hampered and handicapped."[473]

> The final plans for the park system have been submitted to the Park Commissioners by the architects, Olmsted Bros., of Brookline, Mass., to whom the original contracts for constructing the parks were awarded six years ago.
>
> It was supposed when the contract was first awarded that the parks would be finished in three or four years, but the Commissioners have never had enough money on hand to have the work completed.
>
> Olmsted Bros. have been maturing their plans for the parks ever since the work was begun and they are now completed, showing the boundaries, roads and houses that will be in the parks when they are finished. The parks will not be completed for some years, and the work will be carried on in the same manner as heretofore.
>
> "Louisville Park System." *The Courier-Journal*, 19 February 1898.

31
PASSIVE OLMSTED PARKS BECOME MORE ACTIVE (1897)

THE FIRST ANNUAL MEETING of the National Association of Park Commissioners gathered in the men's parlor of the Galt House on 20 May 1897.[474] "Louisville had been intending to call a convention of park men so as to extend the influence of parks," John B. Castleman, president of the Louisville Board of Park Commissioners, told the group.[475] "An organization of park men, built on broad lines and taking in park architects, park commissioners and all persons who are interested in parks, was bound to result in good."

The initial paper, "The True Purpose of a Large Public Park," was delivered by John C. Olmsted, who with his stepbrother, Frederick Law Olmsted, Jr., and Charles Eliot, had taken over the Brookline, Mass., landscape firm made famous by Frederick Law Olmsted, Sr. Echoing the elder Olmsted's philosophy, John C. described a large park as "being large enough to include the different examples of forest trees, the several classes of topography, and with limits extensive enough to allow the thousands of people who wish to take outings in the parks to do so without being crowded." Parks should have a natural appearance, but as he told the group, "many park commissioners are untrue to their trust because they frequently yield to the clamor of the public for some artificial expedient." He then separated the Olmsted camp from many in the crowd. "There should be no ball grounds or golf grounds or unwieldy buildings in large parks. The first object of a big public park is to give its votaries a chance for solitude."[476]

The last paper, "Organization and Notes on Park Planting," was presented by Boston landscape architect Warren H. Manning, who had trained in the Olmsted firm and had represented Olmsted, Olmsted & Eliot the previous year in Louisville, particularly in replanting Southern Parkway.[477] According to landscape architecture historian Lance M. Neckar, after Manning had left the Olmsted firm, he suggested to Charles Eliot the formation of an organization of landscape architects. Eliot did not think the profession was large enough to warrant it, and suggested forming a group with broader interests.[478] Eliot may have had a role in planning for the conference in Louisville, but he died

"Society On Skates: Fun On The Ice In Eastern Park," *The Courier-Journal*, 18 December 1898.

unexpectedly of spinal meningitis two months before it occurred.[479] Manning was named secretary and treasurer of the Park and Outdoor Art Association, the permanent organization formed before the group adjourned.[480] Two years later, Manning would lead the effort to form the American Society of Landscape Architects.

Interviews of conference participants by *The Courier-Journal* were positive about Louisville's parks, although John C. Olmsted thought the city was "a little premature when she called the convention to meet" in Louisville. He considered Minneapolis's park system to have been "more improved" and a better site for the initial meeting. Interestingly, Warren Manning is credited with those parks.[481] "Louisville has no room to be ashamed of her parks," *The Courier-Journal* noted in its wrap-up of the conference.

> When representative park commissioners, engineers and architects from all over the country come to Louisville fresh from their own parks and are enraptured by the wild, rugged beauty of Jacob Park and the splendid forests of Eastern [Cherokee] Park, Louisville, taking everything into consideration, can well be proud of her system of breathing spots. While this city has nothing to compare with the botanical gardens at St. Louis or Central Park, in New York, or Prospect Park, in Brooklyn, she has the ground and the start of parks which can be made in time to outshine any one of these.[482]

A representative from Peoria spoke to the division in park philosophy that had emerged since the Olmsted firm had set the standards decades before. "We do not believe with Mr. Olmsted that a park is a thing simply to look at. We believe in getting as much pleasure out of it as possible."[483] John C. Olmsted's emphatic comment in his prepared remarks that ball fields and golf courses had no place in large parks was directed at the Louisville contingent who on their own had introduced golf at Cherokee Park.

Olmsted had admonished General Castleman a year before, that "no game where balls are propelled so swiftly ought to be allowed in a park so situated, so used, and so small as Cherokee Park."[484] In the fall of 1896, the newly formed Louisville Golf Club had sponsored a practice round on a raw course belonging to the Iroquois Wheeling and Driving Club located on the Grand Boulevard north of Iroquois Park in anticipation of developing a course on the grounds of the "old reservoir park."[485] Ironically, two days after John Olmsted told the national convention in 1897 that large parks should not contain golf "grounds," the Louisville Golf Club opened on River Road on the

"Getting Ready For A Long Drive," illustrating, "The Way To Play Golf" in *Louisville Commercial*, 24 October 1897, listing the 40 rules of golf, adopted from the royal and ancient rules of St. Andrews.

site of the old Water Works Park, near the old reservoir on the bluff overlooking the pumping station.[486] A 1902 article praising outgoing Louisville Golf Club president Marion E. Taylor for making the sport popular in Louisville, noted that the club's links were "considered the finest in the South."[487]

As landscape architect Arthur A. Shurtleff pointed out in 1926: "We cannot meet this demand of physical recreation by ignoring it. We must generously provide space for it in other public grounds dedicated to that physical use. The landscapes of our parks will remain in danger until these provisions are made."[488] If it sounded like Shurtleff was repeating an Olmsted firm theme, he had reason. Initially a protégé of Charles Eliot, he worked at Fairstead from 1896 to 1904, when he struck out on his own. Interestingly, his 1926 paper to the convention of The American Federation of Arts did not invoke the Olmsted name. While Shurtleff recognized the damage being caused by the increased number of visitors to parks, he was retained in 1928 as chief landscape architect for Colonial Williamsburg, which encouraged and promoted visitation.

"A fine park…requires devoted and intelligent care to keep it in perfect condition, to yield the delight it was meant to yield," Shurtleff declared. "It needs protection from the hands and feet of men in order that it may fill their senses with delight. Of all the works of the Fine Arts a fine park in the temperate zone is the most difficult to protect, both from Nature, who would clog it with unneeded plants, and from man, who would destroy it by wear and tear and with clutters of utilities or 'ornaments.'"[489] Shurtleff, who helped Frederick Law Olmsted, Jr., establish the landscape architecture program at Harvard, where he continued to teach, then launched into the meat of his paper. "In these days of rapid transportation there is, however, another danger which threatens to mar the attractiveness of parks which were designed to give delight through compositions of meadows, fields, lawns, woodlands, shrub areas, ponds, lakes and streams. That danger springs from a natural and desirable demand for modern baseball fields, football fields, and for the extensive motor parking spaces which the crowds attending the games upon such fields require." Shurtleff had just joined the firm of Olmsted, Olmsted & Eliot in 1896 when the Louisville Board of Park Commissioners started to grapple with athletic recreation in the system. At the same time, there was no money available to provide additional space for such endeavors that were growing increasingly more popular.

Attorney Robert C. Kinkead was elected to the Board of Park Commissioners in November 1895. During his eight-year tenure, the

Kinkead's brother-in-law, Cary Warren, is now out and Alexander is again superintendent as the Board is now democratic.

Minutes of John C. Olmsted, 11 November 1900. Olmsted firm papers, Library of Congress.

I chanced to meet young Mr. Sneed in Cherokee Park to day and learned from him that it was intended to allow Golf playing there. We would strongly advise against doing so. The reason is that it might be annoying to other visitors to the park especially to mothers and others in charge of young children. There is danger of Golf balls hurting people struck by them and the fear of being hit or of having little children hit would seriously detract from the pleasure of many people strolling in the park. No games where balls are propelled so swiftly ought to be allowed in a park so situated, so used, and so small as is Cherokee Park. It might be reasonable to use the top of the hill at Iroquois Park at certain specified hours of which other visitors ought to be warned so that if they went to the top of the hill they would do so at their own risk…. It is important not to allow Golf to begin in a small way because it is liable to increase both in numbers of players and area required. We can assure you that it is always easier to prevent bad habits or uses in parks in the beginning than it is after they have been going on for some time.

John C. Olmsted to John B. Castleman, 17 April 1896. Board of Park Commissioners Minute Book 5, pp. 205-206.

system would veer from the hardcore Olmsted philosophy that the parks other than Shawnee were scenic retreats only. Kinkead introduced golf at Cherokee in 1897. According to his obituary, "he advocated the use of the parks as playgrounds and insisted upon establishment of tennis courts, baseball diamonds, golf courses and other forms of amusements."[490] Two years before he joined the Board, Kinkead had written the Olmsted firm about creating a zoological garden in one of the parks. When the firm countered that a zoo should be independent of the parks, Cowan assured them that Kinkead was acting in the public good, writing that his idea was not "in the nature of a nuisance scheme" and requesting information for Kinkead about creating independent zoos.[491] Members of the Kentucky Society of Natural History, of which Kinkead was president and Cowan a director, met with the Board of Park Commissioners in June 1894 to discuss establishing a zoological garden in a park. The Board was favorable and referred the matter to the Olmsted firm for advice. Olmsted, Olmsted & Eliot replied early in 1895, counseling the Board against the proposition.[492]

A change was made when Cecil Fraser was hired as park engineer early in 1897.[493] He was born in London in 1859 and worked on the St. Lawrence River locks before coming to America and finally to Louisville as an engineer with the L&N Railroad. He had first been retained by the park commissioners in 1893 to finish up maps of Cherokee Park.[494] One of Fraser's first projects was to work with Kinkead in laying out a nine-hole golf course in Cherokee Park.[495] Later, in 1900, authorization was granted to establish a "Nine Link Golf Course," and a caretaker was hired.[496] Two tents for golfers were to be erected and floored in 1901, and Fraser was authorized "to extend the links if practicable" in the spring of 1902. The next year a permanent shelter was constructed.[497] In 1905, the Board retained well-known Chicago "golf expert" Thomas Bendelow to improve the course.[498] "In accordance with your wish," Bendelow informed the Board, "I went over the ground at your disposal for a golf course at Cherokee Park, and found that it had been very cleverly utilized by Mr. Fraser, and that he had done in great measure, just as well as could be expected. However, with his co-operation we were able to extend the present course to something like over 2,900 yards."[499] Park Commissioner Bonnie suggested the "golf grounds" be extended across the lake, and asked to get estimates for "shaping up the ground." Several years later, John Olmsted responded to president Castleman: "It has been suggested that the ground northwest of the lake could be given over to golf. We believe this would be a mistake, because this ground is likely to come into demand for visitors on foot and may be used for ball games or even in part for tennis." The Board thought otherwise, and in 1908 the lake came into play, along with a green located in a triangle across Cherokee Parkway.[500] The possibility of extending the course to 18 holes was examined by Tom Bendelow in 1911, "but a survey proved it impossible." Plans were made for Bendelow and Ernest Kettig to build a nine-hole course at Iroquois Park instead.[501] Pressure mounted to extend the Cherokee course. A 28 May 1915 *Courier-Journal* editorial taking the park commissioners to task for not providing an adequate course for the "great and growing number of people in Louisville who have taken up the recreation of golf," brought instant relief.

At their next meeting, the park commissioners invited Tom Bendelow back from Chicago to inspect the Cherokee Park site and provide a plan for extending the course.[503] Two weeks later, Bendelow's extension plans were approved and construction was authorized.[504] The new course with drainage and watering improvements opened in September 1915.[505]

In the meantime, the 1911 plans to build a nine-hole course at Iroquois Park did not materialize. Supporters of golf at Iroquois Park submitted a petition to the park board in July 1915 for a public course. Proponents Helm Bruce and A. E. Richards pointed out that Tom Bendelow had made a "sporty outlay in the eastern part of the park" for a nine-hole course in 1911 that was suitable for what they were requesting.[506] At the time, the Olmsted firm told the Board "the topography of Iroquois Park is so rugged that it does not lend itself to sport of this character, and we feel that if your Commission deems it necessary to provide a course in that neighborhood, it would be wisest to purchase a tract of land more suitable for that purpose." In December, Helm Bruce took the matter up with John Olmsted directly.[507] Evidently, when Bruce was informed of the firm's past reservations, he confronted John Olmsted in late 1915. "I am no longer a member of the Board, but still retain my interest in the Parks. A very large number of persons living in the southern part of the City of Louisville, myself included, have been exceedingly anxious to have a golf course established in Iroquois Park. An expert golf engineer has surveyed the ground and said a good course of nine holes could be established, beginning near the entrance at the end of the Third Street car line (Sennings Park), and continuing southwardly along the east side of the Park and around on to the south side…. I heard in a roundabout way that you had expressed the opinion that a golf course could not be located as I have indicated above, and I am simply writing to ask if you have expressed such an opinion."

Olmsted contacted the Board's secretary, Harry S. Smith, to obtain a report on the golf course. Smith could not find any report, but did send a

Concrete tee pad probably in Cherokee Park about 1910. Matlack Collection, University of Louisville Photographic Archives. Golf-course expert Thomas Bendelow had recommended simply tamping the ground to create a tee area. He was critical of the "built-up teeing grounds" at Cherokee Park "made of yellow clay" that "are of an eye-sore to an aesthetic taste."[502]

In time the commissioners may come to understand that there is no form of amusement which can be provided in the parks in which so many of those who own the parks find diversion and benefit. And when the commissioners come to understand this, perhaps they will also understand that it is of more advantage to maintain a golf course in part of the park than to maintain a forest reserve in the whole of the park.

So little have they realized this heretofore that they have stubbornly refused to allow the removal of a single tree in order to make a halfway decent nine-hole course in Cherokee Park.

"Golf Links In Cherokee." *The Courier-Journal*, 28 May 1915.

It should be clearly recognized that most of the existing parks were greatly restricted as compared with what they should have been for so large and growing a city, owing to the entirely inadequate funds available for the acquisition of land. I believe that now is a good time to organize public opinion on this matter.

John C. Olmsted to Helm Bruce, 21 June 1916. Folder 1266, Olmsted firm papers, Library of Congress.

blueprint of a layout by B. G. McAndrews and an old map in dilapidated condition "embodying the general ideas of Mr. Tom Bendelow."[508] After examining the plans, Percy R. Jones drafted a response for Olmsted Brothers. "We deem it our duty to most strenuously protest, as park designers, against the use of this part of Iroquois Park for golf. Without the least desire to bring up any discussion of the question of 'the masses against the classes,' it is necessary for us to design parks fundamentally on the principle of the greatest good for the greatest number. It is primarily because of the flagrant violation of this principle contemplated by these golf plans that we are obliged to run the risk of making ourselves disagreeable to a body of citizens whose particular sport we are most anxious to provide for in the large parks." The firm urged the Board to "secure more park land, open and well adapted to golf" and not ruin "one of the very best and most accessible woods of grand old trees now available in the parks of Louisville."[509]

John C. Olmsted finally responded to Helm Bruce in June 1916 that "it was my duty to give my opinion against the idea of laying out a golf course in Iroquois Park." He advised that "the golfers join forces with others interested to make more adequate provision for baseball and other outdoor games than is in the park system of Louisville."[510]

When the nine-hole golf course at Iroquois Park opened in the summer of 1947, veteran *Courier-Journal* sports columnist Earl Ruby described it as "an enlarged copy of the old Cherokee course." The layout on land added to the north side of the original park was designed by Robert Bruce Harris of Chicago and had been two years in the making. "It is the answer to the adventurous golfer's dream," Ruby noted. "It has everything."[511]

The Shawnee Golf Club, organized in 1925, finally got to play in 1927 on a nine-hole course developed on city property north of Shawnee Park and Fontaine Ferry Park.[512] As early as 1905, golf-course architect Thomas Bendelow examined Shawnee Park with Cecil Fraser and reported to the Board of Park Commissioners. "I was very much surprised to find such a stretch of ground available for this purpose. Of course you may have other things in view for that property, but I should think that nothing else coming up in the near future, in another year or two you could have another golf course in there which would I think, be a very popular proceeding. There is infinitely enough land, for judging from what I saw there are seventy-five acres of open land there available for this purpose, and it would make a rattling good course."[513] While the Board was impressed with Bendelow's suggestion for the system's second golf course, it would not act upon it "for the present." Ironically, as of 1905, Shawnee Park, the only major park approved by the Olmsted firm in 1892 to have athletic fields, still had none. When baseball fields were finally introduced in 1912, Olmsted Brothers protested about "the broad stretches of bare earth for the sake of playing baseball." They suggested switching to grass diamonds like those at Franklin Field in Boston.

By 1915, ten diamonds had already been laid out—five in Shawnee, three in Cherokee, and two in Iroquois—when the Amateur Baseball Federation requested the park commissioners add more diamonds to each park, particularly two in Shawnee Park. The request was forwarded to Olmsted Brothers for its recommendation as to where the diamonds should be established.[514]

The first "turf plots" for tennis were approved for Shawnee Park by the Olmsted firm in June 1896.[515] The next year, the firm was asked to locate five tennis courts in Cherokee Park.[516] Evidently the firm did not specify a space or the parks personnel chose the site without consultation. "The tennis courts in the valley below the first shelter are

It is not only unnecessary but decidedly undesirable to have dirt surfaces for baseball when played in parks, especially in such parks as Shawnee Park where they destroy the fine stretches of meadow view, the equals of which are hard to find.

Olmsted Brothers to Board of Park Commissioners, 20 June 1912. Olmsted firm papers, Library of Congress.

Tennis courts at the bottom of Baringer Hill, 1909. Brenner Collection, University of Louisville Photographic Archives.

exceedingly ugly and conspicuous because they are looked down upon by visitors on all the heights about them," the firm informed Andrew Cowan in the spring of 1908. "They should be removed from this important landscape portion of the park and located on high ground near the boundary where they can be partially screened by additions to the border plantations, or…they should at least be on high ground where they will not be looked down upon."

The clay tennis courts are not only exceedingly ugly in themselves, occurring as they usually do in the midst of what is intended to be a beautiful lawn, but they have conspicuous and ugly back nets, usually without the slightest attempt to mask them by vines, shrubbery and trees. We should be glad if the public could be induced to use a clipped turf tennis court and if the Park Commission would gradually substitute neat iron frame works with small mesh wire netting for the large wooden posts and flimsy-looking poultry netting generally used and to grow vines and plant a few shrubs in connection with these fences. The painting also should be as inconspicuous as can be devised. We have seen high tennis fencing surrounding the whole court and covered with Clematis paniculata, which at the blooming season was a conspicuously beautiful looking object instead of being an eyesore and a destruction of the landscape beauty of the surroundings.[517]

The third annual Cherokee Park tennis tournament will begin this afternoon. The number of entries in the various events reached a total of over sixty, which is the largest number any event in Louisville has boasted of in years.

"Cherokee Park Tennis Tournament Opens To-Day," *The Courier-Journal*, 27 July 1912.

∽ ∽ ∽

View of Hogan Fountain and pavilion by The Detroit Publishing Company, 1907. Library of Congress. A tepee-shaped pavilion designed by local architect E. J. Schickli, Jr., replaced the one shown in the background.

IN 1903, AFTER NEW ORLEANS NATIVE Emma Clara Alter Hogan inherited a fortune from her father's estate, she and husband W. J. Hogan of Anchorage selected from a competition Enid Yandell's design of a drinking fountain for horses and visitors to be located in Cherokee Park.[518] Yandell was present when the fountain was placed in Cherokee Park in the summer of 1905. "I am very much pleased by the site chosen," she told a reporter. "The trees and thick foliage make a beautiful background…. The approaches arranged by the Board of Park Commissioners are fine and will set off the figure to the best advantage."[519] She explained that the statue was a faun, a deity, half-human and half-animal, which in Roman mythology had inhabited the forest until the woods were cut down by man when it took refuge in fountains. Before returning to New York in September, Yandell planned to attend the erection of her statue of Daniel Boone, also in Cherokee Park. She was waiting for the statue's pedestal to be cut.

As Frederick Law Olmsted himself had cautioned, the firm also continued to express reservations about the introduction of sculpture into its parks. The scenic composition would be compromised, giving the "pleasure ground the character of a rural cemetery." One of Olmsted's last official acts regarding the Louisville parks was to advise president Thomas Sherley in the fall of 1894 not to place any commemorative work of "a man who has been lately living" or a piece of sculpture that has not been "formally attested" by a qualified expert.[520] Subsequently, nearly every time the Board of Park Commissioners was offered a statue, the Olmsted firm balked.

Louisville cigar manufacturer C. C. Bickel had Enid Yandell's statue of Daniel Boone, which had been displayed at the 1893 Columbian Exposition in Chicago and later at the Louisiana Purchase Exposition in St. Louis, cast in bronze for the park.[521] John C. Olmsted was asked to locate the site, and he spent some time with Cecil Fraser doing so. "I finally said this Boone Monument is too big to be set down in a casual way, like a little thing, where it will look good," he told Fraser. "It needs approaches and surroundings. So, I finally settled on a site west of the second shelter and on an axis with it and the horse fountain."[522] It was not to be.

When Miss Yandell objected to Olmsted's site selection, he met with her at the location she thought her statue should be displayed. According to Olmsted she did not question her site nor say a word about his, but "simply assumed that as General Castleman had given her this site, I was to help improve it. I thought it useless to enter into an argument with her."[523] When he later inspected the statue, Olmsted thought even though "it was not to my taste to decorate such a naturally beautiful beech wood with bronze monuments," that Fraser had "carried out my instructions for an imitation outcropping of ledge very cleverly but not as boldly as I intended." Fraser explained that he had taken down the top two stone courses at Miss Yandell's request. Just as he had anticipated when he ruled out the elevated site in the beginning, Olmsted "could not see a single feature of the face."[524]

As General Castleman sat "mounted on a splendid charger" at the

Fraser rather sneered at the design, but it did not strike me as bad—only not anything remarkably fine or original. Colonel Cowan said it had been criticized for being bow-legged (which Boone was not) but I did not notice that defect. It may be so in certain points of view.

Notes of John C. Olmsted, Olmsted firm papers, Library of Congress.

unveiling of Yandell's statue in Cherokee Park, 15 June 1906, his son, Breckinridge Castleman, addressed the crowd, concluding: "It is to be hoped that this gift of Mr. Bickel will be followed by others until these charming grounds become a kind of rural art gallery in which will be preserved the statues and busts of Kentuckians who leave imperishable names at their departure from this world."

Not only is it accepted, but assurance is given that it will always occupy a suitable location for its care and display. It vindicates

Enid Yandell's statue of Daniel Boone, 1920. Caufield and Shook Collection, University of Louisville Photographic Archives.

its own propriety of location, as it stands on a foundation of rocks, with primeval forest trees around, apparently guarding it like sentinels of old. If the Park Commissioners had located it upon a bluegrass lawn, gemmed with brilliant flowers, the incongruity would have been patent. The ancient Greeks and Romans increased the loveliness of their forest trees by peopling them with beautiful female forms known as Dryades, but Boone, the rustic philosopher, loved the trees for their own majestic form and silent shade, and needed no wood nymphs to add to his admiration.[525]

Cecil Fraser had so far been able to satisfy the desire of the park board for more athletic activities while representing the Olmsted firm locally as it began to focus on residential and institutional projects, but when John C. Olmsted met with park commission president Castleman in May 1906, he was told that Fraser had been "dropped" as superintendent of Cherokee Park "because he gave too much attention to outside matters and the park was not well cared for." Castleman explained that Fraser "had been granted a long leave of absence when he was ill," and after he returned Castleman told him "he might finish up what works outside he was already under obligations for but after that he would either have to attend exclusively to park business or resign."[526]

After designing suburban Louisville's residential development, Audubon Park, in 1909, Cecil Fraser died a year later following a stroke in the Kentucky governor's office where he was meeting about landscaping the new capitol grounds being undertaken by the Olmsted firm.[527] The list of prominent honorary pallbearers indicated the respect Fraser had garnered.

❧ ❧ ❧

John Charles Olmsted was 62 years old when he appeared before the Board of Park Commissioners in early 1915 for the last time, lauding Louisville's park system, which for the most part was the product of his oversight, diligence, and persistence for two decades. "On the whole," his report read, "it would be difficult to find three large parks in other cities so individual and distinctive, yet so supplementary one to another."

Olmsted recommended that either members of city government undertake a study of the community's needs or else "a permanent board of experts" be created that would "keep constantly before the practical officials those things which are liable to be neglected, or

Mr. Olmsted says the park system is remarkably well balanced in landscape features, yet it must not be assumed that it is finished and that no more park land is required except for playgrounds and ornamental squares…. It hardly need be argued, as it is self-evident, that in the case of a city like Louisville, any comprehensive system of parks that may be devised will prove inadequate in the course of time. The more people there are the more parks there should be and especially the more neighborhood parks and playgrounds there should be, just as there is need for more school houses, more fire engine houses, more branch libraries, more churches and so on.

At present there appears to be a decided lack of foresight in securing vacant land while it can be obtained at reasonable cost for local parks and playgrounds in conjunction with suitable sites for school houses. The mass of the people gives little thought to the needs of the future in these and other respects concerned with making the city a convenient, healthy and agreeable place to live and work in.[528]

to be inadequately provided for." He was suggesting the creation of a planning commission, which had been urged futilely by the city's Engineers and Architects' Club and would not be adopted until 1932.[529] "In the absence of such a comprehensive consideration of the city plan for the future, the Board of Park Commissioners should do the best it can to locate and acquire neighborhood parks where clearly desirable to provide for the future requirements of the rapidly increasing population."[530]

Mr. Olmsted expressed the opinion that playgrounds, tennis courts, wading pools, running tracks, outdoor gymnastic apparatus, children's gardens and like advantages for healthy play in parks should be purely incidental and should not injure the beauty of scenery. He believes the erection of museums and other similar buildings in these parks is undesirable, though he says, every self-respecting city should have them.[531]

John Charles Olmsted had not yet turned seven when his mother married Frederick Law Olmsted, her late husband's brother and best friend. After graduating from Yale University's Sheffield Scientific School, he apprenticed under his stepfather before becoming his partner in 1884 and a partner in F. L. Olmsted & Co. in 1889. He was the senior member of Olmsted, Olmsted & Eliot from 1893-1897, and of Olmsted Brothers from 1898 until his death in 1920. A master of detail, he supervised the firm's increasing office output resulting from his stepfather's national reputation and influence. Although most of the firm's correspondence was not personally signed, his initials are on most of the drafts dealing with Louisville. He ably and faithfully passed on the philosophy of park design he had learned from his stepfather. According to biographer Arleyn Levee, he continued the conceptual work of Frederick Law Olmsted in Atlanta, Boston, Brooklyn, Buffalo, Chicago, Detroit, Hartford, and Rochester, and developed systems in Portland (Maine and Oregon), Seattle, Spokane, Charleston, and Dayton.[532] As in Louisville, his municipal park projects led to many significant individual and institutional commissions. While his stepfather won over clients with broad strokes and grand ideas, John Charles Olmsted excelled in detail, transforming visions into real places.

In reporting his death, *The Courier-Journal* noted that "the roads, bridge locations and planting in Cherokee, Iroquois, Shawnee and Central Parks were arranged by Mr. Olmsted. He also had charge of planning the smaller parks. His last work here was that of locating the position for the new Ahrens Memorial Bridge and indicating the roads approaching it."[533]

BRIDGES BEAUTIFIED (1901-1929)

THE FIRST STONE BRIDGE OVER Beargrass Creek on the boundary of Cherokee Park was erected sometime after 1855 when the Shelbyville Branch Turnpike Road was built as a picturesque alternative to entering the city from the east along Frankfort Avenue and the railroad tracks. Like other stone bridges of the period, it consisted of a single round arch. The earliest Beargrass Creek bridges in the park were eight in number, simple wooden structures subject to the ravages of flooding.

Lexington Road bridge over Beargrass Creek, 1926. Caufield and Shook Collection, University of Louisville Photographic Archives.

View of Bridge Number 1 by Edward F. Brenner about 1908. University of Louisville Photographic Archives.

View appears to be of Bridge Number 1 in 1906. Courtesy of David J. Isaac.

The first stone bridge built by park interests was the Belknap Bridge (see p.18), designed by Shepley, Rutan & Coolidge of Boston, and erected in 1901. Its opening was elliptical and allowed more water to pass under it in flood periods. A dozen years would pass before the Board of Park Commissioners would entertain another such capital investment. When park neighbor Frank Fehr offered to build a bridge in Cherokee Park in 1913, disagreement arose among board members as to what additional costs were entailed. The board recommended that the plans be scrutinized by the Cherokee Park committee as well as Olmsted Brothers. Vice president Louis Seelbach thought the latter unnecessary, stating for a reporter that although he held the firm in "highest regard," he was "satisfied they might be wrong in some instances." He said while he thought the firm's plans for his own house were "the best that could be gotten," his wife did not. Ultimately she prevailed, and according to Seelbach, "Mr. Olmsted himself admitted it would have been a mistake to have built

Mildred Ahrens Howard Memorial Bridge, 2010. Samuel W. Thomas.

Below: "How Hert Memorial Bridge Will Look When Completed," *Louisville Post*, 31 May 1922.

Bottom: "As Hert Memorial Bridge Will Look When Completed," *Louisville Post*, 4 November 1922.

it the way he suggested."[534] Fehr did not wait for a review of his plans and withdrew his offer at the next board meeting.

It was not until after World War I that Theodore Ahrens undertook the next permanent bridge named in memory of his daughter, Mildred Ahrens Howard, who had died in 1919. It replaced wooden bridge number 3. Designed by local engineer James M. Johnson, the stone-faced concrete bridge opened in October 1920.[535]

Wooden bridges 4 and 6 washed out in December 1921. Number 4 was to be replaced by the A. T. Hert Memorial Bridge.[536] In 1922, local architects were instructed to submit designs incorporating stone columns salvaged from the front of the old Galt House. The winning concept, published in May 1922, featured the columns as light standards.[537] But in November a simpler design by the architectural firm of Nevin, Wischmeyer & Morgan, without the Galt House columns, was accepted. The bridge's ornamental balustrade was destroyed by an accident to one side and then in a deliberate act to

the other in 2006. Restoration was completed in late 2008.[538]

Before the Hert Memorial Bridge was completed, plans were being developed by Olmsted firm partner James Frederick Dawson for Olive Speed Sackett to memorialize her mother, Cora Coffin Speed, wife of J. B. Speed.[539] The Speed bridge replaced a wooden bridge destroyed by high water.[540]

Bernheim Memorial Bridge, 1930, soon after completion. Caufield and Shook Collection, University of Louisville Photographic Archives.

The children of Bernard and Rosa Bernheim funded a bridge honoring their parents in 1929. The design of the Beaux Arts bridge was submitted by Walter Wagner, an associate of the local firm of Joseph & Joseph.[541]

Newly constructed bridge connecting Cherokee and Seneca parks, 1929. Caufield and Shook Collection, University of Louisville Photographic Archives.

33

LOUISVILLE'S CENTRAL PARK (1904)

BESIDES OTHER FINANCIAL INTERESTS, Antoine Bidermann du Pont also was president of the Southern Exposition, which opened in 1883 on the present site of St. James Court.[542] When the exposition had run its course, a plan was devised to combine its 16 acres with the adjacent property of Central Park as well as the grounds of the School of Reform by acquiring the mostly vacant land in between. According to one of the plan's supporters, Temple Bodley, Bidermann's brother A. V. du Pont agreed to sell Central Park to the city for 10 percent less than the $150,000 he paid for it, but the city and the Southern Exposition's board did not move forward on the offer.[543] "Mr. du Pont is anxious for us to have the place, and I think that he is inclined to make us a most favorable proposition," Thomas Sherley told the board in May 1891.[544] However, negotiations did not move forward, and A. V. du Pont died

Central Park, looking west toward the du Pont residence. *Louisville Illustrated* (1889), Part 2.

somewhat mysteriously at age 60, the afternoon of 16 May 1893, a week after he had dedicated his gift to the city of the Manual Training High School.[545]

Considered Louisville's wealthiest citizen, he never married and had lived in one room of the Galt House for 23 years. After an elaborate story was concocted about his death occurring in his brother's Central Park residence, when in fact he was visiting in the home of old friend Maggie Payne, rumors spread he had been murdered. The facts, including his relationship with the widow Payne, were divulged several days later by *The New York Times*.[546] "Few people stop to think how generous Mr. du Pont was with Central Park," *The Courier-Journal* eulogized.

> He paid $3,000 taxes on it every year, and employed five or six men to keep it in condition. The grounds have always been open to everyone. He was anxious that the city should buy the property, and he offered to sell it at a price greatly below its actual worth. When the Capital removal question began to be agitated he offered it as a site, the value to be determined by a committee of three, one to be selected by himself, one by the Removal Committee, and another by some third person.[547]

Scene in Du Pont Square. *Art Work of Louisville, Kentucky* (1897), Part 1.

Bidermann du Pont was forced to close the park in 1895 because people persisted in removing the flowers and shrubbery. "I expect that it will be closed for good, though I can not say it will be for certain," a family member said.[548] When Bidermann du Pont moved back to Delaware, he permitted the city to use the property for three years. Warren Manning made an assessment for Olmsted, Olmsted & Eliot of its condition and suggested under the circumstances only minimal changes.[549] At its 1 May 1896 meeting, the Board adopted Manning's recommendations to create additional entrances but maintain "the existing walks and roads with stone surfaces." Because the site "cannot be called a park," the Board decided to rename Central Park, Du Pont Square.[550]

In the spring of 1899, the city reacted to indications that the du Pont heirs were in the process of "cutting up Central Park into building lots." An aldermanic committee was created "to confer with the du Pont heirs and see if some arrangement can be made to save the beautiful tract of land from such a fate."[551] Interest in its purchase was heightened when Isaac and Bernard Bernheim offered to erect a statue of Thomas Jefferson by sculptor Moses Ezekiel, who thought the park would be the most suitable site for his bronze work. The Board of Park Commissioners informed the brothers that the park was not publicly owned and therefore permission could not be granted. The sculptor and the brothers met with the Board and appealed. The Board could only respond that it was pondering acquisition of the park.[552] Board president John B. Castleman suggested that revenue from the sale of the city's Gas Company stock be used to buy the park for the Jefferson statue.[553] The city attorney favored a bond issue, supported by private subscriptions.[554] When the initial issue failed "through lack of interest on the part of the voters," the du Pont estate heirs threatened to subdivide the property.[555] Another bond issue attempt in 1900 passed, but it was challenged in two suits and held up in the courts. Meanwhile, the statue arrived in Louisville in June 1900 and was stored in the old art gallery in Central Park.[556] When the Bernheims asked in May 1901 if the statue's foundation could be set in the park, the Board's response was negative as before.[557] The statue was then erected in front of the Jefferson County Courthouse and dedicated 9 November 1901.

Early in 1903, the du Pont heirs notified the city that the lease, which had been in place for eight years, would be terminated, the park closed, and the property subdivided.[558] The prodding was effective. Castleman informed Olmsted Brothers that du Pont Square "is now practically within our reach," in late 1903. "We are ambitious under your skilled guidance to do something really handsome with this very valuable land and make it an ideal Park and Play Ground."[559] He had instructed Cecil Fraser to forward a survey of the property to the firm.

Will Central Park be secured or lost to posterity of Louisville?... Public sentiment has been called upon, but could not solve it. Like the public library question, the one reply seems "aye," while the taxpayers say "nay." Should the city acquire or relinquish forever a bit of the primeval forest which is located in its very heart and which is the wonder and delight of all strangers who visit the city because of its sylvan beauty?

"Shall Central Park Be Lost to the City," *The Courier-Journal*, 21 October 1900.

Survey of Du Pont Square. 1903. Louisville Metro Archives.

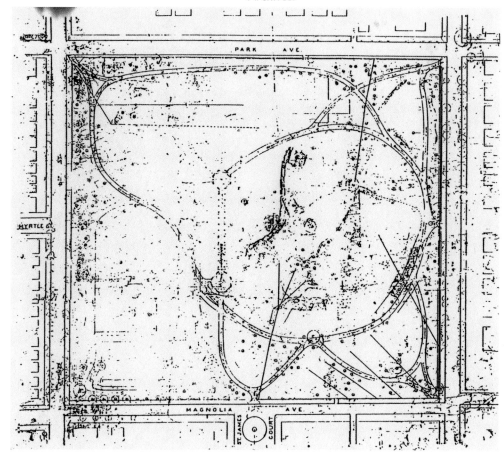

ART GALLERY AND LAKE.

Section of broadside advertising the Southern Exposition: "Louisville, Ky. Closes Oct. 25." Library of Congress.

Olmsted Brothers concurred with the playground concept, suggesting "your Board would do well to make at least a beginning toward the carrying out of a carefully considered scheme for children's amusement apparatus."

The square formerly known as Central Park was acquired finally from du Pont family heirs in early 1904.[560] As the spring planting season approached, the Olmsted firm provided lengthy justifications for tearing down the old Robinson-du Pont house and the art museum that had been erected for the Southern Exposition. Apparently, the firm was under the impression the commissioners were considering creating an art or science museum in the park. The Board was advised "to take the position that it is contrary to their true and rational functions to undertake to provide buildings for art or scientific collections in any of the parks…. A park, aside from its principal and essential characteristic of providing beautiful landscape, is concerned with outdoor recreation, exercise and enjoyment—not with indoor pleasures and occupations and scholastic instruction."[561] Announcing the house was "too large and of the wrong style of architecture for a park," the Board immediately sold it for scrap and ordered the outbuildings and art museum to be demolished.[562] The plan produced by Olmsted Brothers in 1904 envisioned three tennis courts and open air gymnasiums for men and women. The children's amusement apparatus would be added later. The existing walks were retained. A planned connected structure that included a field house, park shelter, and pergola was designed by John Bacon Hutchings and Henry Franklin Hawes.

"As might have been safely predicted," John C. Olmsted wrote after inspecting du Pont Square 3 April 1904, "there was a storm of public opposition both in the newspapers and by petitions and personal interviews, but General Castleman had been polite but decided that our plans were to be carried out." On his subsequent visit 4 June 1904, Olmsted observed: "It has been a matter of much comment how much better the park looks since the trees I marked had been cut and since so many old walks and roads had been dug up, loamed and sodded over and especially since the old art building had been removed."[564]

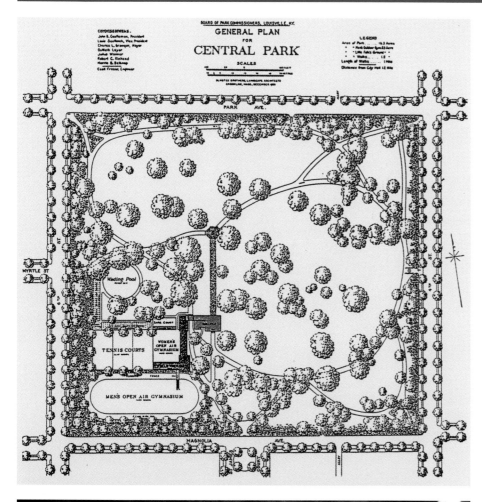

Plan of Central Park, December 1904.

The laying of concrete walks in Central Park will begin this week, and it is expected that the entire park will be ready for use by June 1. The park is open now, but no games are allowed, as they would interfere with the workmen, but after June 1 the children will be given full sway. The new walks will greatly improve the park, both as to general appearance and as to the comfort of the persons using it.

"Central Park To Be Opened On June 1." *The Courier-Journal*, 18 April 1904.

Pergola, 1907.[563] Detroit Publishing Company, Library of Congress.

It is announced that the Board of Park Commissioners will adopt "Kentucky Park" as the official name of du Pont Square…the name of Central Park, by which the square was known during the eight years in which it was kept open by the city, will be officially discarded.

"Central Park Will Be Named 'Kentucky Park.'" *The Courier-Journal*, 12 March 1904.

Additional tennis courts had been placed along Park Avenue by 1907. Detroit Publishing Company, Library of Congress.

Visitors standing in front of the temporary log structure, June 1906. Matlack Collection, University of Louisville Photographic Archives.

Without asking for Olmsted Brothers' consent in May 1906, the Board authorized president Castleman to grant authority to the "Committee on Lincoln Cabin Home Coming" to temporarily erect a cabin in Central Park.[565] As the logs of the cabin in which Abraham Lincoln was born were being loaded on a flatcar in Jersey City to be transported with an escort of honor to Louisville, the announcement was made that the cabin would be erected and exhibited in Central Park.[566] Permission was not a problem. General Castleman's son, Breckinridge, was in charge of the celebration. After the Homecoming Week, the cabin was to be stored in Louisville awaiting plans for "the rehabilitation of the old Lincoln homestead," which had been purchased by Robert J. Collier, editor and publisher of his father's *Collier's Weekly*.[567] He had acquired the Lincoln cabin, which reportedly had been on display in Chicago at the Columbian Exposition in 1893 and the Centennial Exposition in Nashville in 1895, the Pan-American Exposition in Buffalo, and the Louisiana Purchase Exposition in St. Louis. When Collier purchased the homestead, the cabin was on display in New York's Central Park.[568] On the same day the cornerstone was laid for the new capitol in Frankfort, Henry Watterson, whom Breckinridge Castleman described as "the greatest living student of the life of Lincoln," and former vice president Adlai E. Stevenson delivered orations to some 4,000 persons assembled at Central Park for the cabin ceremony.[569] After the Homecoming festivities in 1906, the cabin was dismantled and stored at the Louisville Public Warehouse awaiting Lincoln's centennial celebration in 1909.

While the cabin was on display in Central Park, a memorial was planned to commemorate the birthplace of Lincoln in Hodgenville. Members of the planning group were provided seats on the platform for the unveiling of the Boone statue in Cherokee Park.

Ironically, for all the Olmsted firm's expressed distaste of bronze objects placed within sylvan scenery, the letterheads of the Board of Park Commissioners' stationery displayed first an engraving of Enid Yandell's statue of Daniel Boone and later a depiction of Roland Hinton Perry's statue of General Castleman astride Carolina, which was placed in the circle connecting Cherokee Road and Cherokee Parkway in 1913.[570]

In 1921, Olmsted Brothers was asked its opinion about the placement of a replica of George Grey Barnard's statue of Abraham Lincoln in Central Park.[571] The statue, which originally had been commissioned by the Taft family for Cincinnati, was to be the gift of Mr. and Mrs. Isaac W. Bernheim.[572] The Board had received the firm's response many times before in similar situations, including when Bernheim and his brother had proposed to locate the Moses Ezekiel statue of Jefferson in Central Park. "The question of locating a monument of such a fine character in your parks, or in connection with your parks, is in our minds quite a serious one, and ought to be determined after we have had a chance to actually study the site proposed or any other that might be considered." Olmsted partner James F. Dawson was delegated to come to Louisville to examine the site.

> Central Park, in common with the larger landscape parks of Louisville, was designed to afford recreation to the citizens mainly through the enjoyment of landscapes having distinctive but quiet characteristics of their own. Some landscape compositions are so designed that their highest perfection can only be attained when they are enriched with works of sculpture. The main landscape of these parks are not at all of this character, and to adapt one of them to the effective display of an important work of sculpture would involve a radical change of character, which under all the circumstances, we would deeply deplore.
>
> Frederick Law Olmsted, Jr., to Matt H. Crawford, 26 May 1921.[573]

Yesterday's was a remarkable demonstration. In the center of one of Louisville's beautiful parks had been erected the Lincoln cabin, built of rough logs, held together by notches at their intersections. Their very rudeness brought the vivid contrast of birth and achievement into the mind.

"Watterson Pays Great Tribute To Abe Lincoln," *The Louisville Herald*, 17 June 1906.

We are of the opinion that nothing at all commemorative of a man who has been lately living should be accepted as a gift with the condition that it stand on a public ground, and that no work or sculptural art should be given a place on a public ground the value of which, as a work of art, has not been formally attested to by persons holding positions to which they have been appointed because of their possession of a rare degree of qualities fitting them for so difficult and delicate a duty.

Frederick Law Olmsted to Thomas Sherley, 24 September 1894. Olmsted firm papers, Library of Congress.

Lincoln statue about 1925. *The Courier-Journal* files. Louisville Free Public Library is out of view at right: Fourth Street is at left.

Eventually, the Central Park idea was abandoned, and Barnard's work was unveiled on the grounds of the Louisville Free Public Library 25 October 1922.[574] Interestingly, while Olmsted Brothers had prepared a plan to beautify the library grounds in 1907-1908, it was never implemented, and the firm was not asked about the statue's placement. A year after the Lincoln statue's unveiling, at the behest of its donor, I. W. Bernheim, architect Arthur Loomis wrote Olmsted Brothers to complain that no landscaping had been done and to ask for suggestions. Olmsted partner E. C. Whiting checked the site and reported: "It is a very unpromising problem. The statue is a replica of Barnard's statue about 12 ft. high standing on a rough granite rock about 3 ft. high. It faces 4th St. and its background is the end of the library which contains a framed niche, empty but made for a life-sized statue. The contrast in scale is fierce, making the statue seem ludicrous. Also the space is too small for it."[575] The firm wanted the niche on the end of the building removed, but realizing that would be too expensive, suggested heavy planting between the statue and the building. The next spring, the firm was informed that the planting had been done for $20. "And it looks it!"[576]

John C. Olmsted, who was the firm's primary contact with Louisville, had died in February 1920.[577] Well before then, his stepbrother had inherited the mantle from his father. Olmsted biographer Witold Rybczynski characterized Frederick Law Olmsted, Jr., as an "outgoing and convivial" individual, who "soon eclipsed his older half brother."[578] The two had helped establish the American Society of Landscape Architects in 1899, and a year later the younger Olmsted was asked by Harvard president Charles W. Eliot to initiate, as a memorial to his son, the country's first course in landscape architecture.[579]

Prominent New York architect Thomas Hastings wrote to Frederick Law Olmsted, Jr., 7 May 1924 informing him he had been appointed to design a memorial amphitheater, "something in character with the Arlington [Cemetery] one, for Louisville, Kentucky. I went out there a few days ago and met their committee consisting of about eight very intelligent and influential men…. I found when I arrived that my committee had unanimously voted for what is known as the Central Park site."

I have just received a telegram from the Chairman of my committee saying that he feels that the Park Board would unquestionably be influenced by your opinion in the matter and also saying that your office knows the general park system at Louisville, which is enormously extensive. Their plan is to remove a very large and unsightly construction, a sort of colonnade surrounding a playground and a building of considerable size attached to it. I personally think their project is an excellent one and I wonder if you knew it well enough to express an opinion to me…. I do hope that they will consult with you for an entire new layout of the park. Don't think of me as a park invader! I would like to see you sometime and have a talk with you.

Faithfully yours, Thomas Hastings[580]

After discovering that Olmsted was in New York and not Brookline, Hastings wrote him again the next day, concluding: "Perhaps you can do the "sauce to my pudding" and lay out their park to harmonize with the memorial; it needs it badly." Olmsted's telegrammed responses to Hastings and the Board were not what they wanted to hear.[581]

Mr. G. W. Schardein, President, Board of Park Commissioners, Louisville, Ky.

Thomas Hastings has asked me to commit myself in advance to an opinion about use of Central Park for Memorial Amphitheatre. Stop. Have wired him as follows quote Wisdom or unwisdom of replacing playground et cetera in Central Park Louisville by Memorial amphitheatre seems to depend first on whether the site is really the best possible for performance of the amphitheatre function considering accessibility and the physical conditions of site and surroundings second on whether the local neighborhood has ceased to have a real need for continued maintenance of playground et cetera. Stop. If either question must be answered in negative it becomes a question of the price to be paid for the use of this site for the amphitheatre rather than some other site in terms both of money and of any other values that might have to be sacrificed by the neighborhood or by the City at large. Stop. Without investigation and in the absence of my partners who know present conditions in Louisville closely I cannot answer these questions offhand.

F. L. Olmsted, Jr.

Hastings immediately came to Louisville to meet with the blue-ribbon committee made up of Robert Worth Bingham, chairman,

Thomas Floyd Smith, George C. Burton, P. H. Callahan, Mrs. A. T. Hert, F. M. Sackett, and Henry Vogt. Hastings was familiar with Louisville, having designed Rostrevor near Cherokee Park for James Ross Todd in 1908 before his partner John M. Carrère died. They had both studied at the École des Beaux-Arts and after working briefly in the office of McKim, Mead & White had formed their own firm and would design numerous significant public buildings and private residences. Their first important commissions were hotels for Henry Flagler in Florida, and later his residence Whitehall in Palm Beach. After Robert Worth Bingham married Flagler's widow, he contacted Hastings about designing a memorial building that had been simmering in Louisville for years.[582] Four years later, in April 1924, the announcement was made that Thomas Hastings would design the $1.25 million Louisville Memorial Auditorium.[583]

As Hastings wrote Olmsted after returning from Europe in August, the group was divided, some wanting "a purely aesthetic expression in design," while others desired "a more utilitarian" auditorium seating 6,000 to 8,000. "I brought them all together on a basis of a proposition which made a very strong appeal," he informed Olmsted. "My suggestion was that instead of an auditorium they might build a very simple, open, outdoor amphitheater, such as the one in Berkeley, Calif., perhaps not so much architecture as the one we built at Arlington Cemetery, something which would tie in with the park itself and not occupy much more room than the very unsightly loggias, pergolas, and other things which are now in the park, all of which would be removed, that is to say that it would make a splendid opportunity of a further layout or plan of the park, providing spacious playgrounds for children, approaches, etc." Hastings concluded: "I do hope that we may be able to come together on the work if you so desire, but I am writing to ask if you do not think it safe for you to express an opinion after consulting with those in your office who are familiar with the site, so that I could quote you to my committee."[584]

"I have consulted one of my partners who has been in Louisville more of late than I have, and he has only very general impressions about Central Park," Olmsted replied to Hastings. "For what such general impressions are worth, they do not seem very favorable to the proposition."[585] Despite Olmsted's reservations, the project moved forward quickly with the official selection of Central Park as the site in mid-November. [586] "Central Park has been definitely selected as the site of the City Memorial Auditorium, the Board of Park Commissioners declared yesterday," *The Courier-Journal* reported 19 November 1924 as part of its front-page coverage of Hastings' "Louisville Memorial

Amphitheater" plan. Interestingly, Hastings was planning an amphitheater, while the committee kept calling it an auditorium.

While the main article was headed "Veterans and Women Favor Central Park," a group opposed to the auditorium's construction in Central Park was instructed by the Board of Park Commissioners "to prepare arguments on legal grounds and submit briefs."[587] On the day of *The Courier-Journal* announcement, the managing editor of *The Louisville Post* wired Olmsted: "Park Board has offered Central Park to Memorial Commission as site for large Memorial Auditorium. Please wire us if you were consulted and your opinion as to advisability of such use of Central Park."[588] Olmsted Brothers tersely responded: "Cannot give final opinion without detailed investigation but in general we are strongly opposed to encroachments on dedicated park lands and consequent sacrifice of established park values."[589] A Committee for the Preservation of City Parks quickly formed, also made up of prominent women and men armed with counsel who filed briefs on their behalf.[590] The battle lines had formed, supported by the competing newspapers.[591]

Olmsted Brothers partner Edward Clark Whiting attended a January 1925 meeting of the park board and memorial commission that included E. T. Hutchings, the local architect associated with Hastings. His notes described the latest scheme for "an out-door Auditorium or Amphitheatre with curving colonnades extending from the corners of the Auditorium about half way around the Amphitheatre." The Auditorium would seat about 6,000, the Amphitheater about 10,000. "After some preliminary skirmishes," Whiting wrote, "I asked the President of the Park Board point blank what the situation was. Had they or had they not agreed to allow this development in Central Park? He admitted, a bit sheepishly, that they had given the Memorial Commission permission to use Central Park for this development provided they paid the necessary costs of rearrangement and reconstruction and provided that the plan for location and development was satisfactory to the Park Board. I told Mr. Schardein that I was much disappointed at their decision and that I was even more disappointed at their making the decision without consulting us as they had agreed to do." Despite reluctance on the part of several members of the Memorial Commission to involve a landscape architect, Board president Schardein made it known that "the Park Board would not accept any scheme of development until Olmsted Brothers had been called in on the matter."[592]

Even after the Board of Park Commissioners agreed to employ Olmsted Brothers as a consultant, the firm prepared a formal argument that the project was not a legitimate park use as required by the 1890 act creating the park commissioners. The document, dated 31 January 1925, concluded: "Considering both the sacrifice of park service and the difficulties in making a satisfactory War Memorial on this site, we cannot help feeling on the whole that if this proposed scheme is carried out the people of Louisville will be getting a rather poor bargain." In countering the firm's stand the Board declared, "The arguments in favor of the project greatly out weigh those against it…the Memorial structure will be erected in Central Park unless prevented by Court action." The firm was directed to cooperate with Hastings to the fullest extent possible.[593] In a separate letter to the firm of the same date, the Board made concessions including that "all park and recreational facilities contained in the present buildings are to be duplicated in the Memorial structure, upon the completion of which the present buildings will be razed;" and "no roadways, nor automobile traffic or parking within the Park is to be allowed."

The newspaper war continued to spew misinformation on both sides. "Central Park is neither practical, feasible nor desirable as a site for the proposed memorial auditorium, in the opinion of Olmstead [still frequently misspelled] Brothers," reported *The Louisville Herald*, 30 May 1925. "It is generally believed, however, that in view of the great opposition to the use of Central Park as a site for the auditorium the board will be governed by the advice of Olmstead Brothers, and the negotiations with the Memorial Commission will come to an end within the next few days, and that the latter body will begin negotiations for the purchase of a site nearer the hotel and business section of the city."[594]

The Courier-Journal announced 2 June 1925 that the Board of Park Commissioners and Olmsted Brothers had approved revised plans as well as the use of Central Park for Memorial Auditorium.[595] The Board, which had prodded those disenchanted with the project's use of Central Park to prepare legal briefs against it, got what it did not wish for. Hattie Bishop Speed, widow of James B. Speed, who lived near Central Park, initiated along with others a suit enjoining the Board and Memorial Commission from building the auditorium in Central Park.[596] Jefferson Circuit Court Judge Lafon Allen found in favor of Mrs. Speed and her allies in January 1926.[597] The Board and Commission appealed the decision to the Kentucky Court of Appeals, which concurred with Judge Allen. A more adequate site was found at Fourth and Kentucky streets, and Thomas Hastings revised his plans accordingly. The cornerstone was laid Armistice Day 1927 and the building dedicated 30 May 1929.

Thomas Hastings' Memorial Auditorium, Fourth and Kentucky streets, 1929. Samuel W. Thomas files.

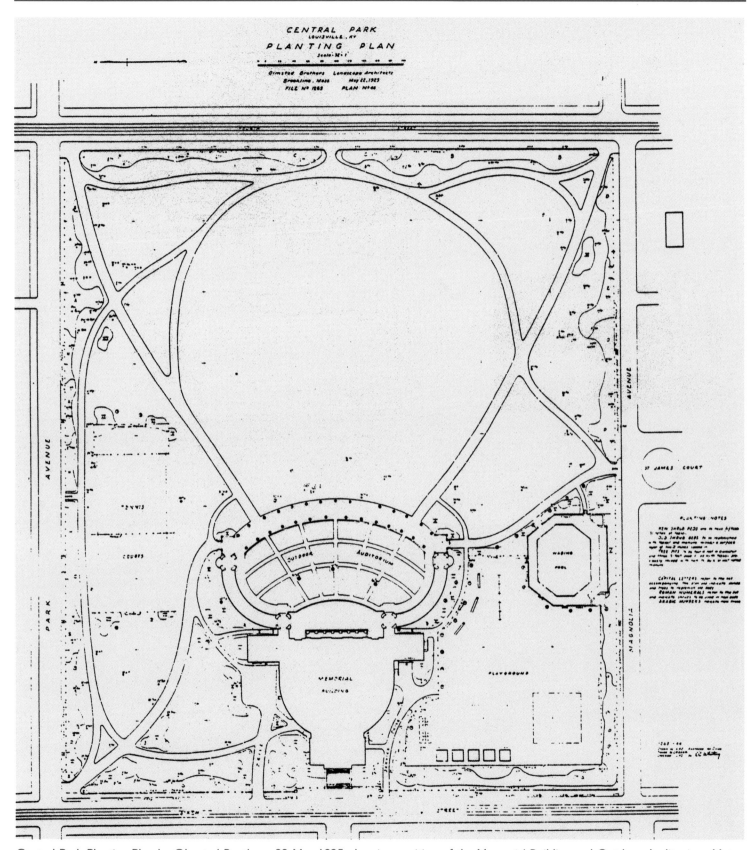

Central Park Planting Plan by Olmsted Brothers, 22 May 1925, showing position of the Memorial Building and Outdoor Auditorium. Metro Parks Archives.

34
PARKWAYS (1889-1917)

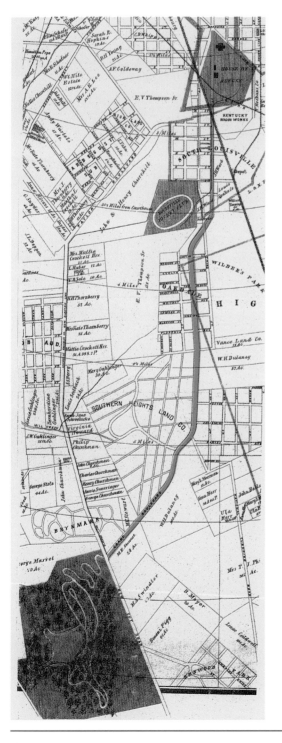

THE FIRST WORK UNDERTAKEN by the Board of Park Commissioners after it assumed control of the City of Louisville's existing park and parkway property on 1 January 1891 was to complete the grading of Grand Boulevard leading from the southern reaches of the city to Jacob Park.[598]

The following year, paving the 40-foot-wide, center driveway of the boulevard with "broken stone and Paducah gravel" a foot thick was begun. "Southern Parkway, leading from the end of Third street to Jacob Park, is ready for public use at last," *The Courier-Journal* announced in June 1893. The job had taken over a year to complete.[599] These improvements were just the beginning of an ever-widening thoroughfare. "On either side will be a grass plot, then a row of trees. A smaller driveway, another row of trees, and a bridle path…. The parkway is to be one of three to be constructed, one of the others going to Eastern Park, and the third to Western Park. It is proposed to connect these three parkways with a boulevard."[600] Due mainly to an economic downturn, parkway planning was suspended until early in 1896 when an east-west parkway connecting Cherokee and Shawnee parks was again investigated, but to no avail.[601]

By 1897, work was underway to complete the three additional divisions of Southern Parkway. Interestingly, the bridle path planned earlier had been replaced by a bicycle path, only to revert to a bridle path years later.[602] A published photograph of Southern Parkway taken in 1896 confirms that no trees had been planted prior to that time.[603] The 1897 Board report provided some history and a description of Southern Parkway.

> In the Southern Parkway Louisville has had for some years, in a semi-finished condition, the nucleus of a truly magnificent drive; what it ultimately can and will be is appreciated by few. The exact length of the drive is 14,100 feet, or two and three-quarters miles, and extends from the end of the brick portion of Third street, in South Louisville, to the entrance of Iroquois

Section of *New Map of Louisville* (1891) showing (in green) extension of Third Street through the House of Refuge and Grand Boulevard from Churchill Downs to Jacob Park.

Park, and is practically an extension of that street, which is itself by far the finest street in the city.

The plans provide, and arrangements are made, for the abutting property holders to give ten feet on each side of the parkway for sidewalk purposes; thus the entire completed width will be one hundred and seventy feet. Messrs. Olmsteds' design for utilizing this entire width forms a portion of this report, and may be briefly described as follows: A main driveway, forty feet in width in the center; the sections on each side of this drive to be occupied each by a bicycle path fourteen feet wide and a carriage way twenty feet wide, for the use of property owners and those who wish to stop for a time along the route, the main center drive to be always kept free from obstruction for the sole use of pleasure drivers.

Each of these drives and paths is to be separated one from the other by a row of trees, planted in a strip of sod seven feet wide, making in all six lines of trees, the effect of which, in a few years, will be more than beautiful.

This general design has never been deviated from; the original allotment of twenty feet on each side of the main drive for bridle purposes has naturally been transferred to the uses of an immensely more numerous and daily increasing body, the bicycle riders, who to day outnumber the pedestrians a hundred to one…. That the park system must be considerably affected is a matter of course; a prompt recognition of this fact by the Board is evidenced in the arrangement of the Southern Parkway.[604]

The illustration published in the *Louisville Commercial* is very similar in appearance to one the Olmsted firm had produced for Boston that also included a railway division. Introducing the term "speedway," the text accompanying the illustration explained that it was "designed for persons who wish to go to the park, and not waste any time on the road."

How Does It Happen? That the Park Commissioners can spend nearly $50,000 on a boulevard to Iroquois Park and entirely neglect the roads leading to the Eastern and Western parks?

The Critic, 11 June 1893.

On June 6, 1893, this Board, by resolution, named the strip one hundred and fifty feet wide, Southern Parkway, heretofore commonly known as "Grand Boulevard," leading to Iroquois Park…. Southern Parkway was opened to the use of the public on the 14th day of June, 1893.

"Annual Report of the Board of Park Commissioners for the Year Ending July, 1893," *Louisville Municipal Reports for the Fiscal Year Ending August 13, 1893* (Louisville, 1894), 194.

Philip Laib with his high wheel bicycle at the Iroquois Wheeling and Driving Club along Southern Parkway about 1900. R. G. Potter Collection, University of Louisville Photographic Archives.

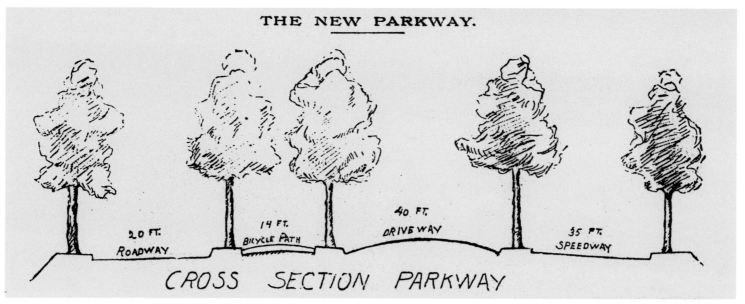

"The New Parkway." *Louisville Commercial*, 3 October 1897. Tree planting along Southern Parkway was completed in December 1897.

The success of your extension of Third Street with a width of 150 feet, all the way to Iroquois Park will surely be a great stimulant to any feasible scheme of making Cherokee Park equally accessible, especially as the distance is so much less. I was much pleased with the main features of that Parkway; and especially with the selection of the several kinds of trees with which it is planted. In 15 or 20 years these trees will have grown sufficiently to make it a magnificent boulevard.

William McMillan to John B. Castleman, 14 February 1898. Louisville Metro Parks.

Southern Parkway or Grand Boulevard about 1910. Caufield and Shook Collection, University of Louisville Photographic Archives.[605]

IN THE MEANTIME, anticipating the 1895 Grand Army of the Republic Encampment in Louisville, the Kentucky Women's Confederate Monument Association sponsored a contest for a monument to Confederate dead that would be erected in a circle at the termination of Third Street at the House of Refuge. The location had been suggested by the Board of Park Commissioners. The selection was made by the executive committee from more than 20 entries. The winning design, one of two entries by Enid Yandell, was a 75-ft Corinthian column topped by a bronze figure, which she called Liberty, holding a Confederate flag.[606] Controversy erupted within the monument association when some members who had wished to vote, protested. A three-man committee of disinterested local architects appointed to choose the design also selected Miss Yandell's. A vote of the membership favored the entry of monument-maker Michael Muldoon.[607]

Design submitted by Enid Yandell. *The Courier-Journal*, 20 September 1894. Yandell's huge Corinthian column was probably based upon the ancient Pillar of Pompey.

Monument designed and erected by Michael Muldoon. Detroit Publishing Company, 1906. Library of Congress.

Adjacent the monument was a popular watering place erected by the Kentucky Humane Society. Atop the water fountain was a bronze figure of Hebe, who periodically would "step off the pedestal and wander away."[608] The recurring costs resulting from the vandalism evidently led to the removal of the fountain from the busy thoroughfare.

❧ ❧ ❧

AT ITS MEETING OF 4 MAY 1891, the Board of Park Commissioners directed its standing committee on boulevards "to investigate" a parkway route from Eastern Park to the Waterworks and then to the House of Refuge. On May 22nd, "Mr. Olmstead entertained the Board in an extended verbal report of his visit here, and investigation of our Parks, and proposed Park and Boulevard system," the minutes record. The firm formalized Olmsted's impromptu advice in an extensive report to Board president Thomas H. Sherley, dated 26 August 1891.[609] However, no mention of parkways was made in the Olmsted firm's written report, reflecting its focus only on parks.

In the fall of 1892, the Board of Park Commissioners instructed Park Engineer Emil Mahlo to prepare preliminary surveys for parkways from Third Street near the House of Refuge to Cherokee Park and another running west to Shawnee Park. "These surveys were completed October 20th [1892] and the corps of engineers was disbanded. Maps and profiles for these two parkways were made in the office."[610] Mahlo did not note, as he did elsewhere, that copies of these surveys had been sent to the Olmsted firm.[611]

It is interesting to note that these surveys were made at the same time that John B. Castleman became president of the Board of Park Commissioners and just after he had purchased property known as Schwartz's Woods, south of St. Louis Cemetery, that he would develop as Castlewood.[612] In 1895, long before the route of Eastern Parkway had been officially determined, Castleman dedicated the divided boulevard through the southern section of Castlewood to the Board of Park Commissioners for public use.[613] It is now the only stretch of Eastern Parkway with planting in the middle.

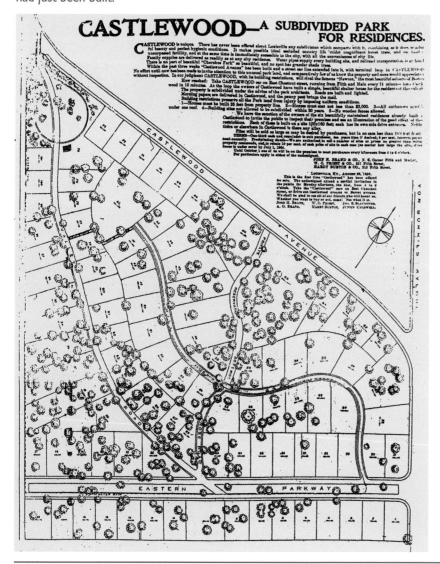

Advertisement for the first public sale of Castlewood lots. *The Courier-Journal*, 30 August 1903. "The property is subdivided under the advice of the park architects." Baxter Avenue replaced Von Borries Avenue at right; Barret Avenue is at left. Castlewood Avenue, cutting diagonally at top, had just been built.

"Surveys have been made for boulevards running from the House of Refuge to East and West Parks respectively, skirting the city limits on both routes and affording the most desirable drives to these resorts," *The Courier-Journal* revealed 28 May 1893. "These new driveways to East and West Parks will be one hundred and twenty [feet] wide, furnishing most commodious and pleasant connections between the larger parks of the system such as few cities aside from Chicago can claim."[614] The Board's third annual report (July, 1893) acknowledged that "while many citizens owning property along the surveyed route have ceded to the Board of Park Commissioners the land making this parkway, others stand in the way of the improvement, and we are thus obliged to rely on the city for the streets."[615]

WHILE NOT CLASSIFIED AS A BOULEVARD, New Broadway (now Cherokee Road) connecting the head of Broadway with Cherokee Park quickly became the most popular drive in the city, according to a well-illustrated *Courier-Journal* article in June 1893. "Many have noticed the remarkable suddenness with which the New Broadway road leading to Eastern Park has sprung into favor with those of the city who are lucky enough to own carriages and other traps in which that most delightful of summer pleasures, a drive, may be taken."[616] About half the length of New Broadway had been macadamized and "a new and splendidly-kept dirt road" extended almost to the park, where "the pleasures of the drive begin in earnest. The driveways have all just been finished and are in perfect condition. They are all amply shaded by the numerous trees of the park, and curve around in all kinds of peculiar shapes. Many of the 'smart set' have deserted the Third avenue boulevard for this new driveway." The reporter described among others Fred Adams in his "dark, high-seated drag, drawn by two well-groomed and spirited bays"; Ed Ferguson's "T" cart drawn by two handsome gray horses; Drudie Ellison driving his chestnut mare "attached to the nattiest of dark green road-carts"; Sallie Ward Downs and her husband in the back seat of "her elegant blue-bodied brougham"; Charles Peaslee in "a spotless, stylish trap"; "the exquisite, prize-winning Castleman turnout"; Mrs. Sebastian Zorn "in her stylish-looking drag, drawn by

"The Proper Thing." Both illustrations from "Fashion Drive." *The Courier-Journal*, 11 June 1893.

two beautiful bay horses, who were well handled by a coachman in livery"; and Morris Belknap's very latest trap "with the extreme high seat and immense top." The reporter remarked that the "handsome vehicles of the society people" could be seen along New Broadway every afternoon. "Few people have an idea of the number of them in Louisville. Especially in the last two years have a great number been purchased in the East and brought to this city."

❧ ❧ ❧

IN THE SPRING OF 1901, Board of Park Commissioners Belknap and Kinkead presented their survey of the secretaries of the "principal park boards of the United States" relative to park use by automobiles. Horseless carriages were just beginning to appear in Louisville, the first one reportedly being delivered to John E. Roche in October 1898.[617] They recommended that "all owners of automobiles of every kind be required to obtain from this office a permit upon which should be presented the rules of the Park Board governing the use of automobiles in the parks & on the parkways." The registered number would be printed on a black leather tag, large enough to be seen at a distance. The speed of automobiles "should be limited to eight miles an hour upon the parkways & in the parks except upon curves when it should not exceed five miles an hour." When horses become "restless and frightened" at an approaching automobile, the vehicle should be brought to a full stop. "The operators of automobiles should not be allowed to sound the gong or bell except at the intersection of drives or streets."[618] By the summer of 1902, when "automobiling is just about three years old in Louisville," some "36 machines" were licensed by the park board.[619] A year later, the park commissioners removed any restrictions against automobiles in any section of a park. "Owners of machines may ride where they please." In addition, to keep down the dust, the board ordered "crude petroleum" be sprinkled on the boulevard as an experiment. If successful, all the park roads would be oiled.[620]

Early in 1902, the mayor and the president of the Board of Park Commissioners were appointed as a committee to secure rights of way for "driveways" from near the Confederate Monument to Cherokee and Shawnee parks.[621] "We have gone with some care over the old surveys made in 1892 by the Board and have instructed the Engineer to enlarge the Engineering Corps to such an extent as may be necessary to resurvey these Parkways," Mayor Charles F. Grainger and John B. Castleman told the Board 1 April 1902. "We find that in the main the routes then surveyed are suitable for today, but some changes need to be effected. These Parkways run approximately three and one half

Work on portions of the new driveway, which will extend from Eastern to Western Park, is in progress at both ends. Mayor Grainger is taking a great deal of interest in the work, and everything that he can do to have the driveway completed within the next year will be done. A committee of citizens who live along the driveway will appear before the Park Commissioners… and will ask that the drive be worked from High street. When finished, the drive will be one of the finest in the State.

"Central Park To Be Opened On June 1." *The Courier-Journal*, 18 April 1904.

miles each."[622] The report estimated the appreciation of the property fronting on the parkways would be about $700,000, while the cost for each would be approximately $100,000. "We see no means of securing these funds except by the issue of bonds by the City of Louisville." The next day's *Courier-Journal* headline read: "Citizens Must Say Whether Parkways Shall Be Built."

"Park Superintendent Cecil Fraser and the engineers under his direction have nearly completed the survey of the two proposed boulevards, one from Eastern Park to the School of Reform and the other from Western Park to the same point," reported *The Courier-Journal*, 15 October 1902. "'These boulevards,' said Mr. Fraser, 'with the one we already have, would give Louisville one of the grandest systems of driveways in the country. The one running to Western Park would be five miles long, and that to Eastern Park about four. It is proposed to make the boulevards 120 feet wide, and according to

Plan of Finzer Parkway, Boundary Road, and Eastern Parkway (Melrose and Ferndale avenues), 1905. Jefferson County Plat Book 1, p. 61.

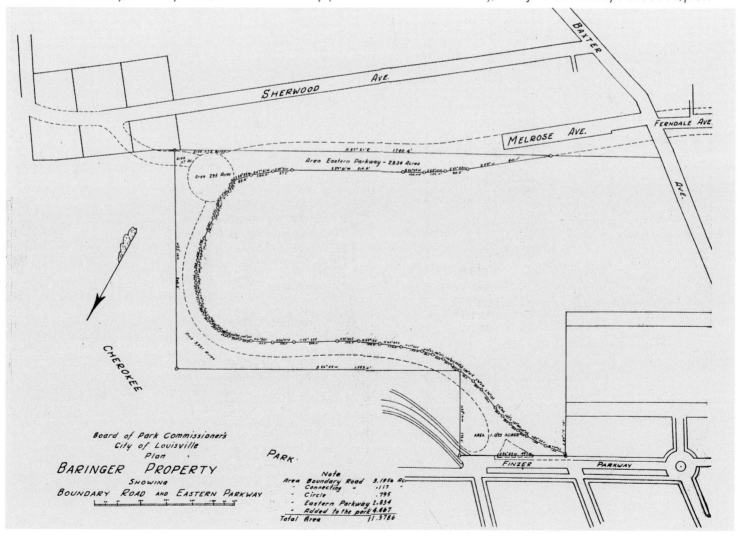

The Eastern Parkway had been surveyed from the circle to Baxter avenue; running parallel to Sherwood avenue, and as the board was able would have been extended west until it joined the Southern Parkway, making one of the most beautiful driveways in the country. The boulevard would have been 120 feet in width and with trees on each side would have been a handsome addition to the city.

"Blocks Purpose To Build Eastern Parkway."
The Courier-Journal, 1 February 1905.

estimates recently made, they would cost about $20,000 a mile, or in round numbers $200,000. They would be constructed after the same plan as the boulevard to Jacob Park.'"[623] There was no correspondence with the Olmsted firm regarding these parkway surveys, which were approved by the Board of Park Commissioners, 21 October 1902.[624] In November, however, the bond issue proposition was voted down.[625]

Fraser's eastern parkway survey called for the widening of Ferndale, a 60-ft wide street that ran between Bardstown Road and Baxter Avenue. East of Bardstown Road it connected to Melrose Avenue. Beyond Baxter Avenue it became a divided roadway (two 25-ft driving lanes with 10-ft sidewalks on the outside separated by a 30-ft planting space in middle) that John B. Castleman had dedicated in 1895 for Eastern Parkway as a section of his Castlewood development.[626] The Board of Park Commissioners proceeded to request contiguous landowners to donate land necessary to widen Ferndale Avenue into Eastern Parkway.[627] But in early 1905 *The Courier-Journal* reported: "Because of the refusal of two property owners to donate forty-foot strips off of their lots, the proposed Eastern Parkway which the Board of Park Commissioners intended eventually to extend to the Southern Parkway leading to Jacob Park, has been abandoned and will not be built."[628]

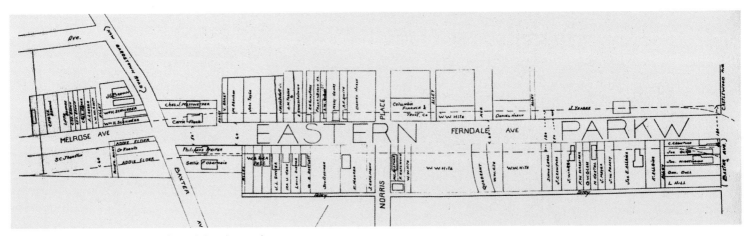

Plat of Eastern Parkway (Ferndale Avenue) showing adjoining property owners, 1905. Jefferson County Plat Book 1, p. 58.

The Board continued to obtain agreements with property owners. A plat of Ferndale Avenue shows the owners and acknowledged their agreements.[629] The Board did announce it was planning to "carry out its intention of extending a boulevard from Everett avenue, and, skirting the edges of Eastern Park, it will end at a circle which is to be made near where Sherwood avenue enters Eastern Parkway."

When the eastern parkway project resumed in 1907, Olmsted partner James F. Dawson asked Board president Castleman if he wished the firm to prepare grading plans. General Castleman declined, stating it would be some time before the commissioners had enough money to build the parkway. "I concluded," Dawson noted, "that he did not want us to prepare grading plans, although he did not seem to have any definite idea as to how he was going to do it."[630] Later, John C. Olmsted sketched ways to ease the flow from the old Ferndale Avenue into Castleman's subdivision west of Baxter Avenue, but requests for parkway plans are not part of the firm records.[631] In the city's 1908 annual report, Board president Cowan reported: "In my opinion no additional roads should be built in the near future, except an extension of Eastern Parkway from Baxter Avenue to Castlewood, work on which was begun by the former Board.... I fear that the cost of maintaining our Park System, with the addition of outside or connecting Parkways, may soon be made a burden too great to merit popular support."[632] The project had proceeded only as far as Beargrass Creek by early 1912 when the firm was requested to submit plans for a bridge. Olmsted requested "blueprints of the property and topographical map of Eastern Parkway with the profile and standard cross section." As he had been instructed to correspond only with Castleman and not the park engineer, he had to spell out the data needed on the documents. Since he had not examined the site, he suggested that the park engineer make the preliminary plan and forward it to him.[633] At the July 1913 meeting, the Board of Park Commissioners agreed to purchase two parcels needed for construction of Eastern Parkway.[634] The Board inspected the completed portion of Eastern Parkway between Castlewood and Floyd Street on 5 September 1913 and, after refreshments at President Castleman's home, deemed the section would open in two days.[635]

Surfacing westbound lanes of Eastern Parkway at Cross Road in Castlewood, 1926. Caufield and Shook Collection, University of Louisville Photographic Archives.

"Autoists and others who love beautiful driveways will have their first opportunity today to inspect the gently rolling Eastern Parkway which traverses a beautiful country to reach Cherokee Park," *The Louisville Herald* observed 7 September 1913. The Board of Park Commissioners ruled that no commercial vehicles were permitted. "The boulevard is for the exclusive use of pleasure seekers." At that point the Brown lumber yard property prevented the parkway from continuing through the old House of Refuge property.

⌇ ⌇ ⌇

WHEN ANNOUNCING THE OPENING of Eastern Parkway in September 1913, *The Louisville Herald* reported: "Work is to be started soon on the Western Parkway which is to extend from Third Street west thru the State Fair grounds, along the river front to Shawnee Park, connecting with the Western Parkway now built to Portland." Plans were underway and most of the right-of-way had been secured to extend the parkway to Shawnee Park, which had already been connected to Portland. The Board of Park Commissioners had settled a case with landowner Sidney J. Blankenbaker that allowed a "public highway" to be opened between Western Park and Fountain (Fontaine) Ferry Park in the fall of 1903.[636] A boulevard connecting Portland and Shawnee Park was surveyed in the following spring.[637] "The survey for the Western parkway from Third street to Shawnee Park through the State Fair grounds" was submitted by park engineers Stonestreet & Ford in July 1913. "The Committee on Parkways was authorized to obtain the right of way for the route planned."[638] The proposed route was prepared too late to appear on the 1913 atlas of Louisville and Jefferson County. The route for Eastern Parkway from west of Preston Street to Cherokee Park was delineated on the atlas. The Broadway to Greenwood section of Western Parkway was ordered graded in late 1916.[639] Work finally began in 1927, but stalled because no provision had been made for a sewer.[640]

Plans had been completed by the Board of Park Commissioners late in 1917 to connect the Eastern and Western parkways by gradually grading more than three miles from "a point near the Ford motor plant on Third street to a point below the State Fairgrounds," if funds were made available.[641] The parkways were never joined.

"It is evident that the city has a very inadequate parkway system," John C. Olmsted pointed out in 1915. He complained that the city's method of park funding was insufficient and too slow to prevent "irreparable loss of opportunities, and if continued will involve great additional cost." He proposed that the Board of Park Commissioners be given what amounted to zoning powers to control development along new parkways to enhance their attractiveness. "The most obvious opportunity for preserving and improving a street as a parkway is that of Broadway," he observed, as the character of the city's major residential thoroughfare was beginning to change. "Of course," he said, "there would be hotels, apartment houses and boarding houses, but their quality could be held up far higher than seems likely to be the case without regulations. With a suitable assessment law the pavement could be improved, the sidewalks repaved uniformly, fresh trees with neat guards and gratings put in as existing trees die out, handsome lighting provided and other improvements made."[642]

Looking east on Broadway at intersection of Third Street, 1923. Caufield and Shook Collection, University of Louisville Photographic Archives.

City Beautiful

THE TERM CITY BEAUTIFUL WAS COINED in 1899 by Charles Mulford Robinson in a series on "Improvement in City Life" for *Atlantic Monthly* that led to his influential and frequently reprinted book, *The Improvement of Towns and Cities*, in 1901. In 1913 Robinson would become the first chair of Civic Design at the University of Illinois. According to William H. Wilson, author of *The City Beautiful Movement*, besides addressing "the need for controlling urban smoke, noise, and billboards," Robinson "underscored the value of natural beauty by advocating street trees, flower gardens, parks, and drives, but was equally concerned with the sculptural, mural, and architectural arts."[643] Although Frederick Law Olmsted's legacy of parks and drives made Robinson's list, the new City Beautiful movement's focus at the turn of the century was broader and broken into smaller components that needed fixing or improvement that would make cities more aesthetically pleasing and therefore more livable. The effect that the huge and expensive parks and boulevards that Olmsted championed could likewise be achieved with a myriad of smaller beautification projects in the city proper.

Map of Callahan's proposed route of canal around city. *The Courier-Journal*, 23 March 1902.

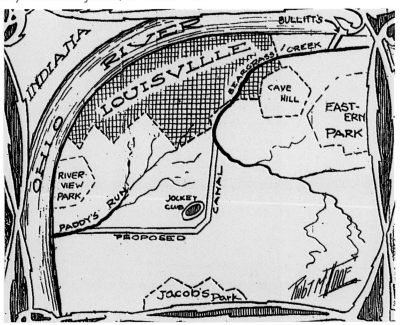

One major project to be located mainly outside the city that was proposed in 1902 did not gain traction perhaps in part because of concerns it would spoil large sections of Beargrass Creek. James Callahan envisioned a drainage and power canal around the outskirts of the city. The canal would be continuously "flushed with pure water" from the Ohio River from about where the Louisville Boat Club now sits to the place where it emptied back into the river at the mouth of Paddy's Run. Callahan projected that the volume of water moving through the canal could generate enough power to operate "several hundred factories."[644] In the three miles of Beargrass Creek that would have been incorporated into the eight-mile-long canal, the natural flow of water would have been reversed, eliminating the need for the cut-off on River Road. While Beargrass Creek had been used as an open sewer since before the Civil War, Callahan's proposal would have doubled the length of that obnoxious system.

In the spring of 1902 at the Galt House, the Louisville branch of the Woman's Auxiliary of the American Park and Outdoor Art Association was organized.[645] It became The Woman's Outdoor Art League in 1907; the name was later simplified to the Outdoor Art League after men became involved. Its expressed purpose was "to promote the conservation of natural scenery; to acquire lands for public parks and reservations; to advance all outdoor art; to design and fit grounds for public and private use and enjoyment; to abolish unsightly billboards; to cultivate artistic ideals in the home; to advance the co-operative interests of parents and teachers in public schools and to further the highest interests of education."[646]

An early project was the creation in 1909 of Duke Place, along Beargrass Creek adjoining the L&N's old Baxter Avenue Station. The small park, named for Mrs. Basil Duke, an activist in beautifying railroad stations, was secured by an impressive iron fence in 1921.[647] When the tracks were elevated over Baxter Avenue in 1936, the urban park was obliterated.

Duke Place. Elevated gate tower in background. *The Courier-Journal*, 13 November 1921.

Baxter Avenue and Garden Street (now Liberty Street), 1935, before railroad tracks were elevated over Baxter Avenue. Duke Place is just beyond Baxter Avenue Station platform. Samuel W. Thomas files.

The successes of the Outdoor Art League spawned similar-minded neighborhood groups such as the Crescent Hill Improvement Club, which in June 1909 entertained architect Brinton B. Davis, chairman of the City Beautiful Committee of the Commercial Club of Louisville, who presented a lecture with stereopticon views on Louisville, Present and Future. One of Davis's illustrations was undoubtedly of a reconfigured Broadway made into a boulevard of grand proportions, lined with Beaux Arts structures, including the recently completed L&N office building between Ninth and Tenth streets. In the lead article in *The Louisville Times* 25th anniversary edition, 31 December 1909, Davis laid out his "Dream of To-morrow: Louisville As a City Beautiful" that put a new Union Station on Broadway as the "city's greatest need." Broadway, Louisville's most impressive residential street after the Civil War, was to be transformed into "our great business street."

Proposal for Broadway by architect Brinton B. Davis. "To-morrow: Louisville As a City Beautiful," *The Louisville Times*, 31 December 1909. View is looking west from Fifth Street (not shown in foreground) toward proposed Union Station with circle and park in front. The rendering resembles Jules Guerin's view of Michigan Avenue for the 1909 Plan of Chicago.

In addition, Davis recommended that the government buildings be set off from "the hum and strenuousness of trade" in a park setting, and the old City Hall be replaced. In the eyes of proponents of the City Beautiful movement like Davis, City Hall's Renaissance Revival style façade did not convey the monumentality that classically designed structures such as the Courthouse did. Davis's proposal remained a dream. Almost a half-century later, a similar plan was put forward by Bartholomew & Associates.[648]

OLMSTED FIRM'S WORKS

AT THE REQUEST OF JOHN G. HEYBURN, president of the Louisville Board of Park Commissioners, the Olmsted firm prepared a list of all the original plans in its files that had been made for the various Louisville projects overseen by the Board through 1925. The list numbered 114 plans on file, although the list of numbers assigned to plans indicated that 292 had been prepared.[649] Perhaps some original plans had been sent to the Board or discarded for some reason. The list is helpful in pinpointing when work was undertaken. For instance, Central Park plans were dated 1904 and 1925. The greatest number of plans were for Cherokee Park, dating from 1892 to 1925. Four plans for Shawnee Park were dated 1893 and 1911, with two for 1915. Only two plans were listed for parkways—Eastern Parkway, both dated 1907.

As Olmsted Brothers' work for the Board of Park Commissioners declined, the firm became more involved in the residential sector. *Louisville's Olmstedian Legacy: An Interpretive Analysis and Documentary Inventory*, published by the Louisville Friends of Olmsted Parks in 1988, listed 191 projects and the identifying numbers assigned by the Olmsted firms. Some exist only as numbers, as no work was actually done. Some jobs progressed only through the planning stage. The group that reached fruition, however, is significant, including: C. B. Robinson/Bonnycot 289 (1902), I. W. Bernheim/Homewood 167 (1900-1902), and Frank Fehr/Braeview 3811 (1909-1924).

ANCHORAGE TOWN PLAN

PERHAPS OLMSTED BROTHERS' MOST AMBITIOUS local effort was the 1916 Anchorage Town Plan, an 88-page printed report. I. W. Bernheim spearheaded the plan through the Anchorage Civic League, of which he was president. John Olmsted studied the community in January 1915, discussing its wants and needs with several of the town's prominent women. While the railroad and railway had been adequate means of transportation, the firm clearly anticipated the impact the automobile would make. A quarter of the study concerned streets, which were divided into four categories—Boulevard, Parkway, Avenue, and Street. Evergreen Road, the town spine, was to be doubled in width from a reported 40 feet to 80 feet—six lanes. It was to have a slow, fast, and parking lane in each direction. (Evergreen Road is now about 20 feet wide and remains one lane in both directions.) "Harmony" was the basic tenet. Housing was to be made more uniform in architecture and color. The firm's pallet consisted of stucco gray. "It would be a pity to continue using yellow, brown, red, and other popular house colors."[650]

By the time the report was received, the Anchorage Civic League was dormant. The First World War drained manpower and interest in capital improvements. The development that Olmsted Bros. outlined was beyond the means even of Anchorage with its sizeable tax base led by the Southern Pacific Railroad headquartered in its midst. The Olmsted firm agreed to a payment of $750 for the extensive plan, although it estimated the cost at $1,500. *The Louisville Times* stated that "copies of the report will be distributed throughout Kentucky in order that other towns may take similar action." Bernheim sent five bound copies to the Louisville Free Public Library. Even though Anchorage is frequently described as an Olmsted-planned community, not one aspect of the plan was ever implemented. The community remains much as it evolved, nurtured by nurseryman Edward Dorsey Hobbs and improved by resident Jacob Lewis Shallcross.[651]

Anchorage Town Plan, December 1915.

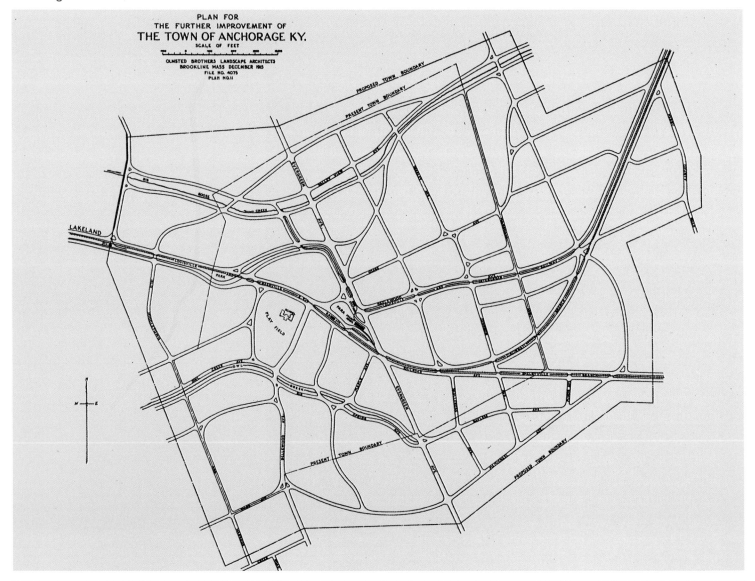

OLMSTED FIRM'S SUBDIVISIONS

IN ADDITION, THE OLMSTED FIRM DESIGNED a number of subdivisions, including: J. B. McFerran/Alta Vista 2064 (1898-1923), J. B. Castleman/Castlewood 2275 (1898), Douglass Boulevard 3225 (1907-1939), Cherokee Gardens 7377 (1925), and Indian Hills 7449 (1925-1926). A year after J. B. McFerran purchased 228.6 acres south of the Shelbyville Road Branch Turnpike from the heirs of W. B. Belknap in June 1890, the Board of Park Commissioners selected an adjacent location for the eastern park. They had been looking at land owned by the Louisville Water Company, but at the last minute Commissioner Andrew Cowan changed the focus to tracts of land available in private hands. While McFerran, successful in a pork-packing business, could not have been aware where Eastern Park was to be located in 1890, he may have influenced the selection process in 1891.

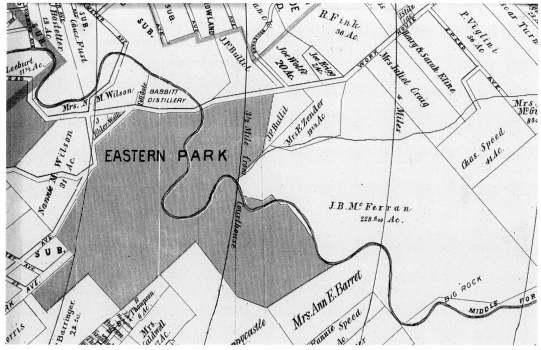

Section of *New Map of Louisville, KY And Environs*, 1891, by Merritt Drane.

Initially, he simply held the land, probably waiting to see how the park was designed and accepted by the public. In 1898, he erected a home on part of the large property, and he contacted Olmsted Brothers to develop a subdivision within the remainder. When his residence was put up for sale following his death, it was described as "the first home site selected" around the park.[652] The subdivision plan, dated March 1900, was devised by the Olmsted firm on a topographical map prepared by Cecil Fraser. The next tract developed in Alta Vista was Norton Hall by George Norton in 1899-1900. It is interesting to note that while modest housing developed quickly along streets near the park, most of the larger homes overlooking the park took well over a decade to come into being. The major holdup in development overlooking the park resulted from the lack of good transportation. McFerran had been in the trotting-horse business with his father, so he was comfortable with that form of transportation. Most others did not move to the country until it was made accessible by the advent of the automobile.

LINCOLN PARK

Lincoln Park has gained notoriety recently from a certain amount of rabid, moblike assembly there. Greater than the frenzied speeches of orators is the voice of the people who go there without any especial purpose in view, sit and tell what they know—that is, if they do not sit and talk too long. It might be a good thing for them to look up occasionally and see the rush of traffic in the street that speaks of busy effort; and to take note of the tall buildings that reach up and send their black smokestacks into the sky and portray great achievement.

Homer Dye, Jr., "Lincoln Park, Our 'Greenwich Village,'" *The Courier-Journal*, 14 September 1917.

Art exhibit in Lincoln Park, 1941. By Norris Mode, *The Courier-Journal* and *The Louisville Times*.

A CONSIDERABLE VACANT SPACE REMAINED adjacent to the U.S. Custom House and Post Office that anchored the northeast corner of Fourth and Chestnut streets after the magnificent stone structure was erected between 1886 and 1892. In 1908, the Women's Outdoor League, through the efforts of its president, Mrs. James A. Leach, obtained permission from the federal government to convert the yard enclosed by a stone wall into a "rest park" beautified by planting flowers.[653] With the celebration of the hundredth anniversary of Abraham Lincoln's birth the next year, the spot took on the name of Lincoln Place, and in 1910, Lincoln Park. By 1917, adjacent structures had been razed in order to extend Guthrie Street from Third to Fourth Street, allowing the Speed Building to be erected fronting the park. The city's first public comfort station was built, topped by a bandstand, designed by local architect Val. P. Collins. Exhibits and events of every sort were held on the only open spot in the downtown, characterized as Louisville's forum, commons, and Trafalgar Square.[654]

Lincoln Park became a site of serious speculation in the early 1920s as Fourth Street solidified its position as the city's retail, office, and entertainment destination.[655] However, the site was not developed, and during the Depression, the Junior Board of Trade planned to transform the site described as "a catch-all for cheap amusements, advertising, a hangout for vagrants, and anything but a beauty spot in the downtown district." The design was made by local landscape architect Carl Berg with the idea that the statue of Abraham Lincoln would be moved to the park from the "inadequate setting" on the lawn of the Louisville Free Public Library.[656]

In time, when starlings had become the principal inhabitants of Lincoln Park as well as the Post Office, the park board was approached with a proposal to place a single-cage zoo in the park, paid for by advertising in lights above the exhibit.[657] Later, Helen Lawton would observe: "As it turned out, the park offered so few attractions that some citizens almost regretted not accepting a 1940 offer to set up a one-cage zoo with changing exhibits at no expense to the City."[658] After

View of Lincoln Park in mid-1949 looking northeast from Fourth and Chestnut streets. By Charles Darneal, *The Courier-Journal* files. Lincoln Park was located in the southwest corner of the former site of Louisville's first park, Jacob's Woods. This became the site of the Louisville Industrial Exposition in 1872 and in 1893, the U.S. Custom House and Post Office, the finest structure built in Louisville before the Humana Tower. It was razed in 1942-1943 and its imprint became part of Lincoln Park.

the building was demolished in 1943 for the scrap metal to be used in the war effort, the City planned to expand Lincoln Park into a war memorial with an underground parking garage. In the meantime, the site was landscaped under the direction of Carl Berg.[659]

It was not to continue as a park for long, as Grady Clay pointed out later in a summary of the land use dispute.[660] To downtown business interests, the space was going to waste. A. J. Stewart, a vice president of the old Citizens Fidelity Bank & Trust Company and a force to be reckoned with in downtown where his bank's trust department managed a great deal of property, advocated selling the land for commercial purposes. "The interests of idle transients, unemployed, unemployables, and the small subversive element in our population would be better served in

The park's days are numbered, ending two years of debates about what kind of trees to plant, about a fountain, about concerts by nonunion singers, about the walks which failed to be timesavers because they didn't cut diagonally across the park, about the lack of benches (some claimed it was a good idea not to have any because they might not attract the right sort of sitters).

Helen Lawton, "Lincoln Park," *The Courier-Journal*, 17 November 1946.

a larger and more scenic park," which could be provided a few blocks away. Based upon reports from other cities with parks in retail sections, Stewart claimed that "such parks are an affliction rather than a blessing." An analysis by St. Louis economist Roy Wenzlick for the Planning and Zoning Commission supported Stewart's contention. Mayor Wilson Wyatt and his successor, Leland Taylor, continued to push for the garage-park, but in October 1946, the property was auctioned off. The successful group, headed by Jules Endler of Newark, NJ, talked in terms of "responsible development," but claimed that parking either above or below ground was too expensive for the retail center.[661] Two years later, the ambitious plans had faded and the Endler group began selling off Lincoln Park piecemeal. In anticipation of new construction, the park was leveled in 1950.[662] J. C. Penney was the first to build on the park site and then W. T. Grant, but ironically, the Fourth and Chestnut corner remained in surface parking for some time, until replaced by a parking garage incorporating a Newberry variety store.[663]

GUTHRIE GREEN

IN THE LATE 1950S, as suburban retail centers began to flourish, cities began to experiment with pedestrian streets. According to Grady Clay, the idea was first broached in Louisville by Yale graduate student Dieter Hammerschlag, and five years later, Louisville Central Area put it to a one-month test on Guthrie Street, adjacent to the former site of Lincoln Park.[664] "It magnetized tremendous public notice," Clay would later write. "It was a great success with the public and it demonstrated that the downtown district would indeed not be 'taken over by bums' if a block-long downtown park was designed."[665] Guthrie Green was deemed successful enough to make it a permanent pedestrian plaza, although initially in 1963, the project allowed limited automobile access.[666] A year later, Guthrie Green, as a pedestrian mall designed by Lawrence P. Melillo, was dedicated.[667]

Experimental pedestrian space on Guthrie Street, 1960. By Al Hixenbaugh, *The Courier-Journal* and *The Louisville Times*.

Park Segregation

On 13 June 1924, an outing of 20 students from Taylor S. Coleridge School for Negroes to Iroquois Park ended when the two accompanying teachers were arrested for disorderly conduct. The three arresting park guards claimed the teachers did not obey their order to move the children from the playground set aside for whites to the area for blacks.[668] The incident set in motion a reaction that formalized a code of conduct that had operated unspoken in the park system for probably a decade. As George C. Wright noted in *Life Behind A Veil: Blacks in Louisville, Kentucky 1865-1930*, "The one area where blacks enjoyed limited equal access was eliminated when city officials passed a resolution segregating the public parks." Dr. Wright later interviewed one of the teachers, Margaret Taylor, as well as the sister of the other, Naomi Taylor, in his thorough recounting of the events.

"Race Segregation In Parks Ordered," announced *The Courier-Journal* headline, 18 June 1924. "Temporary orders prohibiting white persons from using negro parks and playgrounds and restricting negroes from visiting similar places for white people, were issued yesterday by the Board of Park Commissioners following testimony of a clash between park guards and two negro school teachers last Friday at Iroquois Park." A protest meeting was held five days later at Quinn Chapel and funds were raised "to fight in court any measure prohibiting negroes' free use of all parks."[669] At a Board of Education hearing, both teachers "disclaimed that they were aware that the Park Board had ordered segregation in the parks," while Board of Park Commissioners chairman G. W. Schardein claimed that "the restriction had been enforced for years."[670] Had Schardein been correct, there would have been no reason to issue the temporary segregation order or to make "the order preventing mingling of the races in the parks permanent" as of 1 July 1924.[671]

On 4 July 1924, *The Courier-Journal* published in its Point of View column a remarkably insightful letter signed by a cross section of black leaders.[673] Expressed in a very conciliatory tone, "the undersigned colored citizens, representing one-sixth of the voters and taxpayers of our city" declared that "there neither is at the present time nor ever has been a law in the city of Louisville restraining certain groups from visiting certain parks or sections of parks."

It is known and admitted by the Park Commission itself that up to June 13 there did not exist any Park Commission rule or regulation as to what parks or part of parks colored people should occupy. General Castleman, the father of our park system,

This is a gala day of colored society in Louisville. The colored schools are having their picnic at Cherokee Park, and the colored population has turned out in force. Not only the smaller representatives of the race, but their elders are enjoying the day to the utmost.

The happiest people in the city are the darkies who have vehicles. All morning long, growing more and more numerous as the day advanced, parties in buggies, wagons, traps and vehicles of all description, have been whirling toward the park. The dusky beaux and belles have on raiment that makes the green wherewith the park is adorned seem somber. The piece de resistance was a tallyho party that caused a sensation as it moved through the city.[672]

"Colored Society At The Picnic." *The Evening Post*, 11 June 1904.

steadfastly refused to allow any kind of racial segregation in the parks of the city, and this policy has been followed until the present board issued its segregation orders a few days ago. This has been true in theory and in fact, for the colored people have used all the parks of the city, especially Iroquois Park, without let or hindrance through all these years and with little or no trouble of any kind.

Special pains have been taken to make the impression that adequate park and playground facilities are furnished by the city for colored people. Nothing could be farther from the truth. There is not a single swimming pool for colored people in the city of Louisville…there is nothing in the city of Louisville that could be called by any stretch of the imagination an adequate playground, while Chickasaw Park is poorly equipped, poorly supervised, dangerous for children and far removed from the center of negro population.

While the signers of the letter "recognize the fact of segregation as set forth in laws regulating certain phases of our lives, we feel that absolute segregation is impossible" and that included the use of public parks. Use of the parks by both races "has been in vogue for fifty years, and more, [and] in no way involves any kind of social contact." Furthermore, they pointed out, providing and maintaining a double system of parks would be prohibitive and unattainable. But the era of "separate but equal" was formally underway. The "parks set aside for the exclusive use of negroes" were Boone, Ballard, Baxter, and Chickasaw.[674] The Olmsted firm considered Boone and Baxter not to be parks, referring to them as squares. Ballard was even smaller. The old Whallen tract, 53 acres on the Ohio River at the end of Greenwood Road, was acquired by the Board of Park Commissioners in late 1921. With only limited funds, the Board planned to provide picnic grounds, two baseball diamonds, and two tennis courts, while converting the Whallen residence into a shelter house.[675] The preliminary plan prepared by the Olmsted firm in late 1923 showed tennis courts but no baseball diamonds, and the contract for the road system was not let until late in 1928.[676]

In 1951 Federal Court Judge Roy M. Shelbourne began to dismantle the law by ordering the city to allow blacks to play golf on the public courses and to fish in the Cherokee Park lake.

CHEROKEE PARKWAY

IN HIS REPORT TO THE BOARD OF PARK COMMISSIONERS in early 1915, John C. Olmsted lamented that "Louisville lacks radial parkways from the heart of the city to the outer parks and to the country."[677] Creating a parkway along the Middle Fork of Beargrass Creek from Cherokee Park to Eight-Mile House on the Shelbyville Road had long been of interest to those who had visions of developing their landholdings in that area. Eight-Mile House had been known as Howesburg, the site of the Howes family's residence, country store, and barroom on the south side of the turnpike just west of the bridge over the Sinking Fork of Beargrass Creek.[678] Across the turnpike and east of the Sinking Fork was the Eight-Mile House.

The nearby Bullitt family, which had abandoned its Oxmoor property during the Civil War, was the first to see potential development for its 1,029-acre farm if better access were provided. In March 1893, Thomas W. Bullitt requested his brother, Philadelphia lawyer John C. Bullitt, come to Louisville so they could "go together over the road between the Park and Oxmoor."[679] Thomas Bullitt later wrote John's son, William C. Bullitt, that he could not interest the Board of Park Commissioners in undertaking the project, but thought if the adjacent property owners along Beargrass Creek were to provide a right-of-way, the proposal might be acceptable. "There is one public improvement, which if we could obtain, would be of very great value.... If we could get the Park Commissioners to extend the drive from the present terminus of Cherokee Park on Beargrass Creek to or through Oxmoor, it would be most valuable. Heretofore I have not been able to get them to consider the matter. I incline however to believe that, in time, if we can get the intervening property owners to give the right of way along the Beargrass Creek, they will be disposed to take it up. It will cost some money, but I feel sure it would add to the value of Oxmoor property, largely more than the cost of the road."[680] Several years later, Thomas W. Bullitt's son, William Marshall Bullitt, began to reassemble the Oxmoor tract from relatives and to renovate the homestead for his residence. In 1927-1928, the Olmsted firm formalized the parkway plan along Beargrass Creek and made preliminary sketches of its route through Oxmoor, showing how it might allow subdivision of the property.

Olmsted Brothers' 1927 plat of Cherokee Parkway is clearly based upon the 1913 *Atlas of Jefferson County*, which was still valid when the firm received a solicitation from Bethel B. Veech. "We are contemplating locating a road from Cherokee Park...along the meanderings of

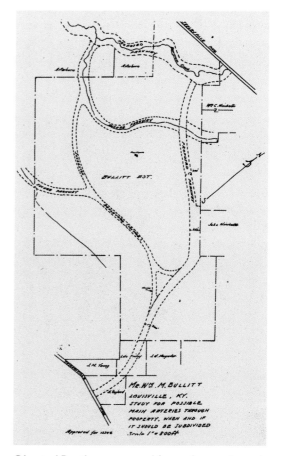

Olmsted Brothers proposal for parkways through Oxmoor for William Marshall Bullitt. Courtesy of the National Park Service, Frederick Law Olmsted National Historic Site.

Plan No. 5, Olmsted Brothers file 7834. Courtesy of the National Park Service, Frederick Law Olmsted National Historic Site. Although dated 20 October 1927, the baseline run by Ben Ford of Stonestreet & Ford was not reviewed on the ground by James F. Dawson until mid-November 1927.[681] The Filson Historical Society.

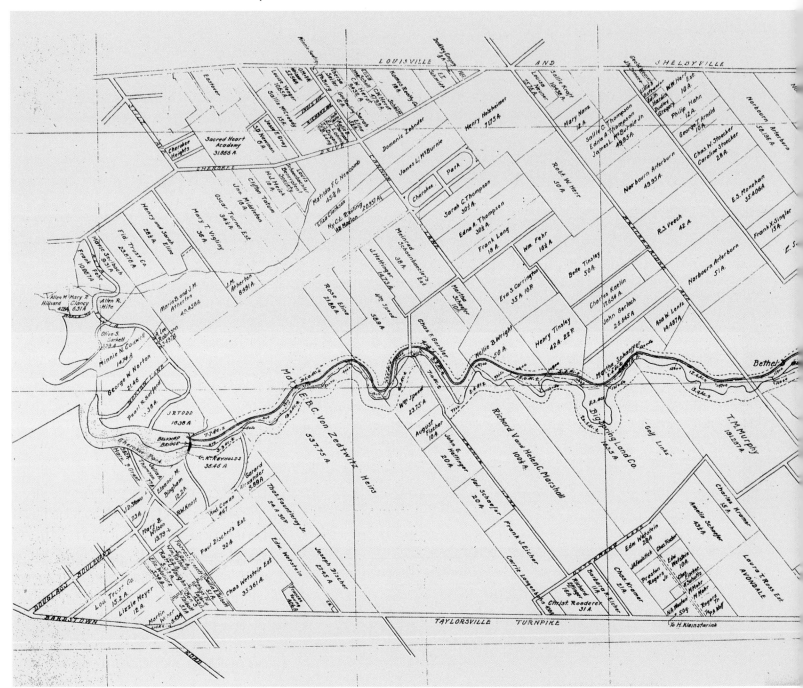

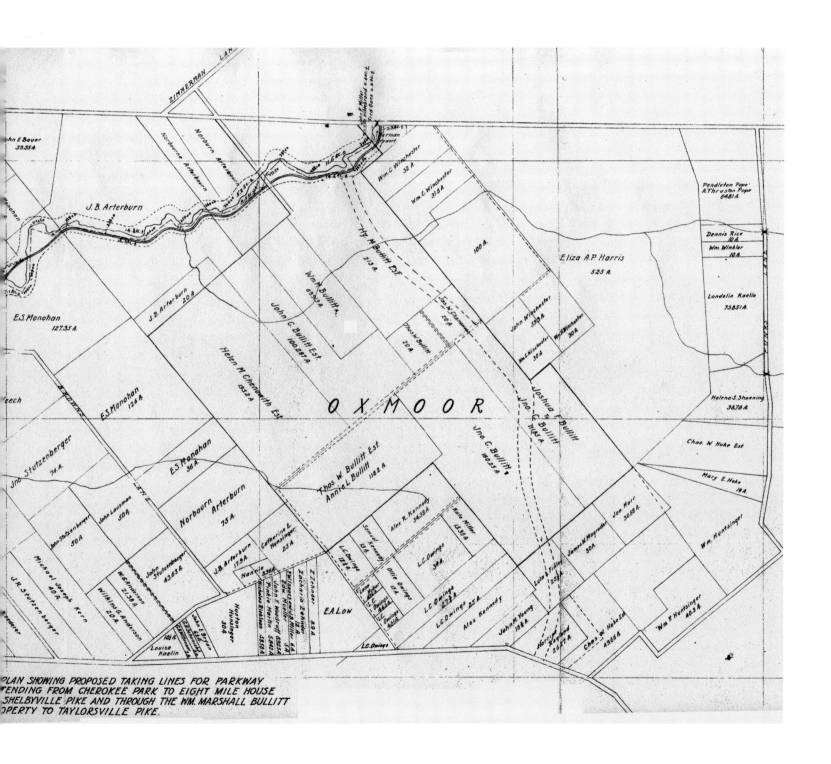

PLAN SHOWING PROPOSED TAKING LINES FOR PARKWAY
TENDING FROM CHEROKEE PARK TO EIGHT MILE HOUSE
SHELBYVILLE PIKE AND THROUGH THE WM. MARSHALL BULLITT
OPERTY TO TAYLORSVILLE PIKE.

Beargrass Creek, which flows through said Park Eastwardly from there to the headwaters of said Creek, which would be a distance of about six miles. It is our desire to employ some one who is competent to locate said road, as it will be necessary to cross said Creek several times in the route because the creek overflows in high water, and it is our desire to get it above the high water mark. We would be pleased to have you write us what would be your probable charge for locating such a road and what preliminary work would be necessary for you to determine the location of same. When do you expect to have one of your representatives in this locality again?"[682] The firm immediately responded that John C. Olmsted could "take up the matter of the Beargrass Creek Parkway," after some park work in New Orleans. "Mr. Olmsted has been very much interested in the general idea of extending the park drive up Beargrass Creek, and has spoken to the Park Commissioners from time to time for a number of years about it. Last winter he described it in his report to the Park Commission."

> Mr. Olmsted has not heretofore gone into the matter at all in detail and has not even traced the line out on a map. Last winter he took occasion to look at perhaps the first half mile or more of the probable route for this drive. This was enough to convince him that while the idea was feasible in a general way, the sides of the valley were so steep and crooked that it would be a somewhat difficult and tedious matter to work out the best possible route for the drive having regard both to appearance and to economy of grading, bridges, etc., and considering also the relation of the proposed drive to the opening up of private properties for suburban subdivisions involving some study of the location for branch drives to reach the more level land at some distance at each side of the creek valley.[683]

The firm suggested that John Olmsted inspect the route with a surveyor and then discuss the matter with Veech and other landowners. The charge for the preliminary visit, which would "no doubt spoil two days," would be $200. The letter then went into some detail as to how the project might unfold and what those costs might be. A preliminary meeting between Veech and Olmsted was held 30 November 1915 at the United States Trust Company where Veech was president. According to Olmsted's notes, the two followed the property tracts and creek meanders on the 1913 atlas, which appeared to have been unknown to Olmsted. "Mr. B. B. Veech said he wrote us simply to get an idea as to how much to ask the various landowners to chip in if they can come to an agreement.... I thought the Board of Park Commissioners would take the land all along up Beargrass Creek as a gift on condition of building a drive on each side from time to time as and when their finances will permit, just as they did further down.... I said a lake somewhere up the Creek would be very desirable, in order to keep a little flow all summer down the Creek below, as well as for its own beauty."[684] On 17 December 1915, the firm sent Veech a recapitulation of Olmsted's suggestions, some blueprints, and a bill for $43.30. In his response to Olmsted, Veech referred to the bill as "a Christmas joke," and while he appreciated Olmsted calling on him, "my object in conferring with you and your office was to get the probable charges in locating the contemplated road; that was my only desire." He returned the blueprints "with compliments of the season."[685] Olmsted cancelled the bill, but the well had been poisoned.

The stumbling point in the Beargrass Parkway venture was the large chunk of land on both sides of the creek that had been the 600-acre Breckinridge property, which later was owned by heirs—the Baroness von Zedtwitz and the Marquise de Merinville—daughters of Mary Eliza Breckinridge Caldwell and William Shakespeare Caldwell. The tract was being held by the U.S. Trust Company of New York for the son of Baroness von Zedtwitz. Veech had not been successful in trying to acquire it for a syndicate of Louisvillians, but he thought if the other large landholders were in agreement, the trust company might provide a right-of-way. At some prior time, Andrew Cowan had been willing to give nine acres of his property to connect Cherokee Park with the sisters' land, which, if they donated part of it for a park, would be called Breckinridge Park. They declined to make the gift, and Cowan lost interest in extending Cherokee Park.[686] However, in 1928, 504 acres of the von Zedtwitz property was purchased by the Board of Park Commissioners. "We would be more interested in developing this new park working in as many golf links as possible, some baseball diamonds, and an aviation field," Board president Berry Stoll informed Olmsted Brothers in March 1928. "I wanted to discuss with you whether or not you would approve such a plan. I do not believe our Board would be interested in buying the property if it were simply to be made an enlargement of the present Cherokee Park. Our only interest in purchasing it is to provide the type of golf links and playground features that Cherokee Park lacks."[687] The plan produced by Olmsted Brothers in 1928 for Seneca Park demonstrated how far the firm had come or could diverge from its initial park philosophy. The entire facility was devoted to sporting activities, including an 18-hole golf course, polo field, tennis courts, and fields for baseball and even football. After New York golf course architect Charles H. Banks

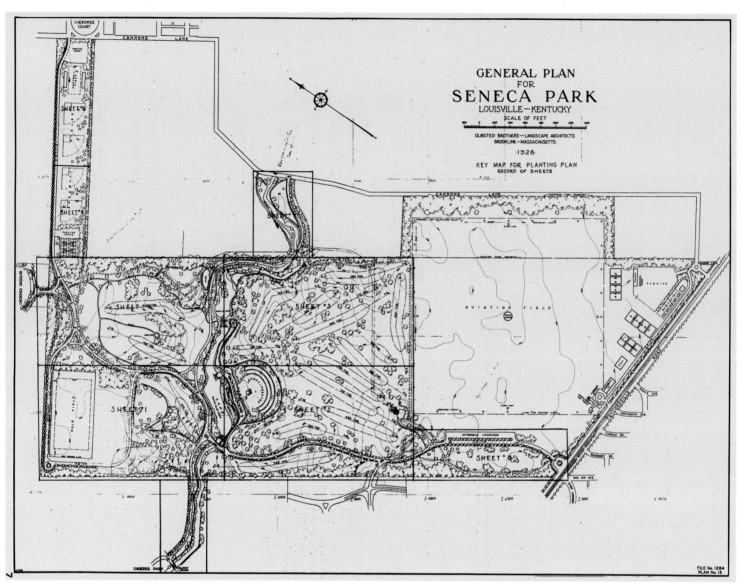

Olmsted Brothers, General Plan for Seneca Park, 1928. The Filson Historical Society.

studied the property, he informed James F. Dawson that "there is a chance to build a first class golf course there…and if the plan is properly handled most of the holes can be made rather outstanding."[688] Due to Bowman Field's requirement for more land, the Banks course plan was abandoned for one by the parks board's planners.[689]

An amphitheater overlooking a lake to be created from Beargrass Creek that John Olmsted had suggested earlier was not built. According to a 1930 *Herald-Post* picture story: "Years from now, canoes may ply the fork of Beargrass creek. A dam will broaden the creek into a long lake. Along a sandy beach to one side will be bath houses. Diving towers will stand in the water near the shore and hundreds of children will swarm the beach."[690]

In September 1928, Marshall Bullitt wrote Olmsted Brothers partner James F. Dawson that he wanted to talk about "carrying out our road plan for the extension of Cherokee Park…. Please let me know what effect the present plans of the City for the development of this air port and the rest of the Von Zedtwitz property, which I understand are being carried on under your advice, will have upon our desire to have a road extended up the creek."

> The Chairman of the Park Board sent word to me the other day that he would be very glad to take into the Park the land along Bear Grass up to my place, provided we would build the road. The Park Board could hardly expect us to go to that expense ourselves, especially as we would be giving them property of great value which would enable them to extend the park system.[691]

"I was told that the present Park Board would never consider such an undertaking," Dawson responded to Bullitt. He thought it such an important project that Jefferson County should undertake it if the city park board would not. "It doesn't matter who builds the road or whether it is not built for years to come; the important thing to do is to acquire the land along the Creek and protect it from being mutilated and cut up into streets and building lots."[692] Here was an early, perhaps first, indication of the city agency not wanting to venture into the county. Up until this time, the large parks and parkways had been beyond the city boundaries.

In any case, the matter was again explored in 1934 by Helm Bruce, Jr., Work Director, Municipal Relief Bureau. In 1951, Mayor Charles Farnsley explored the idea of building a parkway that in the future would be made into the Beargrass Valley Expressway in anticipation of the General Electric plant. By building the cheaper parkway, Farnsley figured at least the city would "sew up" the right-of-way. "Farnsley frequently has said he believes the Beargrass expressway should be one of the first superhighways built," *The Courier-Journal* reported.[693] Two years later, Helm Bruce was still trying to revive interest in the parkway plan before a subdivision proposal put it out of reach.[694] A decade later, *Courier-Journal* Real Estate Editor Grady Clay reported on a meeting of the Louisville-Jefferson County Planning and Zoning Commission slated to discuss the removal of all parkways from the master plan.[695]

On the other hand, the time will come when they will bitterly regret not taking the opportunity when they had it of extending the park system up that creek.

William Marshall Bullitt to James F. Dawson, 20 September 1928. Folder 7834, Olmsted firm papers, Library of Congress.

Louisville, Kentucky, is destined to have the most interesting historical [and] scenic park or park system in the United States—an extension as it were of Cherokee Park, which Almstead [Olmsted] Bros pronounced as the most outstanding park in the U.S. now by extending Cherokee Park (and naming it the George Rogers Clark Memorial Park) eastwardly along both sides of the middle fork of the Beargrass Creek up to and including Hurstbourne Farms, the Mrs. A. T. Hert estate.

Rough draft proposal by Lewis A. Walter, 26 September 1932. The Filson Historical Society. Walter was an accountant before entering the real estate business, specializing in subdivisions. He founded the George Rogers Clark Memorial Association in 1917 and served as its president.

WATERFRONT PARK

Water street and the wharf, between Third and Fourth along the river front of our city, have presented a dilapidated scene for the last few days. Old houses, which had stood looking upon the beautiful Ohio for the last half century, have been pulled down and the ripping off of their roofs and the tumbling of their walls have filled the air with clouds of dust and melancholy sounds.

"And what does this wholesome pulling down of walls along the river front mean?" asks the stranger. It means that the Chesapeake and Ohio Railroad Company has had the wisdom to see that along the river front is the best way to get from the upper part to the lower portions of the city. Any route south of this would be liable to objections in the progress of the city in that direction; but here is a changeless course with the fixed river on one side and the progressive city on the other, as good for all future time as for the present.

The Courier-Journal, 24 June 1883.

PLANS TO IMPROVE LOUISVILLE'S MISERABLE WATERFRONT were first conceived in 1855. Beargrass Creek, which emptied into the Ohio River between Third and Fourth streets, was diverted upstream with the intention of filling in the channel and extending the wharf. According to a 1869 *Courier-Journal*, "In the course of time…the old bed or channel was made the route of a sewer; the bridges at Second and Third streets were torn away; the wharf was extended over a valuable front which Beargrass had so long rendered a nuisance, and finally raised eight or ten feet above its original level."[696] It took so long to fill in the old channel of Beargrass Creek from Third to First that the newspaper estimated it would take until the year 2000 before the entire bed back to the Cut-off would be filled. At the same time, it was suggested that the channels of the three Beargrass Creek forks be made routes for sewer mains, with the cost passed on to abutting property owners. The proposal garnered no support, and the forks continued to serve as open sewers. "Beargrass creek, below the pork-houses, is, at every fifty yards, dammed and boarded in such a manner as to catch the grease which floats on top of the water. When this collects about the dams, the men or women, as the case may be, wade in and skim it off. This they boil down to make soap of."[697]

> Under the head of sewers it will be proper to class Beargrass creek, since the city has grown up on each side of it, and has been making use of it for sewage, etc. Many years ago, this creek was an unimpeded, though crooked, clean stream, fed by pure water from the clouds and the numerous springs along its course. Since, it has yearly become more and more polluted as the city has rapidly built up along its banks, sewers from the older parts of the city have been conducted into it, and numerous slaughter houses and distilleries, etc., have used it as a deposit, until now it has become a regular cess-pool for all the nauseating, if not death-dealing, filth of nearly one-half the city.

"Improvements," *The Courier-Journal*, 19 November 1896.

A major improvement proposed in 1896 by the city engineer was to straighten out and pave the Beargrass Creek beds with a "durable material," so the polluted water would at least flow smoothly and not create "deep, sluggish, stagnant, unwholesome pools." The problem of filling in the old bed of Beargrass Creek left stagnant by the Cut-off was solved mainly with the rerouting of the Louisville, Cincinnati & Lexington Railroad from Jefferson Street to the riverfront, completed in 1881. The LC&L was immediately absorbed by the L&N.[698] Tracks connecting east and west lines were extended across the riverfront in 1883, resulting in the opening of the Short Route in 1884.[699] Start of construction of the Grand Central Union Depot at Seventh north of Main began in 1889. The complexion of the riverfront would soon change as steamboat traffic waned and rail yards expanded.

Right: Wharf at Fourth Street about 1905. James A. Hibben Collection, Kentucky Historical Society.

Below: Bird's-eye view of waterfront in late 1940s. The Filson Historical Society.

Dedication of bird bath and fountain at Stratton Park, 18 April 1931. Samuel W. Thomas files. Railroad trestle in background runs under Clark Memorial Bridge at left. Park site now part of the new arena.

The only bright spot on the riverfront was Mamie Varble Stratton Park, sandwiched between Second Street and the Wharfmaster's office to the west. The park was named in 1923 to honor Mrs. John H. Miller, an activist in the Outdoor Art League. "Large groups of children at play along the river front first directed the attention of the Outdoor Art League to this spot," an organization yearbook noted. "These children could find no other place to play and loitered on the bank of the Ohio River, which was very dangerous."

HARLAND BARTHOLOMEW'S RIVERFRONT PLANS

IN LATE 1928, ALMOST A QUARTER CENTURY after identifying the need, Louisville's new Planning and Zoning Commission sent out requests for proposals to have a comprehensive land use and transportation master plan prepared.[700] Early in 1929, the firm of Harland Bartholomew & Associates of St. Louis was selected.[701] Bartholomew had studied civil engineering at Rutgers before working in Newark as city plan engineer and moving to St. Louis in the same capacity in 1916. He began teaching part-time at the University of Illinois, where City Beautiful advocate Charles Mulford Robinson headed Civic Design. In 1919 Bartholomew formed his firm, which by 1928 had prepared some 40 city plans. He had first come to Louisville in 1926 when Harry Volz, president of the board of aldermen, suggested he study traffic problems.[702]

Shortly after his selection to prepare a master plan, Bartholomew "thrilled" the Louisville Engineers and Architects' Club with a talk on "the new science of city building."

In the history of this country men were more engrossed in the forms of government than the forms of their cities. The Chicago World's Fair produced, he said, for the first time, or rather stimulated the thought of better cities. Shortly afterwards a book produced by an obscure English clerk, "The Garden Cities of Tomorrow,"[703] made its appearance and then came the report of the Committee On Congestion of Population of New York which led to the drafting of the model tenement house laws.

Another factor which Mr. Bartholomew said has affected the American city tremendously was the shift of the rural population to the cities....

The greatest factor which has come in changing the American city, he said, was the automobile. Not only has the character but the living habits of the modern city been changed by the car. The radius of residence of a city a few years ago was five miles; today it is from fifteen to twenty miles.[704]

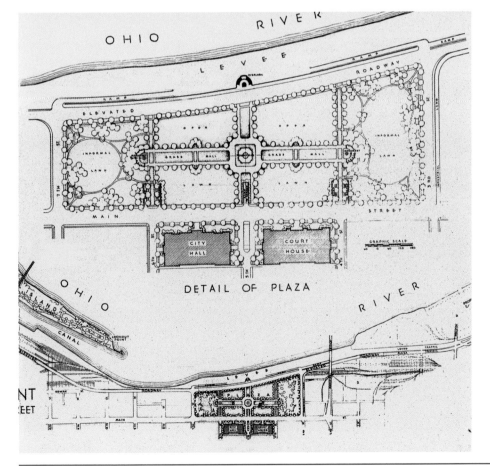

DETAIL OF PLAZA

Rendering of riverfront development plan by Fred Graf, St. Louis. Courtesy of Carl Berg. Sixth Street axis separating the Court House (east) and City Hall (west) is marked on the wharf by an overlook.

One feature of the architect's drawing of the proposed plaza is incongruous. This is the battery of half a dozen chimneys of the Riverside electric plant, which has showered cinders on the retail district for some years and added to the soot and grime. This condition does not fit in well with the park-like plaza, faced with new and beautiful buildings.

"Louisville In 1950?" *The Courier-Journal*, 8 May 1931.

Riverfront development plan by Harland Bartholomew and Associates, 1931.

Part of Bartholomew's overall concept included a mind-boggling transformation of the downtown riverfront. Readers of the local newspapers must have thought they were looking at a different city when they saw the drawing of the proposed change when it was first published in early May 1931. By then, the classical design of City Beautiful monumental buildings were cloaked in the newer Art Deco façades. An impressive new city hall and a courthouse lined the south side of Main Street overlooking a spectacular plaza that included underground parking and railroad tracks. The plan was obviously based upon Bartholomew's 1928 Central Riverfront Plan for St. Louis. The planner who modified it to fit conditions in Louisville was Carl Berg, who had just joined Bartholomew and Associates after graduating from the University of Illinois with a degree in landscape architecture and traveling in Europe for a year through a fellowship. Relocating to Louisville, Berg remained with the new City Planning Commission along with another Bartholomew representative, Harry Alexander. Berg served as planner for the Board of Park Commissioners from 1935-1942 as well as the Louisville Area Development Association, and later held other government planning positions.[705]

The Courier-Journal (8 May 1931) supported the project with an editorial headed "Louisville In 1950?"

> Imagine a landscaped elevated plaza, running from Main Street to the top of the levee and from Third to Seventh Streets. Trees, grass, flowers and shrubbery adorn it, along with fountains, and public memorials. Along its northern edge runs an elevated through east and west highway, with ramps leading down at either end to give access to a great underground parking space beneath the plaza. Facing the park and the river are the new City Hall and Court House, possibly other structures of a civic nature…. A year or two ago, The Courier-Journal discussed the St. Louis plan, also the creation of Harland Bartholomew and Associates, in the consummation of which that city is spending hundreds of millions. This likewise includes utterly changing the squalid Mississippi River front into a thing of beauty, and the laying out of a great civic center.

Fortunately, Bartholomew's ambitious plan never got off the ground, shelved by the Great Depression that had already brought down Louisville's BancoKentucky empire.[706] The local economy and confidence were dashed in 1937 by the worst Ohio River flood in history. The Second World War sucked manpower out of the community, and in 1945, its second worst flood occurred. When the city finally began

St. Louis, Feb. 22 –Mayor Joseph D. Scholtz stood on the Mississippi waterfront here Saturday, looking at forty blocks of demolished houses being removed for the Jefferson Memorial and saw in it a project that Louisville should try to imitate on a smaller scale….

Louisville could very well start studying a similar project as a memorial to George Rogers Clark.

John L. Eschrich, *The Courier-Journal*, 23 February 1941. Scholtz was attending the United States Conference of Mayors in St. Louis.

to protect itself with a massive floodwall, Bartholomew's plan to make over the riverfront became unworkable.[707]

Later the wharf became a massive parking lot. When eminent architectural historian Talbot Hamlin visited in late 1944 to deliver lectures at the University of Louisville, he "discussed the possibility of developing Louisville's ugly riverfront into attractive park sections and riverside driveways."[708] Bartholomew's group returned to prepare a master plan for downtown Louisville including the riverfront in the mid-1950s. The results of this effort were less fanciful along the water but just as unaffordable in the proposed civic center. Bartholomew and Associates also suggested that a countywide park district be created with the power to levy property taxes for purchase of park lands for future improvement. The cost was estimated at $5 million over five years.[709] The firm's presence in Louisville had run its course.

Riverfront proposal by Harland Bartholomew and Associates, 1957.

A SUGGESTED REDEVELOPMENT PLAN OF THE CENTRAL RIVERFRONT AREA

After Republicans took over local government in 1961, riverfront planning took on a more concerted effort that included business leaders, large corporations, and international designer Constantinos Doxiadis. One aspect of the 1950s' Bartholomew plan was brought forward: its "most dramatic proposal for a new downtown riverfront development with a giant three-level underground parking garage, topped by a landscaped plaza north of Main Street."[710] In the hands of Doxiadis, plans for this area in 1965 featured a 450-ft-tall bell and clock tower, "symbolic of the new Louisville."[711] Included in the proposal were a botanical garden, a Reynolds-General Electric complex, wharf area, railroad museum, theater, and underground garage. "Tying downtown to the Ohio River, and holding the plan together, will be a wide plaza between Fourth and Sixth, extending over and hiding the Riverside Parkway and the parallel railroad tracks. The intersection of Fourth and Main would be 'the magnet point into the project area.'" Following the 1968 riots, interest in downtown Louisville projects waned until the Belvedere and Plaza were dedicated 27 April 1973.

As the shifting tide of downtown began to stabilize, attention was focused by Mayor Harvey Sloane and the Louisville Central Area organization on the long-neglected riverfront between the Clark and Kennedy bridges. A task force, with the help of Philadelphia land planners Wallace, Roberts & Todd, made recommendations in 1983. By 1988 a stairway connecting the Belvedere with the wharf had been added to the mix.[712] In early 1990, Hargreaves Associates of San Francisco was selected to prepare a master plan for development of Waterfront Park.[713]

In a large poster celebrating the Waterfront Park's master plan, the Louisville Waterfront Development Corporation stated: "Hargreaves Associates, the architects of Louisville's proposed Waterfront Park, built upon the Olmsted vision and created a park that can host great public festivals and civic celebrations, as well as quiet walks across "broad and tranquil meadow spaces. And because they did, Waterfront Park will be a park for all people, for all time." The park opened 4 July 1999, and has been expanding eastward ever since to include the old Big Four Bridge.[714]

Postcard shows original span of Big Four Bridge about 1895. Samuel W. Thomas files. Incline curves over River Road. Later, shanty boats clustered on the land under bridge.

Olmsted indeed formed a vision of the Ohio River after he visited the site being considered for the western park later named Shawnee, but it bears no relation to the current Waterfront Park. The brilliance of Waterfront Park is its adaptation to its setting—a sand dredging and commercial storage site wedged between two Ohio River bridges. To the south was the old channel of Beargrass Creek, once one of the foulest outflows in the country, that created a bleak area known historically as the Point. Olmsted had rather pristine properties to beautify, while Hargreaves Associates had a reclamation site to work with. The transformation has been stunning—a park worthy of praise in the same breath as Cherokee, Shawnee, and Iroquois. With the inclusion of Waterfront as Northern Park, this triangle of principal parks, long referred to as Eastern, Western, and Southern parks, has become diamond-shaped. While locations of an east, west, and southern park were discussed long before Olmsted came to Louisville to advise the Board of Park Commissioners, there was no deliberation about a park in the prime location accessible to the most people along the Ohio River north of the downtown. It would seem that potential sites had to resemble a park before being selected for a park. By the time in the 1880s that locations of potential parks were being suggested, the riverfront along the wharf in front of the city was so fouled, any thought of making it over into a serene and scenic park seemed ludicrous. The near-miraculous advent of Waterfront Park at last gives visual support to Louisville's long held claim to be the Gateway to the South.

Commerce and a rail yard spoil the riverfront east of First Street in this 1926 view. Caufield and Shook Collection, University of Louisville Photographic Archives. Future site of Waterfront Park is north of curve in River Road. Big Four Bridge is in background.

ENDNOTES

1 "The Park Association." *The Louisville Daily Commercial*, 7 June 1874.

2 Francis R. Kowsky, *Country, Park, & City: The Architecture and Life of Calvert Vaux* (New York, 2003), 5.

3 Joan Riehm, "Frederick Law Olmsted: 'Unknown' U.S. hero…" *The Courier-Journal & Times*, 6 August 1972.

4 "Olmsted: An architect of the land," *The Courier-Journal & Times*, 21 April 1974.

5 Barry G. Jacobs, "Life and work in the shadow of Mr. Olmsted," *The Courier-Journal & Times*, 2 June 1974.

6 Diane Heilenman, "Olmsted imprint on Louisville's landscape is just now becoming clear," *The Courier-Journal*, 29 March 1987.

7 Witold Rybczynski, *A Clearing in the Distance* (New York, 1999), 387.

8 "Charles Eliot." *The New York Times*, 26 March 1897.

9 Rick McDonough, "Boston firm will plot a course for city parks," *The Courier-Journal*, 17 April 1991.

10 In a paper delivered to The Filson Club in 1919, its president Alfred Pirtle noted that Beargrass Creek was named by French explorers who referred to the great reef at the Falls as La Barre Grasse. *The Louisville Herald*, 4 February 1919.

11 Some thought "Rotten C." was a corruption of the French word rattan, meaning cane.

12 J. Stoddard Johnston, *First Explorations of Kentucky*, Filson Club Publications No. 13 (Louisville, 1898), 47-48.

13 Alexander Canaday McLeod, "A Man For All Regions: Dr. Thomas Walker of Castle Hill," *The Filson Club History Quarterly* 71 (April 1997): 169.

14 Otto A. Rothert, "Origin of the Names Beargrass Creek, the Point, and Thruston Square," *The Filson Club History Quarterly* 2 (October 1927): 19-20. Ella H. Johnson, "Beargrass Creek in City's History," *The Courier-Journal*, 6 November 1927. Mrs. Johnson credited Dr. James C. Johnston, William Marshall, and James Harrison with yucca being bear grass.

15 Lawrence J. Fleenor, Jr., *The Bear Grass, A History* (Big Stone Gap, 1991), 2.

16 "Old Spot." *The Courier-Journal*, 17 December 1899. Henry Weedon Gray, who was born in 1819 to a pioneer Louisville family, was a prominent insurance executive. He died at the age of 83. "Old Age," *The Courier-Journal*, 18 July 1903.

17 Born at Farmington in 1812, James Speed was a lawyer and brother of Joshua Fry Speed, a close friend of Abraham Lincoln. James Speed served briefly in Lincoln's cabinet as attorney general. He died in 1887.

18 James Speed (grandson), *James Speed, A Personality* (Louisville, 1914), 124-126.

19 Clarence Boyd was a promising artist when he was shot and killed by his brother-in-law at the age of 28. "Clarence Boyd Dead." *The Courier-Journal*, 9 June 1883.

20 August Carl was principally a portrait painter trained in Europe. He died a young man in 1887. "Carl, The Artist, Dead." *The Louisville Commercial*, 9 October 1887.

21 A photograph of Big Rock, captioned "A Favorite Resort Of Carl Brenner, The Woodland Artist" appeared in *The Courier-Journal*, 26 January 1896. For biographical information see "Speed Museum is showing work of 'beech painter' Carl Brenner," *The Courier-Journal*, 5 June 1983.

22 Capitalist George L. Douglass, who was involved in the development of the Western Union Telegraph Company, lived for many years at Woodbourne on Bardstown Road. He died in 1889 at the age of 89. "Death Of Mr. G. L. Douglass." *The Courier-Journal*, 9 October 1889. Sallie Rutherford Douglass died in 1908 at the age of 73. "Well-Known Woman," *The Courier-Journal*, 20 July 1908.

23 "Old Spot." *The Courier-Journal*, 17 December 1899.

24 Meeting of 20 September 1898. Board of Park Commissioners Minute Book 6, p. 386.

25 "Generous," *The Courier-Journal*, 17 May 1899.

26 "Pastoral," *The Courier-Journal*, 20 May 1900.

27 The specifications for construction of the bridge's arch, dated June 1901, note the Shepley, Rutan & Coolidge architectural firm. Olmsted firm papers, Library of Congress. Interestingly, no mention is made of the bridge in Board of Park Commissioners' minutes.

28 "New Homes." *The Courier-Journal*, 2 March 1902.

29 Jefferson County Plat and Subdivision Book 1, p. 46.

30 Preliminary sketch courtesy of Shepley Bulfinch Richardson & Abbott Architects. Susan T. Steele to Samuel W. Thomas, 19 December 1986. The firm had designed Norton Hall in nearby Alta Vista for George W. Norton.

31 "As To Public Parks." *The Courier-Journal*, 7 August 1882.

32 Samuel W. Thomas, "Document 'Is A Fraud,'" *The Courier-Journal*, 26 March 1990.

33 Reuben T. Durrett, "The Centenary of Louisville: A Paper read before the Southern Historical Association, Saturday, May 1st, 1880," *Filson Club Publication No. 8* (Louisville, 1893), 96.

34 Durrett to Draper, Draper MSS 35J44-48.

35 According to a 24 June 1883 *Courier-Journal* article, "The Old Landmarks," which could only have been written by Reuben T. Durrett, Floyd built a fort at the mouth of Beargrass Creek in the spring of 1779. However, historian of pioneer times Neal O. Hammon states that Floyd and his family did not set out for the Falls from Cumberland Gap until the fall of 1779. William Fleming's 3 December 1779 letter in The Filson Historical Society states that he had visited Floyd on Beargrass Creek "five or six miles from the falls."

36 William Fleming to Nancy Fleming, 3 December 1779. The Filson Historical Society.

37 Durrett to Draper, 21 September 1883. Draper MSS 19J25-26. For other examples of Durrett's fiction, see Jacob F. Lee, "'Whether It Really Be Truth or Fiction,'" *Ohio Valley History* 9 (Winter 2009): 27-47.

38 Clark to Jefferson, 12 October 1783. Historic Locust Grove. Samuel W. Thomas and Eugene H. Conner, "George Rogers Clark [1752-1818]: Natural Scientist and Historian," *The Filson Club History Quarterly* 41 (July 1967): 218.

39 *The Courier-Journal*, 1 December 1894. Edwards was correcting statements made by J. B. C. in a profile of Emma Keats Speed in "People Worth Knowing," *The Southern Magazine* 5 (1895): 312-314.

40 Samuel W. Thomas, *Crescent Hill Revisited* (Louisville, 1987), 55-56.

41 Ibid., 56.

42 Frederick Law Olmsted to Charles Loring Brace, 1 December 1853, Charles E. Beveridge and Charles Capen McLaughlin, eds., *The Papers of Frederick Law Olmsted* (Baltimore, 1981), 2: 232.

43 P. Albert Davies, "Charles Wilkins Short, 1794-1863, Botanist and Physician," *The Filson Club History Quarterly* 19 (July 1945): 148. Deborah Susan Skaggs, "Charles Wilkins Short: Kentucky Botanist and Physician, 1794-1863," M.A. thesis, University of Louisville, 1970. Moses M. Rawlings to Charles W. Short, 20 January 1847 for $32,500, recorded in Jefferson County Deed Book 67, p. 349.

44 "Farm For Sale." *The Louisville Daily Journal*, 30 April 1840.

45 J. Stoddard Johnston, "Hayfield And Its Memories Of Days Long Past." *The Courier-Journal*, 24 May 1908.

46 Will of Dr. Charles Wilkins Short made 25 February 1863 and probated 23 March 1863, and recorded in Jefferson County Will Book 6, p. 70.

47 "Death Came Gently." *The Courier-Journal*, 31 October 1892.

48 "Mansion In The Woods," *The Courier-Journal*, 14 July 1895.

49 Janet Lowell Walker, "An Old Mansion Gives Way to A Hospital," *The Courier-Journal*, 23 October 1949. "Once-Proud Charles Claggett Mansion Will Soon Pass From Louisville Scene," *The Courier-Journal*, 5 April 1954. Martha Elson, "A 'matchless setting,'" *The Courier-Journal*, 24 February 1993.

50 "Fruit Culture—Nursery Business." *The Louisville Daily Courier*, 24 November 1853.

51 "Fruit and Ornamental Trees." *The Louisville Daily Courier*, 24 November 1853.

52 "Centenary Of Old Fontaine Estate," *The Louisville Times*, 24 March 1914. This passage was copied from "Mary Lytle Byers, "The Passing of Fontaine Ferry." *The Evening Post*, 3 October 1903.

53 "A Public Park Site." *The Courier-Journal*, 29 July 1882.

54 "Fontaine And Western." *The Courier-Journal*, 5 August 1894.

55 "Fontaine And Western." *The Courier-Journal*, 5 August 1894. "Ready For Hard Work." *The Courier-Journal*, 29 March 1896.

56 "Mary Lytle Byers, "The Passing of Fontaine Ferry." *The Evening Post*, 3 October 1903.

57 "Old Bike Track Broken Up To Make Driveway." *The Louisville Times*, 3 February 1916.

58 Hugh Hays, "Two Famous Pleasure Gardens," *The Courier-Journal*, 7 May 1882. Hays was a wagon and plow manufacturer who came to Louisville in 1832. His eldest son was Will S. Hays, the celebrated ballad and song writer.

59 "The Willich Festival." *The Louisville Daily Journal*, 23 May 1863.

60 "Amusements." *The Courier-Journal*, 20 May 1877.

61 Samuel W. Thomas and Eugene H. Conner, eds., *The Journals of Increase Allen Lapham for 1827-1830* (Louisville, 1973), 94. The entry was made by Lapham 29 May 1829. Reportedly, Louisville's first amusement park opened 6 June 1829; however, Lapham did not record the event. For a description of the tree construction, see "Elm Tree Garden," *The Encyclopedia of Louisville* (Lexington, 2001), 271.

62 *Memorial History of Louisville* (Chicago, 1896), 1: 73.

63 Hugh Hays, "Two Famous Pleasure Gardens," *The Courier-Journal*, 7 May 1882.

64 Melville O. Briney, "Another Notable Residence On Old Jefferson Street," *The Louisville Times*, 23 September 1954.

65 "Magnolia Garden." *The Louisville Daily Journal*, 15 June 1850.

66 "Wilson's Garden." *The Louisville Daily Journal*, 7 May 1850.

67 A comprehensive description of Père-Lachaise is the centerpiece of *The Architecture of Death* (Cambridge, 1984) by Richard A. Etlin, Ph.D., a Princeton graduate who taught briefly at the University of Kentucky.

68 John Buonarotti Papworth was an English architect and artist of note.

69 Reprinted in John W. Reps, *Town Planning in Frontier America* (Princeton, 1970), 274; and Clay Lancaster, *Antebellum Architecture of Kentucky* (Lexington, 1991), 153.

70 Architect John Notman laid out Laurel Hill. He also prepared the initial plan for Spring Grove Cemetery in Cincinnati, but it was soon rejected and replaced by a design by Howard Daniels. For those plans and an 1838 plan of Green-Wood Cemetery by David Bates Douglass, see Blanche Linden-Ward, *Silent City on a Hill* (Columbus, 1989), 330. Almerin Hotchkiss worked at Green-Wood

Cemetery before moving to St. Louis to design Bellefontaine Cemetery, which was dedicated in 1850. Margaretta J. Darnell, "The American Cemetery as Picturesque Landscape, Bellefontaine Cemetery, St. Louis," *Winterthur Portfolio* 18 (Winter, 1983), 252. Hotchkiss designed Lake Forest in 1856-1857, a dozen years before Olmsted & Vaux designed Riverside not far away.

71 Edmund F. Lee, *Walnut Ridge Cemetery, near Jeffersonville, with some Rules, and Regulations, and an Essay on Public Rural Cemeteries* (Jeffersonville, 1838), 13.

72 Edmund Francis Lee was buried in Western Cemetery. In April 1906 his remains were reinterred in Cave Hill Cemetery. The permit recorded his date of death from cholera morbus as 14 July 1857 at age 57. His obituary in the *Daily Louisville Democrat*, 15 July 1857, noted he was in the "45th year of his age."

73 Samuel W. Thomas, Eugene H. Conner, and Harold Meloy, "A History of Mammoth Cave, Emphasizing Tourist Development and Medical Experimentation Under Dr. John Croghan," *The Register of the Kentucky Historical Society* 68 (October 1970): 334-336.

74 In the subsequent directory of 1848, Lee was residing with real estate agent Thomas G. Addison, whose daughter, Meloria Addison, he had married.

75 27 May 1846, Common Council Minute Book, p. 173.

76 The site had been part of the Cave Hill farm. Jefferson County Deed Book 61, p. 55. "The Eastern Burying Ground," *The Louisville Daily Journal*, 1 June 1843. An announcement that lots were to be auctioned 21 June 1843 appeared in *The Louisville Daily Journal*, 15 June 1843. *The Louisville Daily Journal*, 21 June 1843, noted: "The location is very suitable, and the cemetery will be permanent."

77 11 November 1846, Common Council Minute Book, pp. 279-280.

78 "Women Would Transform Old Cemetery Into Restful Park," *The Courier-Journal*, 15 January 1922. Western Cemetery was established in 1832. It replaced Louisville's first public cemetery, created by 1786, which was converted into Baxter Square beginning in 1872.

79 "We understand that the Trustees are now ready to dispose of lots in the Cemetery grounds, and that they have already commenced selling them. And we are pleased to learn too, that Mr. Ross, superintendent and landscape gardener of the Cemetery, arrived yesterday, and has entered upon the performance of his duties." "Cave Hill Cemetery." *The Examiner*, 19 August 1848.

80 Obituary of Nancy Clarke Ross in "Died." *The Courier-Journal*, 24 April 1876. She was the sister of Robert Clarke, the prominent Cincinnati book publisher.

81 "Robert Ross Dead." *The Courier-Journal*, 5 August 1890. "In Cave Hill," *The Courier-Journal*, 16 June 1895. According to his burial marker, Robert Ross was born at Loch Broom, Scotland, 23 April 1818.

82 Kate Colquhoun, *A Thing in Disguise: The Visionary Life of Joseph Paxton* (London, 2003), 29 and 173. Although several public parks opened in 1846, a year earlier than Birkenhead Park, it is generally credited with being the first in Britain. Cynthia Zaitzevsky, *Frederick Law Olmsted and the Boston Park System* (Cambridge, 1982), 20.

83 9 August 1855, Board of Aldermen Minute Book, p. 359.

84 "Beargrass Cut-Off," *Commercial Review*, 21 December 1855.

85 6 November 1856, Board of Aldermen Minute Book, p. 356. *Daily Louisville Democrat*, 15 July 1857.

86 He was buried in Western Cemetery. On 4 April 1906; his remains along with his wife's were reinterred in the cemetery he designed. Cave Hill Cemetery's permission slip states he died at the age of 57.

87 Surveys plotted by Neal O. Hammon in "The Fincastle Surveyors at the Falls of the Ohio, 1774," *The Filson Club History Quarterly* 47 (January 1973): 20-21. Jefferson County Deed Book AA, p. 274.

88 "Preston's Woods On Sunday." *The Louisville Daily Democrat*, 18 May 1852.

89 This is confirmed on the 1855 bird's-eye view of Louisville.

90 "A Brilliant Ovation to the Little Giant, &c., &c, &c." *The Daily Democrat*, 30 September 1960.

91 "The Execution of David Caution Yesterday," *Daily Louisville Democrat*,

26 January 1861. The hanging process was also described by *The Daily Louisville Journal*, 26 January 1861. After the execution, the body was removed to the Kentucky School of Medicine where "the electrical battery was applied…with the results which are well known to men of science." The skeleton was to be added to the school's museum.

92 William Carnes Kendrick, *Reminiscences of Old Louisville* (1937), 80.

93 Andrew Cowan, "The Public Parks and Parkways," *Memorial History of Louisville* (1896), 2: 339.

94 "Valuable Ground To Lease," *Louisville Public Advertiser*, 11 May 1835. According to the advertisement, by a city council resolution dated 9 May 1835, Bishop Flaget was "authorized and requested to remove the corpse and bones of the deceased persons from the old to the new Catholic grave yard in this city; provided, it is not at the cost and expense of the city, except those graves which are exposed by the grading of 10th Cross street, from Main to Water streets; the city having already agreed to pay the expense of removing same."

95 Isaac Cromie to Charles I. du Pont, Jr., and Alfred V. du Pont, 30 June 1854, Jefferson County Deed Book 89, p. 598. Charles I. du Pont, Jr., conveyed his interest to Alfred V. du Pont, 30 June 1857, Jefferson County Deed Book 98, p. 501.

96 J. Lawrence Smith, *Du Pont's Artesian Well* (Louisville, 1859).

97 According to John Stratton, the well was later located in the basement of the Walker Bag Company, 120 North Tenth Street.

98 "Embellishment of Grounds." *The Louisville Daily Courier*, 8 April 1854.

99 The son of Thomas Joyes, the first child born in Louisville, Patrick Joyes (1826-1904) was raised on the northeast corner of Sixth and Main streets. He graduated from Centre College and studied law at the University of Louisville and Harvard University. "In Old Age," *The Courier-Journal*, 27 April 1904.

100 *Louisville Daily Courier*, 5 January 1868. The writer was simply identified as A Native. When the text was reprinted in *History of the Ohio Falls Cities* (Cleveland, 1882): 1, 286-287, Patrick Joyes was credited.

101 "The Story of James Meaney of Wexford, Ireland, and his Family in America with Personal recollections of Richard Jerome Meaney, His third son," 1898, 67-68. The Filson Historical Society.

102 "Cricket." *The Louisville Daily Democrat*, 14 October 1866.

103 "Ante-Bellum Base-Ball." *The Louisville Commercial*, 24 July 1892. According to E. S. Tuley, who played third base on that team, the club's first field on the northwest corner of the present-day Fourth and Kentucky streets (now occupied by Memorial Auditorium) was cramped by a country road that cut through the outfield, prompting a move to "commons in the suburbs," on the northeast corner of Fourth and Oak streets, which was later the site of a mansion called The Towers. In his synopsis of Louisville baseball, George Yater wrote in "Major-League Memories," *Louisville* (May 1987): 31 that the Louisville Base-Ball Club was organized "apparently in 1856."

104 "Out Door Sports." *Louisville Daily Courier*, 24 September 1858.

105 "'Base Ball on the Brain.'" *The Louisville Daily Democrat*, 14 October 1866.

106 "Base Ball." *The Louisville Daily Journal*, 18 July 1867.

107 The 1867 city directory listed Cedar Hill Park for the first time. Ormsby & Dumesnil were listed as proprietors at Fourth, south of Oak. Mary Ormsby Dumesnil and her husband, Henry A. Dumesnil, had begun to build a large house between Fifth and Sixth streets, Ormsby and Park avenues that later housed the Louisville Collegiate School.

108 Sally Yandell to William Yandell, 7 August 1867. The Filson Historical Society.

109 "The Cricket Match." *The Louisville Daily Journal*, 12 August 1867.

110 "A Description of Floral Park." *The Courier-Journal*, 8 July 1887.

111 Ibid.

112 Richard Deering, *Louisville: Her Commercial, Manufacturing and Social Advantages* (Louisville, 1859), 30. Methodist minister Deering must have seen the Schuylkill River setting in his travels. According to Deering's obituary, he was an agent for the American Tract Society of Philadelphia. "Gone To His Reward." *The Louisville Times*, 16 August 1892.

113 Talbot Hamlin, *Benjamin Henry Latrobe* (New York, 1955), 161. Michael W. Fazio and Patrick A. Snadon, *The Domestic Architecture of Benjamin Henry Latrobe* (Baltimore, 2006), 197.

114 Jane Mork Gibson, "The Fairmount Waterworks," *Bulletin of the Philadelphia Museum of Art* 84 (Summer 1988): 24-25.

115 Harry R. Stevens, "Samuel Watts Davies and The Industrial Revolution in Cincinnati," *The Ohio Historical Quarterly* 70 (April 1961): 116. "Albert Stein, a young man of twenty-five, had already been in the United States for some months. He knew a good bit about steam engines and hydraulics. He had arrived with his skill, but he was unknown…. In the winter of 1817-18 Stein was back in the East looking over steam engines in Philadelphia." Letter from Albert Stein, Germantown (Philadelphia), to editors of *The Western Spy* (Cincinnati), published 7 February 1818.

116 Clifton Potter and Dorothy Potter, *Lynchburg: A City Set on Seven Hills* (2004), 37. In 1840, Stein took on the franchise to supply water to Mobile, Alabama, where he died in 1874.

117 A history provided by James Guthrie in "To the Citizens of Louisville," *Louisville Public Advertiser*, 11 November 1834.

118 "Water Works." *Commercial Review*, 21 March 1856. Scowden was also responsible for the waterworks in Cincinnati, Cleveland, Newport, and Dubuque. He died in Jacksonville at the age of 66 in 1882. "Death Of T. R. Scowden." *The Courier-Journal*, 3 January 1882.

119 "Water Works." *Louisville Daily Courier*, 11 March 1857.

120 The section regarding Scowden's discovery in Charles Whittlesey's paper, "Antiquity of Man in the United States," was reprinted in *History of the Ohio Falls Cities* (Cleveland, 1882), 1: 606.

121 "The Louisville Water Works." *Daily Louisville Democrat*, 24 October 1860.

122 William C. Kendrick, "Reminiscences of Old Louisville," 1937, p. 86.

123 Jefferson County Deed Book 79, p. 536. Oakland Cemetery was platted and considered a city cemetery as noted in an ordinance approved 26 October 1853.

124 26 June 1851, Board of Aldermen Minute Book, pp. 66-67.

125 20 November 1851, Board of Aldermen Minute Book, p. 218.

126 10 April 1854, Board of Aldermen Minute Book, p. 178.

127 28 September 1854, Board of Aldermen Minute Book, p. 472.

128 6 September 1855, Board of Aldermen Minute Book, p. 412.

129 The aldermen were reluctant. 17 June 1857, Board of Aldermen Minute Book, p. 45.

130 6 August 1857, Board of Aldermen Minute Book, p. 77.

131 "House of Refuge." *Louisville Daily Courier*, 22 June 1859. Ordinance titled "House of Refuge," recorded 27 March 1860 in Ordinance and Resolution Book, p. 536. Deed dated 17 April 1860, recorded in Jefferson County Deed Book 107, p. 569.

132 Petition for naturalization of Benjamin Grove, 8 January 1858. City (Police) Court of Louisville Minute Book 26, p. 477.

133 The German Catholic cemetery's name was changed to St. John's Cemetery after 1869.

134 "Map of Cave Hill Cemetery." *The Courier-Journal*, 7 September 1857.

135 "Benjamin Grove, Surveyor Of Cave Hill, Dead At 92," *The Courier-Journal*, 19 March 1915.

136 According to the first annual report of the House of Refuge Board of Directors, 67 acres was set apart by the General Council for the House of Refuge; 40 acres was "intended to adorn and beautify as a park." *History of the Ohio Falls Cities and Their Counties* (Cleveland, 1882), 1: 591.

137 *Third Annual Report of the Board of Park Commissioners* (1893), 62.

138 "Third Street." *The Courier-Journal*, 28 October 1870.

139 "Of Public Interest." *The Courier-Journal*, 29 May 1871.

140 "The New Park Scheme." *Louisville Commercial*, 26 March 1890.

141 "An Interior Park." *The Courier-Journal*, 9 July 1891.

142 Plans were made to abandon the reform school property in 1920. "Modern Building Planned In Merger Of Reform Homes," *The Courier-Journal*, 28 February 1920.

143 Recorded 25 June 1879 in Jefferson County Deed Book 225, p. 639.

144 Reportedly, Grove designed St. Mary's Catholic Cemetery in 1851. However, the cemetery was not listed in a city directory until 1859-1860. In the lower corners of the plan in Grove's collection in The Filson Historical Society are the names Michael Bouchet, secretary, and P. Shelley, sexton. As they are first listed in the 1866-1867 Louisville directory, it would appear that Grove did not record the plan until after that date.

145 Kate Colquhoun, *A Thing in Disguise: The Visionary Life of Joseph Paxton* (London, 2003), 136.

146 "Map of Cave Hill Cemetery." *Louisville Daily Courier*, 31 January 1857. "Map of the unimproved grounds in Cave Hill Cemetery prepared by Benj. Grove," was noted in the Minutes of the Board of Managers, 24 June 1968.

147 Jefferson County Deed Book 139, p. 269.

148 Grove's subdivision plan was not put to record, but it was referred to in deeds from the McFerrans to B. A. May and Alford Whitman for lots they purchased in 1874 on Glenview Avenue directly south of the narrow-gauge station. Whitman sold his property to Philip P. Huston on 11 May 1878 (Jefferson County Deed Book 222, p. 119), so Grove's plan must date between 1874 and 1878.

149 McFerran to McFerran, 1 June 1881. Jefferson County Deed Book 241, p. 266. It is not known why the homestead on Grove's plat is listed as being J. B. McFerran's. For information regarding the sale, see "The Glenview Sale." *The Courier-Journal*, 15 October 1886, and "The Home Of Trotters." *The Courier-Journal*, 17 October 1886.

150 *History of the Ohio Falls Cities and Their Counties* (Cleveland, 1882), 1: 403.

151 Laura Wood Roper, *FLO: A Biography of Frederick Law Olmsted* (Baltimore, 1973), 162.

152 Ibid., 217.

153 Clay Lancaster, *Prospect Park Handbook* (New York, 1967), 51.

154 "Our Parks." *The Louisville Daily Journal*, 4 August 1866.

155 8 June 1866, Louisville Common Council Minute Book, p. 244.

156 "Our Parks." *The Louisville Daily Journal*, 4 August 1866.

157 Ibid.

158 14 June 1867 meeting, Common Council Minute Book, p. 25.

159 Vedette, "To Keep Cool." *The Louisville Daily Journal*, 14 July 1868.

160 "Our Park." *The Louisville Daily Journal*, 27 July 1868.

161 16 July 1868, Common Council Minute Book, p. 385.

162 Reprover, "The Library and Park Questions." *The Louisville Daily Journal*, 17 August 1868.

163 John George Baxter, Jr., a stove manufacturer and Democrat, had served on both the Common Council and Board of Aldermen before being elected mayor in 1870. Defeated in 1875, he was again elected mayor in 1879. "John G. Baxter Dead." *The Courier-Journal*, 31 March 1885.

164 *Louisville Municipal Reports for the Fiscal Year Ending December 31st, 1869* (Louisville, 1870), 15-16.

165 "Board of Aldermen." *Louisville Commercial*, 17 July 1870.

166 "The Park Ordinance Adopted." *Louisville Commercial*, 18 July 1870.

167 "Public Parks—Some Good Suggestions." *Louisville Commercial*, 24 July 1870. "The Parks." *Louisville Commercial*, 30 July 1870. "Our City Parks—Facts and Figures for Fearful Fogies." *Louisville Commercial*, 31 July 1870. "The Parks Discussion." *The Courier-Journal*, 31 July 1870. "The Parks." *Louisville Commercial*, 1 August 1870. "The Parks." *The Courier-Journal*, 1 August 1870.

168 "The Park Ordinance." *Louisville Commercial*, 6 August 1870.

169 "The Parks." *The Courier-Journal*, 2 August 1870.

170 "Parks of Louisville." 1904 city directory, p. 20.

171 Vedette, "To Keep Cool." *The Louisville Daily Journal*, 14 July 1868.

172 "The Crescent Avenue." *The Louisville Daily Journal*, 23 July 1868.

173 Olmsted, Vaux & Co. to Board of Commissioners of Prospect Park, 1 January 1868.

174 Charles E. Beveridge and Carolyn F. Hoffman, eds., *The Papers of Frederick Law Olmsted, Supplementary Series Volume 1, Writings on Public Parks, Parkways, and Park Systems* (Baltimore, 1997), 13.

175 Francis R. Kowsky, "Municipal Parks and City Planning: Frederick Law Olmsted's Buffalo Park and parkway System," *Journal of the Society of Architectural Historians* 46 (March 1987): 56-58.

176 Albert Fein, *Frederick Law Olmsted and the American Environmental Tradition* (New York, 1972), plate 50. Witold Rybczynski, *A Clearing in the Distance: Frederick Law Olmsted and America in the Nineteenth Century* (New York, 1999), 282.

177 "Third Street." *The Courier-Journal*, 28 October 1870.

178 "Of Public Interest," *The Courier-Journal*, 29 May 1871.

179 "The River Road." *The Courier-Journal*, 22 July 1880.

180 "Sale Of Trotting Stock." *The Daily Louisville Commercial*, 13 May 1875.

181 "Sale Of Nutwood." *The Courier-Journal*, 29 September 1881. Nutwood had been foaled at Woodburn in 1870.

182 "A Capital Idea." *The Courier-Journal*, 21-22 March 1869.

183 "The Dead of Half a Century Ago." *Louisville Commercial*, 10 July 1870. *Louisville Municipal Reports for the Fiscal Year Ending December 31st, 1869* (Louisville, 1870), 18. Converting the cemetery into a "very charming little park," had been suggested as early as "Our Parks." *The Louisville Daily Journal*, 4 August 1866.

184 "The Dead of Half a Century Ago." *Louisville Commercial*, 10 July 1870.

185 "Public Park." *Louisville Daily Ledger*, 29 June 1872.

186 "The Graveyard Park," *Louisville Daily Ledger*, 12 May 1873.

187 Naming a park for Mayor Baxter was first discussed perhaps on 9 July 1871 by a *Courier-Journal* reader who suggested that the Fair Grounds in Crescent Hill be made into "one of the most tasteful and beautiful little public parks in the Union." The writer pointed out there had been talk of changing the park's name to Baxter Park to honor "our efficient and worthy Mayor." The Fair Grounds continued to operate, however, until 1875 when the property was subdivided as Fair View and lots on either side of Crescent Avenue were sold.

188 "Baxter Square." *Louisville Commercial*, 15 May 1881.

189 "The New Park," *The Courier-Journal*, 1 May 1881.

190 "Baxter Square." *The Louisville Commercial*, 26 May 1881.

191 "Baxter Square." *The Louisville Commercial*, 15 May 1881.

192 "An Island Park." *The Courier-Journal*, 10 July 1881.

193 Lease dated after the fact, 10 March 1891, recorded in Jefferson County Deed Book 367, p. 135.

194 Gordon Englehart, "Chances for New Produce Market Here Grow Dim," *The Courier-Journal*, 9 June 1952.

195 "As To Public Parks." *The Courier-Journal*, 7 August 1882.

196 For photographs of Baxter Square and other devastation, see Samuel W. Thomas, *Views of Louisville since 1766* (Louisville, 1971), 202-205.

197 "The Park Board." *The Courier-Journal*, 6 May 1891.

198 "Baxter Square Now A Children's Playground." *The Courier-Journal*, 5 May 1901.

199 Margaret M. Bridwell, "The Rebirth of A Park," *The Courier-Journal*, 9 September 1956.

200 "Above Beargrass." *The Courier-Journal*, 9 July 1871.

201 Samuel W. Thomas, *Crescent Hill Revisited* (Louisville, 1987), 27.

202 The 18-acre place cost A. V. du Pont $150,000. Jefferson County Deed Book 160, p. 341. "Public Parks and Drives." *The Courier-Journal*, 26 June 1872. The charter to allow the Central Passenger Railway Company to acquire real estate was approved by the Kentucky General Assembly 21 March 1871. In 1890, the Central Passenger Railway Company merged with the City Railway Company to form the Louisville Railway Company, with Bidermann du Pont as president and Alfred as vice president.

203 "A. V. duPont Dead!" *Louisville Commercial*, 17 May 1893.

204 "A Public Benefit," *Louisville Daily Ledger*, 14 June 1872.

205 A 1,000-acre tract that included Central Park was acquired by Cuthbert and Thomas Bullitt in 1817. The land was divided and Cuthbert built a country home on the 219 acres

he received. His son-in-law, George W. Weissinger, inherited the property, and in 1860, Weissinger conveyed it to Stuart Robinson. See Hugh Bullitt, "Central Park History." *The Courier-Journal*, 27 November 1924.

206 "Central Park." *The Courier-Journal*, 14 June 1872.

207 Q, "Public Parks and Drives," *The Courier-Journal*, 26 June 1872.

208 "A Word about Public Parks." *Louisville Commercial*, 3 February 1872.

209 "A Magnificent Enterprise." *The Courier-Journal*, 25 May 1872.

210 "Falls City Race-Course." *The Courier-Journal*, 20 May 1872.

211 "Woodlawn." *Louisville Daily Ledger*, 13 June 1872.

212 Samuel W. Thomas, *Churchill Downs: A Documentary History of America's Most Legendary Race Track* (Louisville, 1995), 33-34.

213 "The Falls City Association." *The Courier-Journal*, 27 May 1872.

214 His obituary stated he was president of the St. Louis Agricultural Society. "Once Prominent In Kentucky Politics." *The Courier-Journal*, 3 November 1903. "John Richard Barret," *Biographical Directory of the American Congress 1774-1961* (Washington, 1961), 519. He married Matilda Nicholas. After the park venture failed, the Barrets moved to New York, where he died 2 November 1903. He was buried in Cave Hill Cemetery.

215 "Landscape Gardening.—III." *The American Architect and Building News* 23 (7 January 1888): 3.

216 "Maximilian G. Kern," *History of Boone County, Missouri* (St. Louis, 1882), 892-893.

217 Caroline Loughlin and Catherine Anderson, *Forest Park* (Columbia, Missouri, 1986), 15-16, 52. Richard Longstreth, "Maximilian G. Kern" in Charles A. Birnbaum and Robin Karson, eds. *Pioneers of Amercan Landscape Design* (New York, 2000), 209-212. "The Man Who Made St. Louis Beautiful," an undated newspaper article in scrapbook compiled by the Missouri Historical Society, states Kern brought 300 young holly trees from Louisville for Forest Park, which later burned.

218 For an assessment of the importance of the railway to the project, see "The Harrod's Creek Road." *The Courier-Journal*, 20 June 1872. The Harrods Creek and Westport Narrow-gauge Railroad began operation in June 1874. "The Narrow-gauge Road." *The Courier-Journal*, 10 June 1874.

219 Caroline Loughlin and Catherine Anderson, *Forest Park* (St. Louis, 1986), 16.

220 "The Villa Park Sale." *The Courier-Journal*, 31 May 1880. The Villa Park tract was referred to as the Throckmorton subdivision, although neither is indexed as a recorded plat. Ariss Throckmorton purchased 302 acres "about three miles above Louisville near the Ohio River and in the waters of Muddy Fork of Beargrass" from Elias Dorsey in 1835. Jefferson County Deed Book RR, p. 313.

221 Scott Wade, "Options under review for River Road park," *The Courier-Journal*, 23 December 1996. Sheldon S. Shafer, "Country club to shut down; city looks at uses for land," *The Courier-Journal*, 1 February 2005. Sheldon S. Shafer, "Mayor to propose recreation corridor," *The Courier-Journal*, 28 May 2007. Sheldon S. Shafer, "Changes to begin at some River Road parks," *The Courier-Journal*, 5 December 2009.

222 "Standard Club Lease Approved Conditionally," *The Courier-Journal*, 11 June 1952.

223 "'Holiday-Town' Plan Urged For Water Front," *The Courier-Journal*, 9 July 1959.

224 J. Richard Barret, "An Excellent Enterprise." *The Courier-Journal*, 28 May 1874.

225 X.Y.Z., "An Excellent Enterprise." *The Courier-Journal*, 28 May 1874.

226 "The Park Association." *The Daily Louisville Commercial*, 7 June 1874.

227 In his two-volume autobiography, *Marse Henry*, Henry Watterson noted that John R. Throckmorton had traveled to Liverpool before the Civil War.

228 "In Cave Hill," *The Courier-Journal*, 16 June 1895.

229 Laura Wood Roper, *FLO: A Biography of Frederick Law Olmsted* (Baltimore, 1973), 71.

230 Frederick Law Olmsted, "The People's Park at Birkenhead, Near Liverpool," *The Horticulturist*, May 1851: 225-226.

231 Witold Rybczynski, *A Clearing in the Distance* (New York, 1999), 93. Walter L. Creese, *The Search for Environment* (Baltimore, 1992), 46.

232 Francis R. Kowsky, *Country, Park & City: The Architecture and Life of Calvert Vaux* (New York, 2003), 96.

233 "Proposed Racing Park." *The Daily Louisville Commercial*, 19 June 1874.

234 Samuel W. Thomas, *Churchill Downs: A Documentary History of America's Most Legendary Race Track* (Louisville, 1995), 37-41.

235 Although the initial success of Churchill Downs was fueled in part by those expecting to use the track for trotting, that did not happen. See "The Jockey Club Course." *The Courier-Journal*, 25 June 1875.

236 "Where We May Skate." *The Courier-Journal*, 27 November 1874. An earlier skating pond was at Cedar Hill Park.

237 *The Louisville Daily Journal*, 14 April 1865.

238 "Base Ball." *The Louisville Daily Democrat*, 22 July 1865. "President Sherley." *Louisville Commercial*, 11 July 1890.

239 "Destroyed." *The Courier-Journal*, 13 August 1899. Eclipse Park was improved for the 1892 season. "Directors Delighted," *The Courier-Journal*, 21 March 1892.

240 Summary of events in Board of Park Commissioners Minute Book, 7 April 1896. Mrs. T. D. Elliott claimed the city had not passed an ordinance accepting her husband's gift. "Claims Baseball Park." *The Courier-Journal*, 1 July 1900. "City Wins," *The Courier-Journal*, 2 July 1905.

241 "Base Ball." *The Daily Louisville Commercial*, 24 June 1874.

242 "The City's Growth," *The Courier-Journal*, 6 June 1875.

243 For details, see Dennis Charles Cusick, "Gentleman of the Press: The Life and Times of Walter Newman Haldeman," M.A. thesis, University of Louisville, 1987, pp. 120-141.

244 "'Good Enough!'" *The Courier-Journal*, 26 April 1876.

245 "Base Ball." *The Courier-Journal*, 28 April 1878.

246 "Colored League." *The Courier-Journal*, 8 May 1887.

247 "Pete Has 'Lined Out.'" *The Courier-Journal*, 22 January 1890. M. James Doussard, "That Championship Season," *The Courier-Journal Magazine*, 15 April 1984.

248 "Base Ball At The Race Track." *The Courier-Journal*, 11 January 1893.

249 "Louisville Is Out Of It," *The Courier-Journal*, 27 January 1900.

250 In his book, *Crack of the Bat: The Louisville Slugger Story* (Champaign, 2000), Bob Hill relates a number of stories about the making of the first Louisville Slugger bat. One fact is certain: it was made by J. F. Hillerich & Sons Company. Most of the stories say it was made for Pete Browning, starting with the obituary of John Fred Hillerich, the turning company's founder who died 16 January 1924 at the age of 90. *The Louisville Herald* obituary reported that Browning asked Hillerich to turn him a bat, which he liked so much he ordered more. The company then began to manufacture bats. Just months after Hillerich died, *The Courier-Journal* (17 June 1924) profiled his company ("Baseball Bat Industry Brings Fame To City") and detailed Hillerich's making of Browning's bat. When J. Fred Hillerich, Jr., died 16 November 1902 at the age of 30, *The Courier-Journal* noted that J. F. Hillerich & Sons had been in the bat manufacturing business for 14 years, placing its startup date in 1888. When the founder's surviving son, J. A. "Bud" Hillerich, was interviewed at the age of 74 in 1941, marking his 60th year in the business, he claimed that his making a bat for the National League's great hitter Art (Arlie) Latham put the company on the map. (Sherley Uhl, "Bud Hillerich's Business Is the Battiest On Earth," *The Courier-Journal*, 17 August 1941.) Perhaps the Browning bat started the company and the Latham bat made it famous.

251 "Eclipse Park Grandstand Is Razed By Fire," *The Courier-Journal*, 20 November 1922.

252 "Quin Seeks Central Site for Ball Park," *The Courier-Journal*, 12 December 1922.

253 "Parkway's End To Be Relocated," *The Courier-Journal*, 26 December 1922. "Diamond to Span Parkway," *The Louisville Times*, 27 December 1922.

254 *Louisville's Olmstedian Legacy* (1988), 52. Dwayne D. Cox and

William J. Morison, *The University of Louisville* (Lexington, 2000), 66-67.

255 "Plans Are Displayed For Proposed Baseball Park," *The Courier-Journal*, 5 December 1922. The grandstand was razed in 1961.

256 "An Island Park." *The Courier-Journal*, 10 July 1881.

257 "The New Bridge." *The Courier-Journal*, 20 September 1881.

258 "A Bridge Of Size." *The Courier-Journal*, 30 October 1881.

259 "Daisy's First Day." *The Courier-Journal*, 17 October 1886. "The Dandy Daisies." *The Courier-Journal*, 20 October 1886.

260 Samuel W. Thomas and Eugene H. Conner, eds., *The Journals of Increase Allen Lapham for 1827-1830* (Louisville, 1973), 34.

261 "Public Gardens Versus Public Parks." *The Courier-Journal*, 11 June 1875.

262 Reuben T. Durrett, *The Centenary of Louisville: A Paper read before the Southern Historical Association, Saturday, May 1st, 1880*, Filson Club Publication No. 8 (Louisville, 1893), 98-99.

263 Baxter's message, dated 15 December 1881. *Louisville Municipal Reports...1881* (Louisville, 1882), 15.

264 "Mayor's Message." *Louisville Municipal Reports for the Fiscal Year Ending August 31, 1883* (1884), 16.

265 "A Public Park Site." *The Courier-Journal*, 29 July 1882.

266 "The Park Question." *The Courier-Journal*, 1 August 1882.

267 "More Park Suggestions." *The Courier-Journal*, 3 August 1882.

268 "As To Public Parks." *The Courier-Journal*, 7 August 1882.

269 "The Park Question." *The Courier-Journal*, 19 August 1882.

270 Recollection of Temple Bodley. Bodley Collection, The Filson Historical Society.

271 "A Public Park," *The Courier-Journal*, 10 September 1882.

272 Andrew Cowan's remarks, 14 November 1913, for Conversation and Salmagundi clubs. Cowan papers, The Filson Historical Society.

273 *Louisville Municipal Reports...1882* (Louisville, 1883), 54.

274 The committee consisted of Wm. J. Davis, chairman, John E. Green, Andrew Cowan, S. E. Jones, Charles

Hermany, J. H. Lindenberger, C. W. Kelly, A. R. Cooper, B. W. Duke, Edgar Hounsfield, A. P. Humphrey, R. W. Knott, Thomas Speed, J. M. Wright, B. H. Young, W. R. Belknap, John Mason Brown, Geo. M. Davie, Harry Weissinger, Rufus Saxton, and Henry Watterson. See "Public Parks." *The Courier-Journal*, 5 June 1887.

275 Temple Bodley, "Some Park History." *The Courier-Journal*, 31 March 1929.

276 Although the boundaries of East Park were outlined but not identified by roads or other features, it is possible to do so by scaling from particular locations shown on the map such as the boundary notch around the Blind School, the intersection of the Louisville, Harrods Creek & Westport Railroad and the Muddy Fork of Beargrass Creek, and points along the Beargrass Creek Cut-Off.

277 "A Description of Floral Park." *The Courier-Journal*, 8 July 1887.

278 "The Commercial Club." *The Courier-Journal*, 8 July 1887.

279 "Will Frame A Park Act." John Mason Brown to editor, *The Courier-Journal*, 8 July 1887.

280 Andrew Cowan, "Our Parks." *The Louisville Post*, 26 July 1893.

281 "Public Parks." *The Courier-Journal*, 15 July 1887.

282 Andrew Cowan, "Our Parks." *The Louisville Post*, 26 July 1893.

283 Temple Bodley, "Some Park History." *The Courier-Journal*, 31 March 1929.

284 Andrew Cowan, "Our Parks." *The Louisville Post*, 26 July 1893.

285 "Charles D. Jacob Dead." *The Courier-Journal*, 26 December 1898.

286 "The Latest Park Plan." *The Louisville Commercial*, 30 May 1888.

287 "The General Council." *The Courier-Journal*, 7 January 1876. "Mr. R. T. Scowden, City Engineer." *The Courier-Journal*, 7 January 1876. "Scowden, Ransom T." *The Biographical Encyclopædia of Kentucky* (Cincinnati, 1878), 167-168. "Engineer Scowden." *The Courier-Journal*, 17 November 1889. Scowden died at the age of 56 in 1893. "Ransom Scowden," *The Courier-Journal*, 13 December 1893.

288 Paper dated 14 November 1913 by Andrew Cowan read to the Conversation and Salmagundi clubs. Cowan papers, The Filson Historical Society.

289 "How The City Grows." *The Louisville Commercial*, 10 December 1888.

290 Paper dated 14 November 1913 by Andrew Cowan read to the Conversation and Salmagundi clubs. Cowan papers, The Filson Historical Society.

291 "A Measly $100,000," *The Critic*, 23 March 1890.

292 "Jacob Park." *The Courier-Journal*, 12 May 1889.

293 "The City's New Park." *The Courier-Journal*, 9 May 1889.

294 The map was part of a collection given to The Filson Historical Society in 1949 by the Kentucky Title Company. It remained uncatalogued until several years ago.

295 The Board of Park Commissioners did not threaten to abandon the park project, but decided to condemn the land for park purposes. See "Enlarging Jacob Park," *The Courier-Journal*, 30 November 1890.

296 Paper dated 14 November 1913 delivered by Andrew Cowan to the Conversation and Salmagundi clubs. Cowan papers, The Filson Historical Society.

297 Map, located in the Metro Louisville Archives, is reproduced in *Louisville's Olmstedian Legacy* (1988), 37.

298 "Is There No Remedy?" *The Critic*, 10 November 1889.

299 "Jacob Park." *The Courier-Journal*, 12 May 1889.

300 "Mayor Jacob Wins." *The Courier-Journal*, 11 May 1889.

301 "Joseph P. Claybrook, Noted Engineer, Dead," *The Courier-Journal*, 21 June 1921.

302 "Maj. J. P. Claybrook, War Veteran, Dies," *The Louisville Herald*, 21 June 1921.

303 "Forest," *The Courier-Journal*, 6 May 1900.

304 "A Summer Home At Fincastle." *The Courier-Journal*, 22 July 1900. John English Green was the son of Dr. Norvin Green, president of the Western Union Telegraph Company. A banker, about 1900 he moved to New York where he died. "John E. Green Dies At Club," *The Courier-Journal*, 4 September 1909.

305 "The Fincastle Club." *The Courier-Journal*, 22 July 1888. Virginia created

Fincastle County on its western frontier in 1772 and then divided it into Kentucky, Montgomery, and Washington counties in 1776.

306 "Fincastle Club-House And Cottages," *The Courier-Journal*, 6 September 1896.

307 Photographs appeared in *The Courier-Journal*, 1 September 1907.

308 "Nitta Yuma," a paper prepared by Lucy White Booker Burlingame, Christmas 1962.

309 The site was south of the important pioneer salt lick, Mann's Lick. Its northern point on the L & N Railroad was the station and post office known as Old Deposit.

310 "At South Park." *The Courier-Journal*, 12 May 1889.

311 The property was acquired in three tracts recorded in Jefferson County Deed Book 337, pp. 433 and 554; and Jefferson County Deed Book 348, p. 97. The plat was recorded in Jefferson County Deed Book 339, pp. 638-639. This map was later copied in Jefferson County Plat and Subdivision Book 8, p. 29.

312 Advertisement for "South Park Hotel," *The Critic*, 29 June 1890. The hotel was converted into The Pines Sanatorium, operated by E. G. Dick, M.D., specializing in alcohol and drug addictions. *The Courier-Journal*, 25 March 1913.

313 Jefferson County Deed Book 385, p. 557. "South Park Club Now 40 Years Old," *The Courier-Journal*, 3 June 1945.

314 "Balloting For Parks." *The Courier-Journal*, 1 July 1890.

315 R. T. Durrett, "Parks In Louisville," *The Critic*, 29 June 1890.

316 "A Quiet Election." *The Courier-Journal*, 2 July 1890.

317 "President Sherley." *Louisville Commercial*, 11 July 1890. The commissioners drew slips for the lengths of their terms: Finzer and Cowan for three years; Bohne and Castleman for two; and Sherley and Layer for one.

318 "A Victory For Parks." *The Courier-Journal*, 5 August 1890.

319 "Municipal Matters." *The Courier-Journal*, 5 August 1890.

320 "Happy Commissioners." *The Courier-Journal*, 6 August 1890.

321 "Enlarging Jacob Park," *The Courier-Journal*, 30 December 1890.

322 For an example from various issues of local newspapers, see *The Courier-Journal*, 18 December 1890.

323 Ironically, when Albert Fein published *Frederick Law Olmsted and the American Enivonmental Tradition* in 1972, the dust jacket of his book included as background Scowden's layout for Jacob Park.

324 The 26 August 1891 report of F. L. Olmsted & Co. was published in "A Park System." *The Courier-Journal*, 20 September 1891.

325 "Charles D. Jacob Dead." *The Courier-Journal*, 26 December 1898.

326 "Happy Commissioners." *The Courier-Journal*, 6 August 1890.

327 "Where the Trees Are Greenest And the Grass Grows Softest," *The Courier-Journal*, 17 May 1896.

328 "Another New Park." *The Courier-Journal*, 13 May 1891.

329 Col. Boone died in the family residence 24 January 1875 at the age of 61. "Col. W. P. Boone." *The Courier-Journal*, 25 January 1875.

330 "Boone Park." *The Courier-Journal*, 24 May 1891.

331 "The Park Board." *The Courier-Journal*, 6 May 1891. "Another New Park." *The Courier-Journal*, 13 May 1891.

332 "Looking At The Parks," *The Louisville Times*, 21 May 1891.

333 Board of Park Commissioners Minute Book 1, pp. 129, 165, and 207. The Filson Historical Society.

334 A report of the contract being awarded to F. B. Hamilton was noted in *The Courier-Journal*, 12 November 1891.

335 "Progress Of The Parks." *The Critic*, 15 November 1891.

336 Virginia L. Fitzpatrick, "Frederick Law Olmsted and the Louisville Park System," *The Filson Club History Quarterly* 59 (January 1985): 57-58.

337 "Parsons Dead; Woman Sought," *The Courier-Journal*, 17 March 1912. It was determined that Parsons, age 60, had died of natural causes in a house kept by Emma Allen on Pearl Street in an area known as the Chute. He had been accompanied there by a heavily veiled woman, whose identity was not known.

338 Andrew Cowan to Frederick Law Olmstead, 8 January 1891. Letter book file 1260, Olmsted firm papers, Library of Congress. Olmsted was frequently misspelled Olmstead by the Board of Park Commissioners and the Louisville press.

339 In the 4 August 1890 election, 9,961 votes were cast for the parks bill; 2,997 were cast against. Common Council Minute Book, p. 471, 14 August 1890.

340 Salem Howe Wales was an owner and publisher of *The Scientific American* and an active Republican and civic leader who had been a commissioner of New York's Department of Public Parks as well as its president. "Death Of Salem H. Wales." *The New York Times*, 3 December 1902.

341 M. G. van Rensselaer, "Landscape Gardening," *The American Architect and Building News* 22 (1 October 1887): 157-159; 22 (3 December 1887): 263-264; and 23 (7 January 1888): 3-5.

342 M. G. van Rensselaer, "Landscape Gardening," *The American Architect and Building News* 22 (3 December 1887): 264.

343 Clay Lancaster, *Prospect Park Handbook* (New York, 1967), 16-17.

344 Lee Hall, *Olmsted's America: An "Unpractical" Man and His Vision of Civilization* (Boston, 1995), 61.

345 Witold Rybczynski, *A Clearing in the Distance: Frederick Law Olmsted and America in the Nineteenth Century* (New York, 1999), 280.

346 Francis R. Kowsky, "Municipal Parks and City Planning: Frederick Law Olmsted's Buffalo Park and Parkway System," *Journal of the Society of Architectural Historians* 46 (March 1987): 50.

347 Witold Rybczynski, *A Clearing in the Distance: Frederick Law Olmsted and America in the Nineteenth Century*, 288.

348 Francis R. Kowsky, "Municipal Parks and City Planning: Frederick Law Olmsted's Buffalo Park and Parkway System," *Journal of the Society of Architectural Historians*, 63.

349 The most comprehensive and informative study of any Olmsted project is Cynthia Zaitzevsky's *Frederick Law Olmsted and the Boston Park System* (Boston, 1982).

350 Francis D. "Frank" Carley and his brother-in-law, W. E. Chess, operated a paint and oil store on Main Street that became a lucrative business later absorbed by the Standard Oil Company.

351 Culyer had worked at Central Park. Lee Hall, *Olmsted's America* (Boston, 1995), 76. Clay Lancaster, *Prospect Park Handbook* (New York, 1967), 51.

352 Charles E. Beveridge and Paul Rocheleau, *Frederick Law Olmsted Designing: The American Landscape* (New York, 1998), 65.

353 Cowan to Olmsted, 22 January 1891. Olmsted firm papers, Library of Congress.

354 Henry S. Codman was partner in F. L. Olmsted & Co. from 1889 until his death in 1893. "Death of Henry Sargent Codman." *The Inland Architect and News Record* 20 (January 1893): 59.

355 Board of Park Commissioners Minute Book 1, p. 60. The Filson Historical Society.

356 F. L. Olmsted & Co. to Thomas Sherley, 26 February 1891. Olmsted firm papers, Library of Congress.

357 Cowan to F. L. Olmsted & Co., 17 March 1891. Olmsted firm papers, Library of Congress.

358 Board of Park Commissioners Minute Book 1, p. 85. The Filson Historical Society.

359 Sherley to F. L. Olmsted & Co., 17 April 1891. Olmsted firm papers, Library of Congress.

360 "The Park Commissioners." *The Courier-Journal*, 20 May 1891. The newspaper's spellings of Olmstead and Coleman have been corrected to Olmsted and Codman.

361 "Looking At The Parks," *The Louisville Times*, 21 May 1891.

362 "Col. Andrew Cowan," *The Louisville Post*, 21 May 1891.

363 "Laying Out The Parks." *The Courier-Journal*, 24 May 1891.

364 "Looking At The Parks," *The Louisville Times*, 21 May 1891.

365 Board of Park Commissioners Minute Book 1, p. 125. The Filson Historical Society.

366 "A Wise Move." *The Louisville Times*, 23 May 1891. Olmsted continued to be spelled Olmstead. According to the *First Annual Report of the Board of Park Commissioners* (July 1891), 20, the contract was entered into 17 June 1891.

367 Meeting of 9 June 1891, Board of Park Commissioners Minute Book 1, p. 157. The Filson Historical Society.

368 "First Annual Report of the Board of Park Commissioners, July 21, 1891," *The Municipal Reports for the Fiscal Year Ending August 31, 1891* (Louisville, 1894), 632.

369 Folder 1260, Andrew Cowan to F. L. Olmstead, 29 June 1891. Olmsted firm papers, Library of Congress.

370 Folder 1260, F. L. Olmsted & Co. to Thomas H. Sherley, 26 August 1891. Olmsted firm papers, Library of Congress.

371 Folder 1260, F. L. Olmsted & Co. to Thomas H. Sherley, 26 August 1891. Olmsted firm papers, Library of Congress. The report was reprinted in the *First Annual Report of the Board of Park Commissioners* (July 1891), 51-57.

372 "A Park System." *The Courier-Journal*, 20 September 1891.

373 Folder 1260, F. L. Olmsted & Co. to Thomas H. Sherley, 26 August 1891. Olmsted firm papers, Library of Congress. The report was reprinted in the *First Annual Report of the Board of Park Commissioners* (July 1891), 51-57.

374 "Maps To Be Made." *The Courier-Journal*, 27 May 1891. Olmsted was still being spelled Olmstead. *First Annual Report of the Board of Park Commissioners* (July 1891), 20.

375 This topographical map would serve as the basis of future work for 40 years.

376 Michael J. Lewis, "The First Design for Fairmount Park," *The Pennsylvania Magazine of History and Biography* 80 (July 2006): 294-295.

377 Mahlo was employed 26 May 1891 after a letter from Olmsted & Co. was read. Board of Park Commissioners Minute Book 1, p. 127. The Filson Historical Society. Robert C. Kinkead confirmed firm's choice in letter to Olmsted, Olmsted & Eliot, 12 March 1896. Olmsted firm papers, Library of Congress. Mahlo's father-in-law Frederick Leib was a good friend of Board of Park Commissioners E. C. Bohne, Andrew Cowan, and Gottlieb Layer. "Mr. Leib's Funeral, *The Courier-Journal*, 31 October 1895.

378 Frederick Law Olmsted to Andrew Cowan, 26 May 1891. Olmsted firm papers, Library of

Congress. Either the letter was incorrectly dated or it arrived too late to influence the outcome of Mahlo's selection.

379 "A West End Park." *The Courier-Journal*, 10 June 1891.

380 "Progress Of The Parks." *The Critic*, 15 November 1891.

381 *Third Annual Report of the Board of Park Commissioners* (July 1893), 8.

382 Thomas Nord, "Excavation in Cherokee Park gets fresh water flowing again," *The Courier-Journal*, 24 February 1998. Martha Elson, "Glenview club's gift will help restore Cherokee Park spring," *The Courier-Journal*, 18 November 1998. Martha Elson, "Makeover perks up Cherokee Park spring," *The Courier-Journal*, 22 December 1999.

383 "Annual Report of the Park Commissioners for the Fiscal Year Ending August 31, 1892," *Louisville Municipal Reports for the Fiscal Year Ending August 31, 1892* (Louisville, 1893), 666.

384 According to Cave Hill Cemetery records, the Baringer remains were reinterred 11 November 1893 in Section 4, lot 36.

385 "The Park Board." *The Courier-Journal*, 6 May 1891.

386 "How Louisville's Fine Park System Came Into Being—As Written By the Late Colonel Andrew Cowan," *Herald-Post*, 8 October 1925. Morton M. Casseday, the son of Alexander and Nancy Craik Casseday, was educated as a lawyer, but became an editor for *The Courier-Journal* before working for leading papers in the East and then becoming an insurance man. He was 45 when he died. "Found Dead." *The Courier-Journal*, 11 June 1904.

387 John B. Castleman purchased 36.5 acres from Theo. Schwartz & Co. and others on 18 May 1892 for $30,000. Jefferson County Deed Book 388, p. 533.

388 Temple Bodley, "Some Park History." *The Courier-Journal*, 31 March 1929. According to the Board's *First Annual Report* (1891), with the $16,000 donation, the cost of the 259.12 acres exclusive of improvements was $100,317.37.

389 "New Park." *The Courier-Journal*, 8 May 1891. A map of the various tracts being purchased was included in the article.

390 "The Option Closed." *Louisville Commercial*, 9 May 1891. "Will Not Stand It." *Louisville Commercial*, 10 May 1891. "Fighting The Park." *The Courier-Journal*, 10 May 1891. "The Park Fight." *The Courier-Journal*, 11 May 1891.

391 "They Will Fight." *The Louisville Times*, 11 May 1891. "Deserve Credit," *Louisville Commercial*, 12 May 1891.

392 Laura Wood Roper, *FLO: A Biography of Frederick Law Olmsted*, 432.

393 "Annual Report of the Park Commissioners for the Fiscal Year Ending August 31, 1892," *Louisville Municipal Reports for the Fiscal Year Ending August 31, 1892* (Louisville, 1893), 666.

394 F. L. Olmsted & Co. to Emil Mahlo, 1 March 1892. Olmsted firm papers, Library of Congress. The firm thought Olmsted would be in Louisville between March 7 and March 16. He was at Biltmore on March 5th and in New York just after the 16th, so he could have visited Louisville.

395 F. L. Olmsted & Co. to Emil Mahlo, 29 March 1892. Olmsted firm papers, Library of Congress.

396 "Annual Report of the Park Commissioners for the Fiscal Year Ending August 31, 1892," *Louisville Municipal Reports for the Fiscal Year Ending August 31, 1892* (Louisville, 1893), 666-667.

397 Board of Park Commissioners Minute Book 7, p. 81.

398 "Pastoral," *The Courier-Journal*, 20 May 1900.

399 Folder 1260, Andrew Cowan to H. S. Codman, 9 April 1892. Olmsted firm papers, Library of Congress.

400 Folder 1260, T. H. Sherley to F. L. Olmsted & Co., 29 April 1892. Olmsted firm papers, Library of Congress.

401 "The Public Parks." *The Louisville Post*," 7 July 1893.

402 "The West-End Park," *The Louisville Times*, 25 May 1891.

403 "A West-End Park." *The Courier-Journal*, 10 June 1891.

404 "The Tattler." *The Louisville Times*, 23 May 1891. While the bond issue was intended to provide $1 million, the Sinking Fund Commissioners had reduced it to $600,000.

405 "Shawnee." *The Critic*, 17 April 1892.

406 "The West-End Park," *The Louisville Post*, 19 April 1892.

407 Photographs of the Kettig residence appeared in *The Courier-Journal*, 1 July 1900.

408 "A West-End Park." *The Courier-Journal*, 10 June 1891.

409 "The Garr Golden Wedding." *The Courier-Journal*, 21 May 1893. Jacob Gaar purchased 520 acres from Thomas Garland for $10,000 in 1831. Jefferson County Deed Book GG, p. 100.

410 "Shawnee." *The Critic*, 17 April 1892.

411 "Annual Report of the Board of Park Commissioners for the Year Ending July, 1893," *Louisville Municipal Reports for the Fiscal Year Ending August 31, 1893* (Louisville, 1894), 229.

412 F. L. Olmsted & Co. to John B. Castleman, 17 November 1892. Charles E. Beveridge and Arleyn A. Levee, *Olmsted Documentary Resource*, 1992, 355.

413 Charles E. Beveridge and Arleyn A. Levee, *Olmsted Documentary Resource*, 1992, 355.

414 *Sixth Annual Report of the Board of Park Commissioners* (November 1896), 4-5.

415 "Ostrich For Western Park." *The Courier-Journal*, 10 December 1892.

416 Cover letter dated 31 October 1893. Charles E. Beveridge and Arleyn A. Levee, *Olmsted Documentary Resource*, 1992, 359.

417 "Fontaine And Western." *The Courier-Journal*, 5 August 1894.

418 Ibid.

419 Geoffrey Brown, "City completes purchase of old River Glen Park," *The Louisville Times*, 24 February 1977.

420 Robert Emmett McDowell, *City of Conflict: Louisville in the Civil War 1861-1865* (Louisville, 1962), 66. Greenbush is mentioned in an advertisement in *The Louisville Daily Journal*, 30 July 1836.

421 Jefferson County Deed Book 454, p. 208. "Col. Lum Simons Taken By Death," *The Evening Post*, 17 February 1922. "Lum Simons Gone; Figure In Sports And City Politics," *The Louisville Times*, 17 February 1922.

422 "Pretty Riverview." *The Courier-Journal*, 23 May 1897.

423 "Riverview," *The Courier-Journal*, 1 July 1900.

424 L. and Lucy Simons to White City Company, 7 September 1906. Jefferson County Deed Book 647, p. 566.

425 "Thing Of Beauty," *The Courier-Journal*, 28 April 1907.

426 "White City's Sale Set For March 6 Next," *The Courier-Journal*, 16 February 1909. The property was appraised at $91,000. "White City Property," *The Courier-Journal*, 12 March 1909. In May 1909, Simons conveyed the land and assets to the Riverview Park Company. Jefferson County Deed Book 700, p. 568.

427 Information supplied by Bill Carner, University of Louisville Photographic Archives. The photograph was published in *Views of Louisville since 1766*, 216.

428 "Chickasaw Park Opens In Spring," *The Courier-Journal*, 19 February 1922.

429 Sheldon S. Shafer, "Riverview Park work imminent," *The Courier-Journal*, 16 January 2010.

430 "Shadows." *The Courier-Journal*, 2 August 1891. Andrew Cowan's scrapbook (The Filson Historical Society) identified the writer as Maj. J. M. Wright.

431 An attorney, former newspaper editor, and president of The Filson Club, Reuben T. Durrett had been elected to the Board of Park Commissioners to replace the late John Finzer, 13 February 1891.

432 "Given Indian Names." *The Courier-Journal*, 14 August 1891.

433 *The Critic*, 16 August 1891.

434 "Park Nomenclature and Geology." *The Evening Post*, 18 June 1904. By then, Baxter Square had been converted into a playground. For a layout, see "Baxter Square Now A Children's Playground," *The Courier-Journal*, 5 May 1901.

435 Common Council Minute Book, 501, 11 September 1890.

436 "F. F. Lutz Dead," *The Courier-Journal*, 13 August 1915.

437 Meeting of 21 April 1891. Board of Park Commissioners Minute Book 1, pp. 92-93. The Filson Historical Society.

438 Meeting of 13 August 1891. Board of Park Commissioners Minute Book 1, pp. 214 and 215. The Filson Historical Society.

439 Meeting of 25 August 1891. Board of Park Commissioners Minute Book 1, p. 221. The Filson Historical Society.

440 Meeting of 1 December 1891. Board of Park Commissioners Minute Book 1, p. 268. The Filson Historical Society.

441 Meeting of 5 January 1892. Board of Park Commissioners Minute Book 1, p. 290. The Filson Historical Society.

442 Meeting of 16 February 1892. Board of Park Commissioners Minute Book 1, p. 311. The Filson Historical Society.

443 Meeting of 5 April 1892. Board of Park Commissioners Minute Book 1, p. 350. The Filson Historical Society.

444 "Formally Dedicated." *The Courier-Journal*, 16 August 1892.

445 "Small Parks," *The Courier-Journal*, 14 February 1900.

446 Meeting of 20 April 1897. Board of Park Commissioners Minute Book 5, p. 409. The Filson Historical Society. Meeting of 4 April 1899. Board of Park Commissioners Minute Book 6, p. 369. The Filson Historical Society. "Small Parks," *The Courier-Journal*, 14 February 1900.

447 Meeting of 20 September 1898. Board of Park Commissioners Minute Book 6, p. 331. The Filson Historical Society.

448 Castleman was elected president by the board, 2 August 1892. "President Castleman." *The Courier-Journal*, 3 August 1892. Sherley was elected vice president.

449 Olmsted firm papers, Library of Congress.

450 "The Tattler." *The Louisville Times*, 23 May 1891.

451 "Annual Report of the Board of Park Commissioners for the Year Ending July, 1893," *Louisville Municipal Reports for the Fiscal Year Ending August 31, 1893* (Louisville, 1894), 260. The bond referendum was not voted on until November 1894.

452 Ibid, 261.

453 F. L. Olmsted, Sr., to John C. Olmsted, 27 October 1893. Olmsted firm papers, Library of Congress.

454 C. B. Robinson to F. L. Olmsted, 14 March 1894. Olmsted firm papers, Library of Congress.

455 Olmsted never saw Bonnycot, but the firm laid out the grounds in 1902-1903.

456 Olmsted to firm partners, 15 March 1894. Reproduced in Olmsted Associates, "Journal of the Development of Cherokee Park, Louisville, Kentucky, 1891-1974."

457 F. L. Olmsted & Co. to John E. Green, 1 March 1892. Olmsted firm papers, Library of Congress.

458 Laura Wood Roper, *FLO: A Biography of Frederick Law Olmsted* (Baltimore, 1973), 467-468.

459 Susan L. Klaus, *A Modern Arcadia: Frederick Law Olmsted, Jr. and the Plan for Forest Hills Gardens* (2002), 24-25.

460 "Fred. Law Olmsted." *The Courier-Journal*, 29 August 1903.

461 Board of Park Commissioners Minute Book 7, p. 321. The Filson Historical Society.

462 "Report of Park Commissioners, November 30, 1894," *Louisville Municipal Reports for the Fiscal Year Ending August 31, 1895* (Louisville, 1896), 786-787.

463 Board of Park Commissioners Minute Book 5, p. 18. The Filson Historical Society.

464 Board of Park Commissioners Minute Book 5, pp. 93-94. The Filson Historical Society.

465 "Fred Leib Dead." *The Courier-Journal*, 30 October 1895.

466 Robert C. Kinkead to Olmsted, Olmsted & Eliot, 12 March 1896. Olmsted firm papers, Library of Congress.

467 Due to insufficient collections from city tax assessments, the Board teetered on insolvency much of the fiscal year and ended with an overdraft of $4,038.23, "which we hope to liquidate at an early date." *Sixth Annual Report of the Board of Park Commissioners* (November 1896), 51.

468 Olmsted, Olmsted & Eliot to John B. Castleman, 16 April 1896. Olmsted firm papers, Library of Congress.

469 Jefferson County Marriage Register 16, p. 236. A notice of the wedding appeared in *The Courier-Journal*, 12 October 1893.

470 Mahlo's death notice in the Washington *Evening Star*, 1 September 1904.

471 "Park Bonds Win." *The Courier-Journal*, 7 November 1894. Belknap v.

City of Louisville et al., *Kentucky Reports* 99 (April Term, 1896), 474-490.

472 Folder 1260, John C. Olmsted to John B. Castleman, 27 April 1896. Olmsted firm papers, Library of Congress.

473 *Louisville Municipal Reports... 1896*, 685.

474 "Everything Ready." *The Courier-Journal*, 19 May 1897. "Park Work," *The Courier-Journal*, 20 May 1897.

475 Notice to call national meeting made at Board of Park Commissioners meeting 20 April 1897. Board of Park Commissioners Minute Book 5, p. 411. Castleman was elected president succeeding Thomas Sherley, 2 August 1892. "President Castleman." *The Courier-Journal*, 3 August 1892. "Col. Sherley Retires." *The Courier-Journal*, 17 August 1892. Sherley died in 1898 at the age of 55. "Stricken," *The Courier-Journal*, 1898.

476 "Park Talk." *The Courier-Journal*, 21 May 1897.

477 Warren H. Manning to Olmsted, Olmsted & Eliot, 1 and 5 August, and 1 October 1896. Warren H. Manning to John B. Castleman, 1 October 1896. Olmsted firm papers, Library of Congress.

478 Lance M. Neckar, "Developing Landscape Architecture for the Twentieth Century: The Career of Warren H. Manning," *Landscape Journal* 8 (Fall 1989): 82.

479 "Charles Eliot." *The New York Times*, 26 March 1897.

480 "Organized," *The Courier-Journal*, 22 May 1897. "Planning Group Meeting This Week Had Its Foundation In Louisville," *The Courier-Journal*, 18 May 1952.

481 "W. H. Manning Dead; Designer Of Parks," *The New York Times*, 6 February 1938.

482 "Our Parks." *The Courier-Journal*, 23 May 1897.

483 O. F. Dubois quoted in "Our Parks." *The Courier-Journal*, 23 May 1897.

484 John C. Olmsted to Castleman, 17 April 1896. Board of Park Commissioners Minute Book 5, p. 205. Olmsted had just learned that golf was about to be played in Cherokee Park. According to a 1932 souvenir issue of *Shawnee Golfer*, the course at Cherokee had been laid out in 1895.

485 "Golf Is Here." *The Courier-Journal*, 19 November 1896. According to Julia A. Muldoon, "Kentucky Golf," *The Kentucky Magazine* 1 (July 1917): 181, the first course in Kentucky consisted of six holes set out by George C. Patten along with a clubhouse on Third Street boulevard in 1886. However, the first golf course in the United States was not established until 1888 in Yonkers, New York. Muldoon must have been confusing the Iroquois Wheeling and Driving Club, which did not have a golf course in May 1895, when it opened. By November 1896, it did have a very rough course that the Louisville Golf Club played a practice round on.

486 "Golf Ushered In." *The Courier-Journal*, 23 May 1897.

487 "Harry R. Phillips Elected President Of The Golf Club, *The Courier-Journal*, 2 December 1902.

488 Arthur A. Shurtleff, "Park Scenery In Relation to the Fine Arts and to Physical Recreation," *The American Magazine of Art* 17 (August 1926): 399.

489 Ibid.

490 "Kinkead Services Wait As Son Due," *The Louisville Times*, 14 May 1932.

491 Cowan to F. L. Olmsted & Co., 28 February 1893. Olmsted firm papers, Library of Congress.

492 Correspondence was included in the *Fifth Annual Report of the Board of Park Commissioners* (1895), 57-62.

493 Fraser was updating maps of the three large parks in early 1897, although he had no contract with the Board. He was officially hired as park engineer effective 1 March 1897 for $2,100 annually at the 6 April meeting of the Board. Board of Park Commissioners Minute Book 5, pp. 402-403. Mahlo's leaving was never acknowledged.

494 Meeting of 3 October 1893. Board of Park Commissioners Minute Book 3, p. 289.

495 Souvenir edition of *Shawnee Golfer* (1932) stated the Cherokee course was first laid out in 1895, but did not receive much play until 1897.

496 Meeting of 1 May 1900. Board of Park Commissioners Minute Book 7, p. 111. Olmsted Associates, Inc., "Journal of the Development of Cherokee Park, Louisville, Kentucky, 1891-1974," 43-44.

497 Board of Park Commissioners Minute Book 7, pp. 168, 280, 312, and 322.

498 Committee on Cherokee Park was authorized to extend the golf links at meeting of 7 February 1905. Board of Park Commissioners Minute Book 8, p. 1.

499 "Park Golf Links." *The Courier-Journal*, 17 April 1905.

500 Samuel W. Thomas, *Cherokee Triangle*, 38-39.

501 "New Course For Local Golfers," *The Courier-Journal*, 22 November 1911.

502 "Park Golf Links." *The Courier-Journal*, 17 April 1905.

503 "Will Plan Course For Cherokee Park," *The Evening Post*, 2 June 1915.

504 "Extension Of Cherokee Links To Begin At Once," *The Courier-Journal*, 16 June 1915.

505 "Golf," *The Courier-Journal*, 6 September 1915. Scenes At Formal Opening Of The New Eighteen-Hole Golf Course At Cherokee," *The Courier-Journal*, 7 September 1915.

506 "Bendelow Staked Off Iroquois Golf Course." *The Evening Post*, 8 July 1915.

507 Folder 1266, Olmsted firm to Castleman, 4 May 1911, Olmsted firm papers, Library of Congress.

508 Folder 1266, Smith to Olmsted Brothers, 27 March 1916. Olmsted firm papers, Library of Congress.

509 Folder 1266, Jones to Board of Park Commissioners, 31 March 1916. Olmsted firm papers, Library of Congress. Later, John C. Olmsted's letter to Helm Bruce, 21 June 1916, stated the report to the commissioners was "my report."

510 Folder 1266, Olmsted to Bruce, 21 June 1916. Olmsted firm papers, Library of Congress.

511 "Ruby's Report," *The Courier-Journal*, 1 August 1947. The course had been expected to open 4 July 1946. "New Links to Open," *The Courier-Journal*, 12 July 1945.

512 "Plan Golf Club For Residents Of Shawnee," *The Courier-Journal*, 15 February 1925. "Plan of new Shawnee Golf Club links," *The Courier-Journal*, 10 October 1927.

513 "Park Golf Links." *The Courier-Journal*, 17 April 1905.

514 Folder 1269, Harry S. Smith to Olmsted Brothers, 19 March 1915. Olmsted firm papers, Library of Congress.

515 Meeting of 16 June 1896. Board of Park Commissioners Minute Book 5, p. 252.

516 Meeting of 20 April 1897. Board of Park Commissioners Minute Book 5, p. 404.

517 Olmsted Brothers to Andrew Cowan, 12 March 1908. Olmsted firm papers, Library of Congress.

518 "Fountain," *The Courier-Journal*, 19 May 1903. Samuel W. Thomas, *The Village of Anchorage* (Louisville, 2004), 174-175.

519 "Pleased." *The Courier-Journal*, 27 August 1905.

520 Frederick Law Olmsted to Thomas Sherley, 24 September 1894. Olmsted firm papers, Library of Congress.

521 "Fifty Thousand Do Honor To Kentucky's Backwoodsman," *The Courier-Journal*, 16 June 1906. "Kentucky." *The Courier-Journal*, 2 June 1893.

522 Folder 1263, report of J. C. Olmsted, Olmsted firm papers, Library of Congress.

523 Folder 1263, notes of John C. Olmsted, 29 September 1905. Olmsted firm papers, Library of Congress.

524 Folder 1263, notes of John C. Olmsted, 15 May 1906. Olmsted firm papers, Library of Congress.

525 "Fifty Thousand Do Honor To Kentucky's Backwoodsman" *The Courier-Journal*, 16 June 1906.

526 Folder 1263, notes of J. C. Olmsted, 15 May 1906. Olmsted firm papers, Library of Congress.

527 Plan of Audubon Park, The Filson Historical Society. "Suffers Stroke," *The Courier-Journal*, 29 March 1910. "Cecil Fraser Dies," *The Courier-Journal*, 31 March 1910.

528 "Greater Park Areas Advised," *The Courier-Journal*, 20 January 1915.

529 For a comprehensive account, see Carl E. Kramer, "James C. Murphy and the Urban Planning Movement in Louisville, 1901-1934," *The Filson Club History Quarterly* 64 (July 1990): 317-359.

530 From the report of John Charles Olmsted quoted in "Greater Park Areas Advised," *The Courier-Journal*, 20 January 1915.

531 "Greater Park Areas Advised," *The Courier-Journal*, 20 January 1915.

532 Arleyn Levee, "Olmsted, John Charles (1852-1920)," *Pioneers of American Landscape Design*, Charles A. Birnbaum and Robin Karson, eds. (New York, 2000), 282-284.

533 "J. C. Olmsted, Designer of Park System, Dies In East," *The Courier-Journal*, 26 February 1920.

534 "Gift For Park," *The Courier-Journal*, 2 July 1913. This is probably the first recorded break with the firm's omnipotence.

535 "Theodore Ahrens To Erect Bridge In Beautiful Cherokee Park As Memorial To His Daughter," *The Courier-Journal*, 14 September 1919. "Ahrens Bridge In Cherokee Is Opened Today," *The Courier-Journal*, 3 October 1920.

536 "Bridge In Cherokee Park, Out 16 Months, Is Still Unrepaired," *The Courier-Journal*, 3 April 1923.

537 "One Architect's Idea For Hert Memorial Bridge." *The Louisville Times*, 14 February 1922.

538 Martha Elson, "Costly bridge repair will have to wait," *The Courier-Journal*, 26 September 2007. Sheldon S. Shafer, "Cherokee Park bridge restoration nears completion," *The Courier-Journal*, 23 November 2008.

539 "Get Bids On Park Bridge," *Louisville Post*, 11 April 1923. "Mayor Gets Plans For Cherokee Park Bridge," *Louisville Herald*, 12 April 1923. James Frederick Dawson had been mentored by John Charles Olmsted and was living in California.

540 "Bridge In Cherokee Park, Out 16 Months, Is Still Unrepaired," *The Courier-Journal*, 3 April 1923.

541 Mention of the bridge plans was contained in article headed "Shawnee Park To Get Stand," *The Courier-Journal*, 20 February 1929.

542 "Bidermann DuPont Dies In Delaware," *The Courier-Journal*, 23 October 1923. About 1898, Bidermann du Pont moved back to Delaware, where he died at the age of 86.

543 Recollection of Temple Bodley. Bodley Collection, The Filson Historical Society.

544 "The Park Board." *The Courier-Journal*, 6 May 1891.

545 "A. V. Du Pont." *The Courier-Journal*, 17 May 1893.

546 "Was Millionaire DuPont Shot?" *The New-York Times*, 19 May 1893. "DuPont Was Not Murdered," *The New-York Times*, 20 May 1893.

547 "A. V. Du Pont." *The Courier-Journal*, 17 May 1893. For an account of the capital removal episode (1891-1893), see Robert M. Ireland, "Capital Question: Efforts to Relocate Kentucky's Seat of Government," *The Register of the Kentucky Historical Society* 104 (Spring 2006): 260-282.

548 "Central Park Closed," *The Courier-Journal*, 29 April 1895. The *Critic* erroneously announced 1 May 1892 in "A Grand Surprise" that "the park commissioners will purchase Central Park from A. V. Du Pont for $200,000."

549 Warren Manning to John B. Castleman, 16 April 1896. Olmsted firm papers, Library of Congress. Manning's report was copied into the minutes of the Board of Park Commissioners, 1 May 1896.

550 Meeting of 1 May 1896. Board of Park Commissioners Minute Book 6, p. 202.

551 "Effort," *The Courier-Journal*, 10 March 1899.

552 Meetings of 19 September 1899 and 3 October 1899. Board of Park Commissioners Minute Book 7, pp. 70 and 79.

553 Meeting of 19 December 1899. Board of Park Commissioners Minute Book 7, p. 92.

554 "Bond Issue," *The Courier-Journal*, 12 March 1899.

555 "Park Will Be Sold." *The Courier-Journal*, 1 August 1900.

556 "Jefferson Statue Due To-Day," *The Louisville Times*, 15 June 1900. This article states the statue was to be erected in front of the Courthouse and dedicated 4 July 1900.

557 Meeting of 7 May 1901. Board of Park Commissioners Minute Book 7, p. 174.

558 "Lease," *The Courier-Journal*, 24 January 1903.

559 Castleman to Olmsted Brothers, 22 December 1903. Folder 1265, Olmsted firm papers, Library of Congress.

560 After some haggling, the agreed-upon price was $297,500.

561 Olmsted Brothers to Castleman, 4 March 1904. Folder 1265, Olmsted firm papers, Library of Congress.

562 "By Auction Sale." *The Courier-Journal*, 29 May 1904. "Home Of Famous Minister To Be Torn Down." *The Courier-Journal*, 30 May 1904.

563 The pergola was refurbished in 1999. Anne Eldridge, "Central Park pergola is given a fresh look," *The Courier-Journal*, 30 June 1999.

564 Folder 1265, Olmsted firm papers, Library of Congress.

565 Meeting of 3 May 1906. Board of Park Commissioners Minute Book 8, p. 80.

566 "Lincoln's Cabin Homeward Bound," *The Louisville Post*, 7 March 1906.

567 "Lincoln's Birthplace Sold." *The New York Times*, 29 August 1905. "Lincoln's Home For Park." *The New York Times*, 8 October 1905. "R. J. Collier, Originator Of Plan To Buy Lincoln's Birthplace, Dies," *The Louisville Times*, 9 November 1918.

568 "The Lincoln Farm." *The Courier-Journal*, 22 April 1899. "The Sale of Abraham Lincoln's Home." *The Courier-Journal*, 27 August 1905. "Lincoln Cabin," *The Courier-Journal*, 16 March 1906.

569 "Honor Memory Of State's Great Son, Abraham Lincoln," *The Courier-Journal*, 17 June 1906.

570 Samuel W. Thomas, *Cherokee Triangle* (Louisville, 2003), 169-171.

571 Folder 1265, Harry G. Evans to Olmsted Brothers, 5 May 1921. Olmsted firm papers, Library of Congress.

572 "Statue Of Lincoln To Arrive In April," *The Courier-Journal*, 24 December 1920.

573 Folder 1265, Olmsted firm papers, Library of Congress. Matt H. Crawford was president of the Board of Park Commissioners.

574 "Thousands See Flag Drop From Lincoln Statue Gift at Impressive Unveiling Ceremonies," *The Louisville Times*, 26 October 1922. Olmsted Brothers had prepared a plan to beautify the library grounds in 1907-1908.

575 Folder 1289, report of E. C. Whiting, 16 November 1923. Olmsted firm papers, Library of Congress.

576 Folder 1289, note on Seelbach Hotel stationery to Olmsted Brothers, 16 April 1924. Olmsted firm papers, Library of Congress.

577 Olmsted died 24 February 1920 at the age of 67. "J. C. Olmsted, Landscape Architect." *The New York Times*, 26 February 1920.

578 Witold Rybczynski, *A Clearing in the Distance*, 410.

579 Laura Wood Roper, *FLO: A Biography of Frederick Law Olmsted* (Baltimore, 1973), 475.

580 Folder 1265, Hastings to Olmsted, 7 May 1924. Olmsted firm papers, Library of Congress.

581 Folder 1265, Telegrams from Olmsted to Hastings, 9 May 1924 and from Olmsted to Schardein, 9 May 1924. Olmsted firm papers, Library of Congress.

582 When Bingham discussed the project initially with Hastings is not known, but in Bingham's letter of 4 March 1920 to Hastings he says: "I am so grateful for your interest in this matter and so sure that we shall have something very fine and very beautiful through you." Bingham family papers, The Filson Historical Society.

583 "Name Architect For Memorial," *The Louisville Herald*, 18 April 1924.

584 Folder 1265, Hastings to Olmsted, 27 August 1924. Olmsted firm papers, Library of Congress.

585 Folder 1265, Hastings to Olmsted, 16 September 1924. Olmsted firm papers, Library of Congress.

586 "Memorial Body Discusses Plans," *The Courier-Journal*, 14 November 1924. "Central Park Picked For Auditorium," *The Courier-Journal*, 18 November 1924.

587 "U.S. Legion Head O.K.'s Memorial Site," *The Courier-Journal*, 19 November 1924.

588 Folder 1265, Telegram from George E. Newman to Olmsted, 19 November 1924. Olmsted firm papers, Library of Congress.

589 Folder 1265, Telegram from Olmsted Brothers to Newman, 19 November 1924. Olmsted firm papers, Library of Congress.

590 "Committee To Protect City Parks," *The Louisville Post*, 26 November 1924. "Objectors To Park Site For Memorial File Brief," *The Courier-Journal*, 26 November 1924.

591 *The Courier-Journal* carried an interview 21 November 1924 with former park commissioner Louis Seelbach supporting the project and the park location "if there were no legal obstacles." The Republican *Louisville Herald* and Democratic *Louisville Post* had been acquired and merged in early 1924 by banker James B. Brown, who used them to vent his dislike of Robert Worth Bingham.

592 Folder 1265, notes of E. O. Whiting, 8 January 1925. Olmsted firm papers, Library of Congress. On 13 January 1925, the Board of Park Commissioners resolved to employ Olmsted Brothers to consult on the project.

593 Folder 1265, Schardein to Olmsted Brothers, 9 February 1925. Olmsted firm papers, Library of Congress.

594 "Park Site For Memorial Hit," *The Louisville Herald*, 30 May 1925.

595 "Park Board O.K.'s Auditorium Site," *The Courier-Journal*, 2 June 1925. "Park Experts Co-Operate In Memorial Plan," *The Louisville Times*, 2 June 1925.

596 "Protection Of Parks Urged By Mrs. Speed," *The Louisville Herald*, 7 March 1925. "Suit To Save Central Park Is Instituted," *The Louisville Herald-Post*, 26 July 1925.

597 "Court Bars Auditorium In Central Park, *The Courier-Journal*, 17 January 1926.

598 "First Annual Report of the Board of Park Commissioners, July 21, 1891," *Louisville Municipal Reports for the Fiscal Year Ending August 31, 1891* (Louisville, 1892), 620.

599 "Park Engineer's Report," *Louisville Municipal Reports...1893*, 230.

600 "Boulevard Opened." *The Courier-Journal*, 11 June 1893.

601 At a Board meeting 18 February 1896, a special committee was authorized to confer with mayor, Board of Public Works "as to making a Boulevard or Parkway East and West from Cherokee Park to Shawnee Park." Board of Park Commissioners Minute Book 5, p. 156. The Filson Historical Society.

602 "The New Parkway." *Louisville Commercial*, 3 October 1897.

603 "The Beauty of Louisville's Southern Parkway," *The Courier-Journal*, 10 August 1902.

604 *Annual Reports City of Louisville...1897*, 491-492.

605 R. G. Potter later superimposed automobiles and a pony in this photograph and published the scene in *Memories: Louisville's Family Album* (Louisville, 1976).

606 The concept was displayed in *The Courier-Journal*, 20 September 1894. For a biographical sketch of Enid Yandell, see Nancy D. Baird, "Enid Yandell: Kentucky Sculptor, *The Filson Club History Quarterly* 62 (January 1988): 5-31.

607 "Mr. Muldoon Says A Word." *The Courier-Journal*, 5 October 1894.

608 "Hebe Back On Her Pedestal At Third-Avenue Drinking Fountain," *The Courier-Journal*, 9 June 1906.

609 The report was published in "A Park System." *The Courier-Journal*, 20 September 1891.

610 "Park Engineer's Report," *Louisville Municipal Reports...1893*, 229-230.

611 Mahlo had been in Brookline meeting with the Olmsted firm in August 1892, so presumably the firm was aware the parkway surveys were underway or about to be undertaken. Report from Mahlo in "Col. Sherley Retires." *The Courier-Journal*, 17 August 1892.

612 Theodore Schwartz et al to John B. Castleman, 18 May 1892. Jefferson County Deed Book 388, p. 533.

613 Plats recorded 28 March 1895 and 27 March 1896 in Jefferson County Deed Books 444, p. 640 and 474, p. 640.

614 "The Park System." *The Courier-Journal*, 28 May 1893.

615 *Third Annual Report of the Board of Park Commissioners* (July 1893), 68-69. The list of expenditures for 1893 record "West Parkway, $412.80 and East Parkway, $329.80." Ibid, 91.

616 "Fashion Drive." *The Courier-Journal*, 11 June 1893.

617 Charles Swearingen, "The Conquest Of The Automobile In Retrospect," *The Courier-Journal*, 5 November 1911. According to a report in *The Evening Post*, 2 January 1909, the first car in Louisville was delivered to Roche by boat in June 1900.

618 Meeting of 16 April 1901. Board of Park Commissioners Minute Book 7, p. 171.

619 "Automobiling In And About Louisville," *The Courier-Journal*, 8 June 1902.

620 "Elects," *The Courier-Journal*, 19 July 1903.

621 Meeting of 18 February 1902. Board of Park Commissioners Minute Book 7, p. 226.

622 Meeting of 1 April 1902. Board of Park Commissioners Minute Book 7, p. 232.

623 "Survey For The Belt Boulevard Nearly Completed," *The Courier-Journal*, 15 October 1902.

624 Meeting of 21 October 1902. Board of Park Commissioners Minute Book 7, p. 253.

625 "Decisive," *The Courier-Journal*, 5 November 1902.

626 "Castlewood," Jefferson County Deed Book 444, p. 640. Corrected plat of Castlewood, 8 December 1896, recorded in Jefferson County Deed Book 474, p. 640.

627 Plat of Ferndale Avenue property owners recorded in Jefferson County Plat and Subdivision Book 1, p. 58. A list of the concessions to property owners was recorded in Jefferson County Deed Book 620, p. 290.

628 "Blocks," *The Courier-Journal*, 1 February 1905.

629 Recorded in Jefferson County Plat Book 1, p. 58 and as Ferndale in Jefferson County Deed Book 620, p. 290.

630 Folder 1272, notes by J. F. Dawson, 20 April 1907. Olmsted firm papers, Library of Congress.

631 Folder 1272, sketches by John C. Olmsted, dated 10 November 1907. Olmsted firm papers, Library of Congress. "Castlewood—A Subdivided Park For Residences." *The Courier-Journal*, 30 August 1903.

632 *City of Louisville Annual Reports…1908* (1909), 202.

633 Folder 1272, Olmsted to Castleman, 6 January 1912. Olmsted firm papers, Library of Congress.

634 "Gift For Park," *The Courier-Journal*, 2 July 1913.

635 Meeting of 5 September 1913. Board of Park Commissioners Minute Book 10, p. 57.

636 "Highway Open," *The Courier-Journal*, 29 August 1903. For information about Fontaine Ferry Park, see "Fontaine And Western,"

The Courier-Journal, 5 August 1894.

637 Survey authorized at meeting of 19 April 1904. Board of Park Commissioners Minute Book 7, p. 361.

638 "Gift For Park," *The Courier-Journal*, 2 July 1913.

639 "Parkway Work Ordered Begun," *The Courier-Journal*, 6 December 1916. "City Will Extend Western Parkway," *The Louisville Herald*, 20 March 1918.

640 "Work Rushed By City Boards," *The Courier-Journal*, 22 June 1927.

641 "Would Connect City Parkways," *The Courier-Journal*, 15 December 1917.

642 "Greater Park Areas Advised," *The Courier-Journal*, 20 January 1915.

643 William H. Wilson, *The City Beautiful Movement* (Baltimore, 1994), 47.

644 "A Proposed Drainage and Power Canal around Louisville," *The Courier-Journal*, 23 March 1902.

645 The movement was spearheaded by Miss Margrethe Koefoed Christensen, who recognized her mother with a fountain in Cherokee Park.

646 Constitution of The Outdoor Art League of Louisville, Kentucky.

647 "Louisville's New Memorial Park," *The Courier-Journal*, 13 November 1921.

648 Samuel W. Thomas, *Louisville since the Twenties* (Louisville, 1978), 188-189.

649 14 May 1926. Folder 1260, Olmsted firm papers, Library of Congress.

650 Samuel W. Thomas, *The Village of Anchorage* (Louisville, 2004), 191-203.

651 "How Olmsted Brothers Intended to Transform the Town Edward Dorsey Hobbs Built," Talk by Samuel W. Thomas, The Filson Historical Society, 8 November 2005.

652 "Historic Estate To Be Put On Block," *Louisville Herald*, 21 June 1921.

653 "Outdoor League Gets Use of Customhouse Yard," *The Courier-Journal*, 19 July 1908.

654 Homer Dye, Jr., "Lincoln Park, Our 'Greenwich Village,'" *The Courier-Journal*, 14 September 1919.

655 "Over $400,000 Is Offered For Park," *The Louisville Times*, 18 July 1922. "Eastern Firm Wants To Buy Lincoln Park," *Louisville Herald*, 18 July 1922.

656 "Transformation of Lincoln Park Into Beauty Spot Planned By Junior Board," *The Courier-Journal*, 23 December 1934.

657 "Lincoln Park Zoo Proposal Given Board," *The Louisville Times*, 30 July 1940.

658 Helen Lawton, "Lincoln Park," *The Courier-Journal*, 17 November 1946.

659 "Wyatt Plans Lincoln Park Expansion," *The Courier-Journal*, 9 May 1944.

660 Grady Clay, "Park Dispute Is Recalled," *The Courier-Journal*, 19 March 1959.

661 Robert Doty, "Highest Bidder On Park Plans 4-Story Building," *The Courier-Journal*, 3 October 1946.

662 "City Begins Clearing Lincoln Park," *The Courier-Journal*, 21 April 1950.

663 The pavilion was torn down to make way for the J. C. Penney store in 1950. Grady Clay, "Bid-Opening Set Friday For New Penney Store On Site In Lincoln Park," *The Courier-Journal*, 24 December 1950.

664 Grady Clay, "Guthrie Green Enters Realm Of Probability," *The Courier-Journal*, 24 June 1962.

665 Grady Clay, "Guthrie Green: Short Step On A Long Road," *The Courier-Journal*, 6 September 1964.

666 Peter Milius, "Green Light," *The Louisville Times*, 25 June 1963.

667 "Public Places," *Louisville* 15 (September 1964): 62.

668 "Outing Stopped By Teachers' Arrest," *The Courier-Journal*, 14 June 1924.

669 "Negroes To Fight Park Segregation," *The Courier-Journal*, 23 June 1924.

670 "Hearing Given To Negro Teachers," *The Courier-Journal*, 22 June 1924. For a recounting of earlier park use by blacks, see Jonathon Free, "'What is the Use of Parks,': The Debate over Parks and the Response of Louisville's African-American Community to Racial Segregation, 1895-1930," *Ohio Valley History* 9 (Spring 2009): 25-33.

671 "2 Negro Teachers Draw Reprimand," *The Courier-Journal*, 2 July 1924.

672 "Colored Society At The Picnic." *The Evening Post*, 11 June 1904.

673 "The Negroes And The Parks," *The Courier-Journal*, 4 July 1924.

674 "Race Segregation In Parks Ordered," *The Courier-Journal*, 18 June 1924.

675 "Chickasaw Park Opens In Spring," *The Courier-Journal*, 19 February 1922.

676 "Road Contracts Let For Chickasaw Park," *The Courier-Journal*, 5 December 1928.

677 "Greater Park Areas Advised," *The Courier-Journal*, 20 January 1915.

678 The Howes country store and barroom were advertised for sale in *The Courier-Journal*, 19 February 1882.

679 Thomas W. Bullitt to John C. Bullitt, 30 March 1893. Bullitt family papers, The Filson Historical Society.

680 Thomas W. Bullitt to William C. Bullitt, 31 January 1903. Bullitt family papers, The Filson Historical Society.

681 Folder 7834, Olmsted Brothers to Ben Ford, 21 January 1930. Olmsted firm papers, Library of Congress.

682 Folder 1278, Veech to Olmsted Brothers, 13 November 1915. Olmsted firm papers, Library of Congress.

683 Folder 1278, Olmsted Brothers to Veech, 15 November 1915. Olmsted firm papers, Library of Congress.

684 Folder 1278, notes of John C. Olmsted, 30 November 1915. Olmsted firm papers, Library of Congress.

685 Folder 1278, Veech to Olmsted, 21 December 1915. Olmsted firm papers, Library of Congress.

686 "Sisters Refused To Give Any Land Toward A Park," *The Louisville Post*, 24 April 1919.

687 Folder 1284, Berry Stoll to Olmsted Brothers, 22 March 1928. Olmsted firm papers, Library of Congress.

688 Folder 1284, Charles H. Banks to Dawson, 2 August 1928. Olmsted firm papers, Library of Congress.

689 Folder 1284, report of Helm Bruce, Jr., 9 April 1935. Olmsted firm papers, Library of Congress.

690 "Nature Wields Fairy Wand In City's New Park Link Addition," *Herald-Post*, 30 March 1930.

691 Folder 7834, Bullitt to Dawson, 20 September 1928. Olmsted firm papers, Library of Congress.

692 Folder 7834, Dawson to Bullitt, 26 September 1928. Olmsted firm papers, Library of Congress.

693 "City Ponders Beargrass Parkway," The Courier-Journal, 3 August 1951.

694 Folder 7834, various letters, Olmsted firm papers, Library of Congress. Samuel W. Thomas, Oxmoor: The Bullitt Family Estate Near Louisville, Kentucky, Since 1787 (Louisville, 2003), 160-161.

695 Grady Clay, "Fading Parkways," The Courier-Journal, 15 December 1963.

696 "Beargrass Creek," The Courier-Journal, 11 December 1869.

697 Item in The Courier-Journal, 9 December 1869.

698 "The Short-Line," The Louisville Commercial, 7 July 1881. "The Latest Scoop." The Louisville Commercial, 8 July 1881. "The Short-Line Purchase." The Courier-Journal, 9 July 1881.

699 "The Short-Route Transfer." The Courier-Journal, 28 December 1881. "Opening The Short Route," The Louisville Times, 13 May 1884. A comprehensive history of the extension is presented.

700 "Need of a City Plan," The Courier-Journal, 11 October 1914. "City Plan Items Sent To Bidders," The Louisville Times, 26 December 1928.

701 The contract to prepare a comprehensive city plan was dated February 1929. "Rebuilding of City Is Aim Of Planning, Zoning Commission," Herald-Post, 7 July 1929.

702 "City To Employ Traffic Expert," The Courier-Journal, 9 April 1926.

703 Ebenezer Howard, Garden Cities of To-morrow (London, 1898). For a comprehensive study of English garden cities, see The Search for Environment by Walter L. Creese (Yale University Press, 1966). A graduate of Brown and Harvard universities, Dr. Creese taught at the University of Louisville from 1946 to 1958 and then the University of Illinois. He served on the Louisville Planning and Zoning Commission, 1951-1955. Paula Burba, "Architectural historian Creese dies," The Courier-Journal, 1 May 2002.

704 "Modern Magic Thrills Club," The Courier-Journal, 20 March 1929.

705 Douglass Nunn, "The City 'Hires Brains,'" The Courier-Journal, 5 April 1959. "Berg, former planning official for city, county commission, dies," The Courier-Journal, 4 August 1986.

706 Samuel W. Thomas, "Death of a city planner," Readers' Forum, The Courier-Journal, 25 January 1990.

707 A floodwall was proposed in 1913 only weeks before Louisville experienced the second highest flood up to that time. "Another Meeting Is Held In Interest of Wall as Guard Against Floods," The Courier-Journal, 17 February 1913. The worst flood up to that point had occurred in 1884. The worst flood of all time occurred in 1937 followed by the 1945 deluge. While a bond issue had been passed in 1939, and the city had done some planning, no protection was in place when the 1945 flood crested on 9 March. Richard Renneisen, "It's the City's Move, But the Flood Wall Awaits End of War," The Courier-Journal, 4 March 1945. With the two highest floods occurring within eight years, construction of the floodwall became a priority.

708 "Buildings Here Are Praised By Art Scholar," The Courier-Journal, 10 November 1944.

709 "Planners Ask County-wide Park Agency," The Courier-Journal, 13 July 1956. A subcommittee of the Committee of 100 recommended Bartholomew's proposal. John V. Collis, chairman of the subcommittee, and his family had given Jefferson Fiscal Court the land along River Road along with $50,000 to create Carrie Gaulbert Cox Park in 1951.

710 "Giant Downtown Reorganization Proposed for Louisville of 1980," The Courier-Journal, 7 December 1956.

711 Gerald Henry, "New Riverfront Plan Features Bell Tower," The Courier-Journal, 28 August 1965.

712 Alan Judd, "Louisville group seeks to reunite city and its river," The Courier-Journal, 4 September 1983. Sheldon Shafer, "Officials turn over plans for riverfront to experts," The Courier-Journal, 3 October 1983. Sheldon Shafer, "Riverfront plans show office towers, lake, amphitheater," The Courier-Journal, 29 September 1983. Al Cross, "Railroad's exit expected to lead to redevelopment of riverfront," The Courier-Journal, 30 April 1986. Rick McDonough, "Plans for riverfront park grow, doubling the cost," The Courier-Journal, 12 April 1988.

713 Rick McDonough and Sheldon Shafer, "Three private donations will pay for top designer to draw waterfront plans," The Courier-Journal, 1 June 1989. "Sheldon Shafer, "Firm picked to design 'vibrant' riverfront," The Courier-Journal, 28 February 1990. Tom Spalding, "Designers tour waterfront, promise it can be one of best," The Courier-Journal, 6 June 1990. Sheldon Shafer, "Revised design adds apartments, activities, wins officials' praise," The Courier-Journal, 21 December 1990. Sheldon Shafer, "Briefing on riverfront master plan draws a wave of acclaim," The Courier-Journal, 22 March 1991. George Hargreaves and Glenn Allen, "A Waterfront plan," The Courier-Journal, 28 July 1991. Sheldon Shafer, "Cascading 'canal' a key part of revised plan for riverfront," The Courier-Journal, 19 January 1993.

714 Sheldon S. Shafer, "Work to begin this month to expand Waterfront Park," The Courier-Journal, 14 July 2001. Sheldon S. Shafer, "'Adventure Playground' takes shape," The Courier-Journal, 2 February 2003. Sheldon S. Shafer, "Waterfront Park deal gets land for last phase," The Courier-Journal, 29 December 2004. Joseph Gerth, "Work starts on last piece of park's puzzle," The Courier-Journal, 27 September 2005. Sheldon S. Shafer, "Gradual ramp will lead up to Big Four Bridge," The Courier-Journal, 17 June 2006. Sheldon S. Shafer, "Waterfront Park nears final phase," The Courier-Journal, 5 November 2006. Sheldon S. Shafer, "Work continues on Big Four ramp," The Courier-Journal, 6 March 2008. Sheldon S. Shafer, "Big Four Bridge walkway about to be a step closer," The Courier-Journal, 16 May 2007.

INDEX